# South Asia

Post-colonial and post-partition South Asia, one of the fastest growing and yet one of the least integrated regions of the world, is marked by both optimism and pessimism. This intriguing dichotomy of strength and weakness, security and insecurity, hope and fear, connections and disconnections underpins South Asia's regionalism conundrum and gives birth to borders and boundaries – both material and mental – with a complex territoriality. The Janus-faced nature of South Asian borderlands – the inward nationalizing impulses entangled with the outward regional frontier-orientations – is a stark reminder that history of mobility in this eco-geographical region is much older than the history of territoriality and colonial cartography and ethnography. This collection of meticulously researched, theoretically informed, case studies from South Asia provides useful insights into bordering, ordering and othering narratives as practices and performances that are intricately entangled with identity politics and security discourses. It shows how a sharper focus on subterranean subregionalism(s), border communities, popular geopolitics of enmity and transborder challenges to sustainability could open up spaces for new multiple (re)imaginings of borders at diverse scales and sights including sub-urban neighbourhoods, school textbooks/cinema and trans-border conservation initiatives.

The chapters in this edited volume have been contributed by both renowned and young emerging scholars, looking into the borders and boundaries in South Asia. Each chapter offers new perspectives and insights into themes like trans-Himalayan borderlands, India-Pakistan physical and mental borders, Afghanistan-Pakistan border and numerous social boundaries that we see in everyday South Asia.

The chapters in this book were originally published as a special issue of the *Journal of Borderlands Studies*.

**Dhananjay Tripathi** teaches International Relations at South Asian University, New Delhi. He specializes in South Asian Borders. He has authored one, edited one and co-edited one book, and also contributed in several edited volumes and reputed international journals. He is editorial board member of prestigious journals like *Journal of Borderlands Studies* (Routledge); *Alternatives: Global, Local, Political*; and *BIG Review*.

**Sanjay Chaturvedi** teaches International Relations at South Asian University, New Delhi. He has extensively written on South Asian borders, partition, critical geopolitics and maritime South Asia. He has authored two, co-authored three and co-edited eight books. Chief Editor of *Journal of the Indian Ocean Region* (Routledge), he serves on the editorial board of several reputed international journals.

# South Asia
Boundaries, Borders and Beyond

*Edited by*
**Dhananjay Tripathi and Sanjay Chaturvedi**

LONDON AND NEW YORK

First published 2022
by Routledge
2 Park Square, Milton Park, Abingdon, Oxon, OX14 4RN

and by Routledge
605 Third Avenue, New York, NY 10158

*Routledge is an imprint of the Taylor & Francis Group, an informa business*

© 2022 Association for Borderlands Studies

All rights reserved. No part of this book may be reprinted or reproduced or utilised in any form or by any electronic, mechanical, or other means, now known or hereafter invented, including photocopying and recording, or in any information storage or retrieval system, without permission in writing from the publishers.

*Trademark notice*: Product or corporate names may be trademarks or registered trademarks, and are used only for identification and explanation without intent to infringe.

*British Library Cataloguing-in-Publication Data*
A catalogue record for this book is available from the British Library

ISBN13: 978-1-032-11356-2 (hbk)
ISBN13: 978-1-032-11362-3 (pbk)
ISBN13: 978-1-003-21954-5 (ebk)

DOI: 10.4324/9781003219545

Typeset in Minion Pro
by codeMantra

**Publisher's Note**
The publisher accepts responsibility for any inconsistencies that may have arisen during the conversion of this book from journal articles to book chapters, namely the inclusion of journal terminology.

**Disclaimer**
Every effort has been made to contact copyright holders for their permission to reprint material in this book. The publishers would be grateful to hear from any copyright holder who is not here acknowledged and will undertake to rectify any errors or omissions in future editions of this book.

# Contents

*Citation Information* — vii

*Notes on Contributors* — ix

Introduction – South Asia: Boundaries, Borders and Beyond — 1
*Dhananjay Tripathi and Sanjay Chaturvedi*

1 Re-engaging the "International": A Social History of the Trans-Himalayan Borderlands — 10
*Nimmi Kurian*

2 Borders and Bordering Practices: A Case Study of Jaisalmer District on India–Pakistan Border — 22
*Krishnendra Meena*

3 Portraying the "Other" in Textbooks and Movies: The Mental Borders and Their Implications for India–Pakistan Relations — 34
*Dhananjay Tripathi and Vaishali Raghuvanshi*

4 Pakistan's Border Policies and Security Dynamics along the Pakistan–Afghanistan Border — 50
*Lacin Idil Oztig*

5 The Status of Durand Line under International Law: An International Law Approach to the Pakistan-Afghanistan Frontier Dispute — 66
*Fawad Poya*

6 No Mountain Too High? Assessing the Trans-territoriality of the Kailash Sacred Landscape Conservation Initiative — 81
*Jayashree Vivekanandan*

7 Analysis of a Parallel Informal Exchange Rate System in Indo-Bhutanese Border Towns — 95
*Ankur Sharma*

# CONTENTS

8   Gaining a Ghetto: The Resettlement of Partition-affected Bengalis in New
Delhi's Chittaranjan Park        108
*Anubhav Roy*

*Index*        127

# Citation Information

The following chapters, except chapter 7, were originally published in the *Journal of Borderlands Studies*, volume 35, issue 2 (2020). When citing this material, please use the original citations and page numbering for each article, as follows:

**Chapter 1**
*Re-engaging the "International": A Social History of the Trans-Himalayan Borderlands*
Nimmi Kurian
*Journal of Borderlands Studies*, volume 35, issue 2 (2020) pp. 243–254

**Chapter 2**
*Borders and Bordering Practices: A Case Study of Jaisalmer District on India–Pakistan Border*
Krishnendra Meena
*Journal of Borderlands Studies*, volume 35, issue 2 (2020) pp. 183–194

**Chapter 3**
*Portraying the "Other" in Textbooks and Movies: The Mental Borders and Their Implications for India–Pakistan Relations*
Dhananjay Tripathi and Vaishali Raghuvanshi
*Journal of Borderlands Studies*, volume 35, issue 2 (2020) pp. 195–210

**Chapter 4**
*Pakistan's Border Policies and Security Dynamics along the Pakistan–Afghanistan Border*
Lacin Idil Oztig
*Journal of Borderlands Studies*, volume 35, issue 2 (2020) pp. 211–226

**Chapter 5**
*The Status of Durand Line under International Law: An International Law Approach to the Pakistan-Afghanistan Frontier Dispute*
Fawad Poya
*Journal of Borderlands Studies*, volume 35, issue 2 (2020) pp. 227–241

**Chapter 6**
*No Mountain Too High? Assessing the Trans-territoriality of the Kailash Sacred Landscape Conservation Initiative*
Jayashree Vivekanandan
*Journal of Borderlands Studies*, volume 35, issue 2 (2020) pp. 255–268

viii CITATION INFORMATION

## Chapter 7

*Analysis of a Parallel Informal Exchange Rate System in Indo-Bhutanese Border Towns*
Ankur Sharma
*Journal of Borderlands Studies*, DOI: 10.1080/08865655.2019.1635515

## Chapter 8

*Gaining a Ghetto: The Resettlement of Partition-affected Bengalis in New Delhi's Chittaranjan Park*
Anubhav Roy
*Journal of Borderlands Studies*, volume 35, issue 2 (2020) pp. 269–286

For any permission-related enquiries please visit:
http://www.tandfonline.com/page/help/permissions

# Notes on Contributors

**Sanjay Chaturvedi** Department of International Relations, South Asian University, New Delhi, India.

**Nimmi Kurian** Centre for Policy Research, New Delhi, India.

**Krishnendra Meena** Centre for International Politics, Organization and Disarmament, School of International Studies, Jawaharlal Nehru University, New Delhi, India.

**Lacin Idil Oztig** Department of Political Science and International Relations, Yildiz Technical University, Istanbul, Turkey.

**Fawad Poya** Faculty of Legal Studies, South Asian University, New Delhi, India.

**Vaishali Raghuvanshi** Assistant Professor (Political Science), MMV, Banaras Hindu University, Uttar Pradesh, India.

**Anubhav Roy** Faculty of Social Sciences, Department of Political Science, University of Delhi, Delhi, India.

**Ankur Sharma** Department of International Relations, South Asian University, New Delhi, India.

**Dhananjay Tripathi** Department of International Relations, South Asian University, New Delhi, India.

**Jayashree Vivekanandan** Department of International Relations, Faculty of Social Sciences, South Asian University, New Delhi, India.

# Introduction – South Asia: Boundaries, Borders and Beyond

Dhananjay Tripathi[1] and Sanjay Chaturvedi[2]

## Post-Colonial and Post-Partition South Asia

South Asia as a post-colonial as well as a post-partition region has a lot to offer to those interested in the geopolitical triad of bordering, ordering and othering (Houtum and Naerssen, 2002). Several of these practices – that feed into and are in turn fed by boundary producing formal and popular narratives – continue to unfold on a sub-continent that eminently qualifies as ecologically-geographically connected but remains geopolitically partitioned, and is yet to be theorized. The Janus-faced nature of South Asian borderlands – the inward nationalizing inclinations entangled with the outward regional frontier-orientations – is a stark reminder of the reality that is often overlooked: the history of mobility in this part of the world is much older than the history of territoriality.

The geopolitical triad or triangle mentioned above (i.e. bordering, ordering and othering) comes with a heavy price tag for the inhabitants of the sub-continent, especially for those communities whose homeland landed in a suddenly erupted borderland in the wake of the 1947 partition of British India, which caused the death of nearly one million people and more than ten million were displaced. Whose territory was being partitioned in 1947 (Chaturvedi, 2005) is a question that remains unanswered even today.

It is useful to acknowledge at the outset that contemporary South Asia is, paradoxically, both a rich and poor region due to the mismatch between opportunities and capacities. It is a region where people across borders are culturally and socially interrelated but this commonality is not reflected in state-to-state relations of two nuclear powers – India and Pakistan. South Asia is both one of the fastest growing and one of the least integrated regions of the world. It is also a region of contrasts, marked by both optimism and pessimism, and features many intricacies. This dichotomy of strength and weakness, security and insecurity, hope and fear with connections and disconnections is a remarkable, if not unusual, feature of South Asia and gives birth to borders and boundaries with different kinds of territoriality. Some of the enduring legacies of this partition include truncated territories, economies, cultures, and unforgettable memories. As pointed out by Ranabir Samaddar (2005: 95), there was "[N]ot one partition, not even two, not even three…but several partitions…partitions of several territories, several units, several identities and several visions".

How does one capture the *idea* of South Asia? On its radical side, social theorist Ashis Nandy would even question the idea of South Asia. For Nandy,

> [T]he idea does not fit the self-image and ambitions of the states in the region. South Asia's constituent nation-states are modelled on the pre-Second World War nation-states of Europe, the kind that builders of nation-states in South Asia came to know during their formative years in colonial times. (Nandy, 2005: 541)

The political acrimony in South Asia continues to overshadow the prospects of economic linkages and trade flows, despite occasional sparks of hope. More than politics and economics, it is the cultural moorings that unite South Asia. Ironically, South Asian states ignore the cultural affinity while making efforts for political and economic integration (Ahmed, 2012). The negation of socio-cultural linkages further eclipses the prospects of overcoming political divisions. Thus, in South Asia, boundaries and borders acquire utmost prominences, confining societies to the lines of separations drawn by the power elites. At times there are notional changes but again territoriality bounces back in one form or the other. In the words of Passi, "de-and re-territorialization occur in various institutional practices and discourses and display economic, cultural and political power relations" (Passi, 2011: 18). This is true in the case of South Asia as well.

With existing boundaries and borders adding substantially to adversities faced by the South Asians, especially border communities, many would hope on both the sides of the dividing line that hopefully, in not too distant a future, South Asian states would bridge the borders and blur the political boundaries. Some simple statistics do strengthen the argument in support of integration. Despite a decline in poverty in South Asia it is next to Sub-Saharan Africa in the terms of numbers of poor (Deyshappriya, 2019). As many as 130 million South Asians live in informal settlements. Except for Sri Lanka – ranked 71 – none of the South Asian countries are in the top 100 on Human Development Index. South Asia is also one of the most disaster-prone regions in the world with high vulnerability to global warming and climate calamities (Chaturvedi and Doyle, 2015, Chaturvedi and Sakhuja, 2016). These realities of South Asia pose a question: Can we remodel or even reimagine contemporary South Asia with fewer borders and boundaries?

There are material conditions that kindle hope, and the economic growth experienced by the region is a silver lining (World Bank, 2017). This positive economic growth in the form of sustainable development is likely to receive support from young South Asians. The demographic dividend of South Asia is a natural advantage in comparison to many regions on the face of the globe. In simple terms, "more than 12 million new workers will join the labour force every year, for the next two decades" (Ghani, 2012). South Asia today is at a crossroads, facing huge opportunities as well as complex challenges. Integration across national boundaries and borders through trade, cooperative diplomacy, and people-to-people contacts is steadily turning into a matter of necessity rather than choice.

## South Asian Boundaries and Borders: Comparative and Critical Perspectives

Hard borders embody and represent political anxieties between neighbours. Likewise, boundaries – both mental and material – are indicators of socio-political divides between the people. In South Asia borders and boundaries affect the everyday life of millions in profound manner. South Asia borders are "agents of active politics" (Banerjee, 1998: 191). At times, it is these borders that solely influence foreign and security policies of the states in South Asia (Tripathi, 2019). In South Asia, borders acquire a political shape and remain integral to domestic political discourses (Tripathi, 2015). To understand the criticality of these borders in South Asia we also need to explore, in a geo-historical perspective, how borders were created in the region. Borders are like human beings having their histories that are region specific (Tagliacozzo, 2016). As observed by Schendel and Maaker "[M]any of Asia's borders owe their existence to colonial state making and the violent histories that this involved" (Schendel and Maaker, 2014: 3). In South Asia, most of the present-day borders were demarcated by the British to overcome their security anxieties. These borders, therefore, are the result of war, conflict and victories while sometimes they were drawn as an outcome of diplomatic efforts and administrative convenience.

India-Nepal border is a good example of how initially war and then diplomacy led to the creation of a border between these two countries. The formal demarcation of India-Nepal borders started after the Anglo-Nepali war in 1814. Later, the border between India and Nepal was consolidated, owing to Nepal's help to British during the 1857 'mutiny' in India, and Nepalese troops joining the British in the World War-I (Tripathi, 2019). There are other examples showcasing how social realities were ignored and arbitrary lines drawn in South Asia. The controversial Durand line is another reflection of British strategic interests in South Asian border making process. Durand line between Pakistan (Pre-1947 United India) and Afghanistan politically divided people of the same ethnicity, turned Afghanistan into a 'buffer state', thereby consolidating the British control over India.

In South Asia, some of the colonial political themes are not only retained but also refurbished. The "cartographic anxiety" (Krishna, 1994) that is quite visible in South Asia can be described as a legacy of the British colonial rule. In the case of India, we can see how borders continue to play a central role in contemporary national politics and remain a cause for concern and contestation both for the state and for the people. India's international border is the third longest in the world, and she shares both her land and maritime borders with almost every South Asian country. Immediately after independence from the British Colonial rule India had witnessed a violent partition. British India was divided into two countries: India and Pakistan. Not satisfied with the partition, Pakistan expressed its discontent over the drawing of borders and to this date makes claims on Kashmir. Moreover, the setback to India in the 1962 war with China only added to India's distress and concerns over the security of her borders. It is important to note that "[T]he theme of perceived indispensability of 'secure' or 'inviolate' borders for national development, in fact for nationality itself is not limited to politics. In the Indian society it is a recurring theme" (Krishna, 1994: 511).

The most prominent expression of obsession with borders in South Asia manifests in the form of militarization of Siachen glacier, which in all respect is exceptionally hostile for human habitation. The Indian army during the operation codenamed as 'Meghdoot' (1984) sent troops to set up bases on the glacier. India blamed Pakistan for provocation by allowing mountain expedition to the Siachen glacier and by distributing maps showing it as a part of Pakistani territory. While Pakistan's intentions could be questioned, India's policy of keeping troops at a place that is almost 18,000 ft above the sea level is considered equally questionable by many (Nair, 2009). Ignoring humanitarian concerns, such as casualties due to frost bites, India has justified the presence of its troops on the Siachen glacier. This is a good example of how national security concerns completely dominate border issues in South Asia.

India-Bangladesh border is another illustration of border politics in the region. These two neighbours do not have hostile political relations but border problems at times make things acrimonious. India-Bangladesh border is the fifth longest land border in the world with some unique characteristics like conclaves. Owing to its geographical stretch, large numbers of people are directly and indirectly dependent on this border region. As true for many other parts of the world, India-Bangladesh border has its peculiar economy connecting the dwellers of both sides. Sometimes these ground realities are ignored by states. India is fencing the border on its side with Bangladesh citing security concerns to check infiltration. New Delhi decided to fence the India-Bangladesh land borders in 2012, and as per the official report, "[T]he total length of Indo-Bangladesh border sanctioned for fencing is 3326.14 km; out of which about 2731 km of fencing has so far been completed (31.12. 2016)" (Government of India, 2016: 37). These fences again symbolize the general sensitivity, bordering anxieties, towards borders in South Asia. In South Asia, borders are overwhelmingly viewed as a matter of national security.

It is a truism that it takes two to make a boundary, and a 'secure' and securitizing border cannot be sustained for a long time without convincing justification from either side. In a region that is culturally so connected it is even harder to keep people apart and divided. This is where psychological-mental borders become so important to territorially bounded statecraft and boundary-sustaining practices. Once 'we' are convinced about an impending threat, we view people on the other side of the border with suspicion. This is also true in the case of South Asia where states have devised several methods to keep people separated from each other. Nationalist and populist rhetoric by the political leadership of different South Asian states appears to be a daily affair. Some of the popular methods for creating mental borders include state-sponsored propaganda through media and other means. A closer analysis further reveals how several boundaries are created by societal practices that surround everyday life in South Asia. Caste discrimination, religious fundamentalism, patriarchy, economic deprivation, etc., are some of the common visible boundaries that exist throughout the region.

## In This Special Issue

As Guest Editors of this special issue, we feel highly privileged to introduce this rich, diverse and insightful collection of meticulously researched articles on South Asian borders by South Asian scholars. Even a cursory glance at the *Journal of Borderlands Studies (JBS)*, since its inception in 1986, should suffice to reveal that Border Studies, in general, have come a long way with several theoretically robust, conceptually innovative and thought-provoking contributions, including case studies. In a seminal contribution, David Newman, one of the leading experts on the subject, wrote:

> [B]order studies have come a long way during the past decade. From the study of the hard territorial line separating states within the international system, the contemporary study of borders focuses on the process of bordering, through which territories and peoples are respectively included or excluded within a hierarchical network of groups, affiliations and identities. (Newman, 2003: 13)

In the same article Newman invited attention to the fact that contrary to the prevalent long-standing impression, borders need not always be rigid and can be quite flexible,

> reflecting new territorial and aspatial patterns of human behavior. While modern technologies, particularly cyberspace, have made the barrier role of borders redundant in some areas, they have also served to create new sets of borders and boundaries, enclosing groups with common identities and interests who are dispersed throughout the globe, lacking any form of territorial compactness or contiguity. (Newman, 2003: 13)

Despite – or perhaps due to – the nearly omnipresent and overwhelming presence of both physical and mental borders in the region, Border Studies is still an emerging field of study in South Asia. This is not a new subject for South Asian scholars, who in their individual intellectual-academic explorations have been in conversation with western scholarship from time to time. But as a collective enterprise the South Asian Border Studies can be considered as still a work in progress. Europe, due to the integration process, that necessitates dealing with the borders and boundaries both at the epistemological and ontological levels remains a fertile ground for Border Studies discussions. Similarly, the US-Mexico border continues to shape the contours of debate related to borders and boundaries. The US-Mexico border represents several divides, some of which have become more evident in the recent past. The border questions in West Asia too have fascinated many scholars. Every border, irrespective of the region in which it is located, has certain resemblances or commonalities with other borders with respect to 'control' and 'purpose'. Yet each region has its own distinct character and understanding. In South Asia, borders are primarily linked to national security, often described by intellectuals of statecraft as a sensitive issue, and thus perceived as inappropriate for open academic discussion. Critiquing such notions, several scholars from within and outside the region have made a remarkable contribution to Border Studies by going beyond the realm of Security Studies (Aggarwal, 2004; Menon and Bhasin, 1998; Samaddar, 1999; Schendel, 2005). Undoubtedly, there is plenty of scope for Border Studies in South Asia. Moreover, well-researched, theoretically informed, case studies from South Asia are likely to enrich Border Studies. We sincerely hope that this special issue will serve this objective well, while outlining agenda for future research on South Asian boundaries and borderlands.

The first article of this special issue by Nimmi Kurian underlines the importance of approaching border regions not as a passive peripheral location but as agentive sites. While drawing attention to the paradoxical nature of Delhi's emerging border narratives that invoke the sub-regional imagery of borders as bridges, she refuses to give up at the same time the reductionist logic of borders as barriers. Kurian takes Dharchula, an ancient trading town in northern India located on the trans-Himalayan trading routes with Nepal and China, and everyday lived-in geographies of 'borderlands as homelands' as her primary cases to question disciplinary International Relations (IR) and cartographic imprisonment, and reveals the socially constructed nature of borders. Extending some of the arguments made in her outstanding book titled *India-China Borderlands: Conversations Beyond the Centre* (Kurian, 2014), Kurian shows how the focus on 'subterranean subregionalism(s)' is likely to reveal multiple ways of imagining, understanding and interpreting borders.

In South Asia, borderlands are in most cases considered as homelands. It has been rightly pointed out that "to study borders as dynamic institutions, it is therefore important to study the 'bottom up'" process of change, emanating from the daily practices of ordinary people living in these borderland regions. There should also be as the traditional "'top down' approach which focuses solely on the role of institutional actors, notably – but not only – the governments" (Newman, 2003: 15). Krishnendra Meena in his paper makes this point quite evident by bringing data from his case study of Jaisalmer district of Rajasthan in India that shares a border with Pakistan. Jaisalmer district is a major tourist attraction, and India-Pakistan border in this area is known as a 'peaceful border'. Meena in his paper brings specifics from these adjoining villages of Jaisalmer district and shows how, beyond the imagery of a peaceful border, the security anxieties of the Indian state continue to and express and assert themselves in various forms. The "peaceful border" is fenced, and everyday life of ordinary villagers remains under constant state surveillance.

It is argued by Emmanuel Brunet-Jailly that to "understand borders and borderlands, social scientists need to focus on lenses of analysis that underscore the tug of war between agency and structural processes" (Brunet-Jailly, 2011: 1). Further, Emmanuel added that "complex social processes that establish borders" (Brunet-Jailly, 2005: 643). We can witness these complex social processes that are clearly visible in the case of India-Pakistan borders. Both India and Pakistan continue to grapple with the unfinished task of welding together post-colonial and post-partition states into contemporary nation-states. Consequently, one finds within these two estranged neighbours a multitude of formal and popular geopolitical narratives on how to secure the national self from the threats posed by the 'alien' other. The hegemonizing and homogenizing process of othering, in both its material and discursive manifestations, continues to dictate and drive not only bi-lateral relations between the two neighbours but also the internal majority-minority dynamics, along with the path of mutual mistrust and friction (Chaturvedi, 2002). The spatial scale of states is certainly not the only scale where territorial strategies of ordering, bordering and othering often take place.

The third paper in this issue by Dhananjay Tripathi and Vaishali Raghuvanshi shows how nation-building projects of India and Pakistan continue to generate practices of inclusion and exclusion and are sustained discursively through flagging differences, including those that are religious in nature. Tripathi and Raghuvanshi deconstruct and critically examine the formidable mental borders that exist between India and Pakistan. Their critique of the popular geopolitics of enmity between India and Pakistan, taking examples of school textbooks and cinema, reinforces their contention that "the political existence of the border is not sufficient in itself; for the processes of Othering to have maximum effect a performance of it is required" (Athique, 2008: 477). As believed "national identities have been created after borders are more or less in place" (Agnew, 2018: 83), this is exactly the case of India and Pakistan, and articulated in this article.

Each 'border dispute' has a complex geography and history to it. Also compressed in this term is some kind of entanglement between the legal and geopolitical factors and forces. Any discussion on South Asian borders will remain incomplete without the mention of Afghanistan-Pakistan border. The Durand line, which has a legacy of its own, remains a matter of discord between Afghanistan and Pakistan. The geopolitical security dynamics along this contested border, with special reference to Pakistan's diverse border strategies, have been examined at length in Oztig paper, where she argues that "Pakistan's defensive and offensive border strategies at its Afghan border are closely related to the security dynamics of the region generally and its national security priorities and domestic policies against militant groups particularly". However, borders are also legal entities, and the contribution of Fawad Poya to this special issue skilfully unpacks the legal status of the Durand line in international law. Poya's argument that "mere denial of parties to rebuff a dispute, shall not affect the existence of a dispute", is thought-provoking indeed. This article, well researched and grounded in the discipline of international law, is also an excellent example on the multidisciplinary character of the Border Studies.

The next paper by Jayashree Vivekanandan reiterates the interdisciplinary nature of the Border Studies and shows how regional initiatives, involving both national and local actors, and are directed at preserving specific mountain landscapes, while questioning the existing state-centric discourses and practices of territoriality. Her paper focuses on the Kailash Sacred Landscape Conservation Initiative (KSLCI), involving India, Nepal and China. Established in 2009, this initiative is aimed at conserving an area of shared cultural heritage and rich biodiversity. Vivekanandan illustrates that despite the rhetoric of sustainability there are significant challenges to transboundary approaches to governance including the entanglement between the logic of the market and the logic of sustainability. She raises profound questions about the rights of the people of these border regions over the space that naturally belongs to them.

"Difference in national economic policies, regional resources, and monetary currencies makes borders lucrative zones of exchange and trade, often illicit and clandestine" (Flynn, 1997: 313). "Borders are created and creative spaces" (Brambilla, 2009: 583), and this is so well presented by Ankur Sharma. In his well-researched paper Ankur Sharma, taken a case study of India-Bhutan borders, presented how informal exchange rates exist and how it cannot be controlled. This border economic in this way is different from the form structures established by the states. The last paper by Anubhav Roy is a relevant contribution to post-partition Border Studies aimed at broadening as well as deepening the meaning of borders and boundaries. Roy draws attention to what he describes as 'borderscaping', which includes "imagined and microcosmic borders (including mental) within, and not peripheral to, states". This intriguing concept is based on the assumption that cities, especially post-partition, may not be as borderless as some analysts would like to believe. Roy takes as his case Chittaranjan Park – a sub-urban neighbourhood or colony of New Delhi granted as a ghetto to the Bengalis displaced by the formation of East Pakistan. Roy addresses a very important question in his extremely well-written contribution: "…could a part of city, such as a colony – especially one initially carved out as a mono-ethnic ghetto, such as Chittaranjan Park – also be imagined as a bordered landscape?"

This special issue is the outcome of a two-day international conference organized by the Department of IR, Faculty of Social Sciences of South Asian University (SAU) in partnership with Association for Borderlands Studies (ABS), Borders in Globalisation (BIG) and Maulana Abul Kalam Azad Institute of Asian Studies (MAKAIAS). On behalf of the Department of IR, we would like to thank our partners. We would also like to take this opportunity to sincerely offer our thanks to all those who supported this academic endeavour. It is due to their encouragement and support that we have reached this final juncture of finalizing a special issue on South Asian borders. We are truly beholden to President of SAU, Dr. Kavita Sharma for her visionary support and encouragement for this project. We also offer our sincere thanks to Vice President Prof. Santosh Panda, Vice President Prof. Sasanka Perera, Registrar Dr. A. K. Malik and other members of the administrative staff at the SAU for all their valuable assistance. Needless to say, all this would not have been possible without the help of our truly wonderful colleagues of the IR department and our dear scholars and students of the IR department. We are equally beholden to participants from different parts of the world for adding so much of value to the conference deliberations.

One of the key purposes behind this special issue was to invite further critical reflection and research on South Asian borders. It was undoubtedly most heartening to see such high-quality papers emanating from a very well-attended international conference at SAU, whose motto is 'Knowledge without Borders'. It was not an easy task to short list papers for consideration of publication in the one and only, highly coveted *JBS*, and under the prestigious imprint of Routledge. We eventually decided to give preference to papers with thematic reflections and having a regional focus. We are hopeful that students of Border Studies, the world over, will receive this special issue on South Asian borders with keen interest and provide us with their highly welcome critical feedback.

## Notes

1. Assistant Professor, Department of International Relations, South Asian University, New Delhi. Orcid Id: https://orcid.org/0000-0003-3984-270X
2. Professor, Department of International Relations, South Asian University, New Delhi.

## References

Alggarwal, Ravina (2004) *Beyond Line of Control: Performance and Politics on Disputed Borders of Ladakh, India*. Durham, NC: Duke University Press.

Agnew, John (2018) *Globalization and Sovereignty beyond Territorial Trap*. London: Rowman & Littlefield.

Ahmed, Imtiaz (2012) "Regionalism in South Asia: a Conceptual Note", *Millennial Asia*, 3 (1).

Athique, Adrian M. (2008) "A Line in the Sand: The India–Pakistan Border in the Films of J.P. Dutta", *South Asia: Journal of South Asian Studies*, 31 (3), 472–499.

Banerjee, Paula (1998) "Borders as Unsettled Markers in South Asia: A Case Study of the Sino-Indian border", *International Studies*, 35 (2), 180–191.

Brambilla, Chiara (2009) "Borders: Paradoxical Structures between Essentialization and Creativity", *World Futures*, 65 (8), 582–588.

Brunet-Jailly, Emmanuel (2005) "Theorizing Borders: An Interdisciplinary Perspective", *Geopolitics*, 10 (4), 633–649.

Brunet-Jailly, Emmanuel (2011) "Special Section: Borders, Borderlands, and Theory: An Introduction", *Geopolitics*, 16 (1), 1–6.

Chaturvedi, Sanjay (2002) "Process of Othering in the Case of India and Pakistan", *Tijdschrift Voor Economische En Sociale Geografie*, 93 (2), 149–159.

Chaturvedi, Sanjay (2005) "The Excess of Geopolitics: 'Partition of British India" in Stefano Bianchini, Sanjay Chaturvedi, Rada Ivekovich and Ranabir Samaddar (eds.) *Partitions: Reshaping Minds and States*. London: Routledge: 106–137.

Chaturvedi, Sanjay and Doyle, Timothy (2015) *Climate Terror A Critical Geopolitics of Climate Change*. Houndmills: Palgrave Macmillan.

Chaturvedi, Sanjay and Sakhuja, Vijay (2016) *Climate Change and the Bay of Bengal Evolving Geographies of Fear and Hope*. New Delhi: Pentagon Press.

Deyshappriya, Ravindra N.R (2019), "Examining Poverty Trend in South Asian Countries: Where Is Sri Lanka among Its South Asian Counterparts?" Retrieved August 3, 2019, from South Asia @ LSE https://blogs.lse.ac.uk/southasia/2018/07/31/examining-poverty-trends-in-south-asian-countries-where-is-sri-lanka-among-its-south-asian-counterparts/

Flynn, K. Donna (1997) "Identity, Exchange and the State along the Benin-Nigeria Border", *American Ethnologist*, 24 (2), 311–330.

Ghani, E. (2012). What Will South Asia Look Like in 2025? Retrieved July 10, 2017, from The World Bank: http://blogs.worldbank.org/endpovertyinsouthasia/what-will-south-asia-look-2025.

Government of India. (20016). *Ministry of Home Affairs Annual Report 2015–16*. New Delhi: Ministry of Home Affairs.

Houtum, Henk Van and Naerssen, Ton Van (2002) "Bordering, Ordering and Othering", *Tijdschrift Voor Economische En Sociale Geografie*, 93 (2), 125–136.

Krishna, Sankaran. (1994) "Cartographic Anxiety: Mapping the Body Politic in India", *Alternatives: Global, Local, Political*, 19 (4), 507–521.

Kurian, Nimmi (2014) *India-China Borderlands: Conversations beyond the Centre*. New Delhi: Sage.

Menon, Ritu and Bhasin, Kamla (1998) *Borders and Boundaries: Women in India and Pakistan*. New Delhi: Kali for Women.

Nair, P. (2009). "The Siachen War: Twenty-Five Years On", *Economic and Political Weekly*, 44 (11), 35–40.

Nandy, Ashis. (2005) "The Idea of South Asia: A Personal Note on Post-Bandung Blues", *Inter-Asia Cultural Studies*, 6 (4), 541–545.

Newman, David. (2003) "On Borders and Power: A Theoretical Framework", *Journal of Borderlands Studies*, 18 (1), 13–25.

Passi, Anssi (2011), "A Border Theory: An Unattainable Dream or a Realistic Aim for Border Scholars", in Doirs Wastl-Walter (ed.) *The Ashgate Research Companion to Border Studies*. Surrey: Ashgate Publishing Company: 11–32 .

Samaddar, Ranabir (1999) *The Marginal Nation: Transborder Migration from Bangladesh to West Bengal*. New Delhi: Sage Publications.

Samaddar, Ranabir (2005) "The Undefined Acts of Partition and Dialogue", in Stefano Bianchini, Sanjay Chaturvedi, Rada Ivekovich and Ranabir Samaddar (eds.) *Partitions: Reshaping Minds and States*. London: Routledge: 78–105.

Schendel, William van (2005) *The Bengal Borderland: Beyond State and Nation in South Asia*. London: Anthem Press.

Schendel, William van and Maaker, Erik De (2014). "Asian Borderlands: Introducing Their Permeability, Strategic Uses and Meanings", *Journal of Borderlands Studies*, 29 (1), 3–9.

Tagliacozzo, Eric (2016) "Jagged Landscapes: Conceptulizing Borders and Boundaries in the History of Human Societies", *Journal of Borderlands Studies*, 31 (1), 1–21.

Tripathi, Dhananjay (2015) "Interrogating Linkages between Borders, Regions, and Border Studies", *Journal of Borderlands Studies*, 30 (2), 189–201.

Tripathi, Dhananjay (2019) "Influence of Borders on Bilateral Ties in South Asia: A Study of Contemporary India-Nepal Relations", *International Studies*, 56 (1-2), 186–200.

World Bank (2017) The World Bank in South Asia. Retrieved July 10, 2017, from The World Bank: http://www.worldbank.org/en/region/sar/overview

# Re-engaging the "International": A Social History of the Trans-Himalayan Borderlands

Nimmi Kurian

**ABSTRACT**

The paper critically interrogates a central paradox in India's emerging border discourse. Although a feel-good narrative of rethinking borders as bridges, it has been curiously resistant to step away from the reductionist logic of borders as barriers. The paper argues that this dualism can be traced to conflicting geopolitical and sociological notions of the international that have resulted in a range of contradictions and distortions at the borders. The paper will engage with the puzzle as to why the trans-Himalayan trader, historically the central protagonist has today become a rather forlorn metaphor of a conflicted discourse. It will draw inferences based on field observations in Dharchula, an ancient trading town in northern India located on the trans-Himalayan trading routes with Nepal and China. These offer interesting insights on how state power and regulation as well as new border alignments have affected everyday lives at the borders. The paper concludes by arguing for discursive cross-fertilizations as first steps towards recognizing the borderlands as the agentive sites that they are.

## A Discursive Border is Crossed

At the core of Delhi's "new" reading of the borders stands a liberal vision of borders as bridges. This in turn is part of a longer shift-in-the-making in Indian foreign policy and marks a subregional turn in Indian diplomacy towards the Asian neighborhood (Kurian 2014).[1] These shifts are bringing interesting methodological and conceptual insights that nudge a rethinking of the border region not as a passive location but as an actor with agency. The idea of subregionalism has gained increasing recognition in discourses of development and offers new insights to mainstream theories of regionalism. Subregional cooperation represents a novel extension of this larger idea, in that the unit of cooperation becomes the geographically proximate subregions within two or more countries as important sites of transnational cooperation.[2] While regional trading blocs and arrangements have been a common phenomenon, both the bilateral and the regional levels have tended to bypass the subregional level with its local governance particularities and stakeholders (Kurian 2016).

The paper identifies biases in the construction of borders in Indian IR and argues that the manner in which scholarship frames many of these questions has reduced the borderlands to virtually becoming research peripheries (Kurian 2010). Far from offering alternative imaginaries, IR has largely tended to faithfully mirror the "cartographic anxiety" of the state (Krishna 1994). The mainstream discourse has been structured to peripheralize these spaces and from this conceptual peg it has been but a small leap to micro managing and the parachuting problem solving models from a distant center. A privileging of the formal and intergovernmental scales coupled with a capital-centric notion of space has also left it virtually incapable of acknowledging the quotidian dynamism that characterizes the borderlands. It is this shortcoming that renders it intellectually inept at understanding how human geographies have reconstituted social and symbolic practice, transforming borderlands into multiple sites of interactions. Such linear narratives effectively rob the border of its rich and varied cultural, historical and social layers of identity. The geoeconomic and the geopolitical narratives have by and large tended to engage each other parenthetically, often with wary resignation. It is this tension at the heart of India's subregional imaginary that the paper attempts to push and foreground.

A focus only on the formal is clearly inadequate for understanding the drivers of cross-border functional and institutional interdependence (Sohn, Reitel, and Walther 2009; Brunet-Jailly 2010; Blatter 2003; Perkmann and Sum 2000) Without connecting with the lives of the people who inhabit these physical spaces, Indian IR's theoretical agendas will remain both unimaginative and irrelevant. If IR is to make itself relevant to borderlands, disciplinary IR will in turn need to find a viable interface with new discourses that are engaging with the international in imaginative ways, bringing fresh insights into its domain be it critical geopolitics (Ó Tuathail 2000; Ó Tuathail and Dalby 1998) cultural geography (Jackson 1989; Mitchell 2000) political geography (Taylor 1994; Johnston 2001). The field of border research has also covered much ground over the decades, with itinerant inquiries stepping away from the reductionist logic of conceiving borders as territorial dividers and bringing with it a whole new lexicon of approaching these spaces as dynamic and socially constructed (Kurian 2014). Dissident writings that seriously interrogate spatial and territorial assumptions (Ashley and Walker 1990; Weldes et al. 1999; Booth 2005; Appadurai 2006; Varadarajan 2010; Jones 2011; Bilgin 2012) now overlap with inquiries in political geography, border studies, and ethnic theory on the state, identity and difference (Middleton 2013). Many of these cross-disciplinary insights can help to problematize disciplinary IR's "fixed representation of territorial or structural space" and underline the spatial and socially constructed nature of borders (Agnew 1994, 55). These will in turn allow Indian IR to engage with themes of identity, culture and the like which have been relegated to its disciplinary borders. Doing so could also help it effectively address the charge of ahistoricism and also help find ways to make "past history continuous with present experience".[3] By doing so, it can also fundamentally redefine scale as a category of practice, as Brubaker and Cooper argue, define it as "categories of everyday experience, developed and deployed by ordinary social actors" as against "experience-distant categories used by social scientists" (Brubaker and Cooper 2000, 4).

Privileging only formal intergovernmental processes has also resulted in a highly distorted and partial understanding of the quotidian dynamism of the borderlands. The underlying power shifts and assumptions that such a cross-border remapping entails also remain subsumed in mainstream visions. These remappings are no impartial imaginaries and it will be pertinent to invoke William Callahan's warning that these could well result in "a new set of borders-which would have a different logic of exclusion and inclusion, creating new centres and peripheries- rather than a borderless region" (Kurian 2014). IR as a discipline is likely to increasingly struggle with the contradictions of maintaining its analytical focus on relations between territorially bound sovereign states as it faces up to the overwhelming reality of social, economic and cultural flows that bear declining relevance to territory. Far from offering alternative imaginaries, mainstream IR has tended to faithfully mirrored the "cartographic anxiety" of the state. IR scholarship has often taken the cue from statist frames, disinterested in the everyday struggles and contestations of the borderlanders, preferring instead esoteric systemic battles. A politico-military reading of border landscapes is conspicuous by what it leaves out of its research remit; that there is also an anthropology, a history and a sociology of borders to negotiate (Lynch 1999). By presupposing the irrelevance of sub-systemic actors to state behavior, mainstream IR theory tends to flatten out differences and effectively block voices and representations from the margins.

## Suboptimal Subregionalism

These dichotomies represent a classic instance of suboptimal subregionalism at work, a discourse with neither the capacity nor the incentive to operationalize what is a potential foreign policy innovation (Kurian 2015). These dichotomies have also made for a highly confused narrative rendering its political signaling contradictory and virtually unintelligible. For instance, while Prime Minister Modi's Neighborhood First policy appeared to set the right tone with high-profile visits to South Asian capitals,[4] the then Chief Economic Advisor Arvind Subramanian publicly argued that "regional economic integration in South Asia is not a first priority for India" (*The Hindu*, 2015). This double-speak constitutes a classic instance of the paradoxes at the heart of India's border discourse as well as explains the range of contradictions and distortions that one sees in India's borderlands. While India's Act East policy ostensibly builds a narrative of rethinking borders as bridges, there has been an almost pathological fear of open borders. For instance, India's border fencing project is a stark metaphor of this conflicted discourse. The trade-off between border mobility and border security being struck has often strengthened the security state while eroding human security. A case in point is the fencing of a 10-km long stretch on the India-Myanmar border at the border town of Moreh, Manipur in India's Northeast. Meant to ostensibly prevent militants from using the road to procure arms from international gunrunners, the fence has today resulted in a grave livelihood crisis and drastically disrupted the lives of villages situated along the border. After the construction of the fence, the border village of Muslim Basti today finds itself without any access to freshwater with the Lairok and Khujariok rivers now falling across the international border in Myanmar. Similarly, among the changes that India's border wars with China in 1962 and with Pakistan in 1965 brought were a series of land use changes that came into effect almost immediately. In Garhwal Himalayas, following the war with China, 10% of all forest land was acquired by the government for defence purposes (Rangan 1996). These were further compounded by India's Fourth Five Year Plan of 1969–1973 that effectively granted the State Forest Department rights over all forest and open lands owned by states (Rangan 1996). The most deleterious of these changes was the abrupt ending of border trade with Tibet, the mainstay of border communities without any viable alternatives to fall back on.

The effects of these dualisms can also be seen in the low intra-regional trade levels in South Asia when compared to East Asia. As per a recent study, South Asia's intra-regional trade, one of the lowest in the world, accounted for a mere 5% of the region's total trade compared to 50% for East Asia and the Pacific. (*Asia Times* 2018) India's trade with South Asia makes for only 3% of its global trade. While India's trade with the world accounts for $637 billion, its trade with South Asia makes for only $19.1 billion (Press Information Bureau 2018). An Indian exporter to Bangladesh has to reportedly obtain as many as 330 signatures on 17 documents at various stages, which includes cumbersome procedural requirements (De and Ghosh 2008).[5] It is not surprising then that the reopening of traditional border markets or *haats* along the India-Bangladesh border after a gap of 40 years in 2011 has today ended up becoming an exercise in choreographed trade (Kurian 2016). Barter trade has been tightly regulated with a pre-selected list of vendors and vendees carrying out trade in a pre-selected list of goods and operating within a pre-demarcated radius of 5 kms on either side of the border. The discretionary powers wielded by agents of state have also sharpened several of these dichotomies at the borders. These agents of state or "petty sovereigns," as Judith Butler calls them, wield enormous discretionary powers, "performing their acts unilaterally and with enormous consequence" (Butler 2004, 65). The role of "lineman" or facilitators who enable illegal border crossings is a highly institutionalized one, with the willing connivance of border guards (Carney, Miklian, and Hoelscher 2011). An illustrative example of this is the well-coordinated chain of financiers, traders, middlemen and the couriers involved in cattle smuggling across the India-Bangladesh border with an estimated annual turnover of Rs. 5000 crore.

What is also problematic about India's border discourse is that it remains an economic narrative without any meaningful engagement with social history. The teleological reading of the Himalayas as a self-contained bounded territorial space is a case in point. Powerful but misleading metaphors such as "natural frontier," "barrier," and "bulwark" end up flattening a highly complex, mobile, ethno-cultural landscape and undermine the role that the Himalayan borderlands have historically played as a territorial interface. What is ironic is that while the discourse celebrates the idea of borders as bridges, it all but neglects the protagonist, the pastoral Bhotias who played an important "bridge and buffer" role between Tibet, northern India, and Nepal. This absence has, however, neither been voluntary nor anticipated but instead can be traced to fundamental flaws in India's subregional discourse with its bias toward state-led formal institution building. Many of the old trading passes today remain in disuse with governments disinterested in restoring connectivity that could spur trade.[6] Lack of efficiency of border corridors has been another factor hindering competitiveness and trade expansion. The trade office at Gunji, a border village in Uttarakhand, a Himalayan state in northern India lacks even the most basic amenities such as drinking water, accommodation and warehouses. The lack of a currency exchange facilities also has meant that Indian traders end up paying more to buy yuan at Taklakot in Tibet. An erstwhile trader, Pradyuman Garbiyal whose family had a shop in Tibet in Tukhar and Taklakot *Mandis* (market) till 1962, noted how the odds were today stacked against the trans-Himalayan trader due to the steep transportation costs. He noted that mule carriage costs had now exorbitantly risen to

Rs 4000 per quintal making it highly unprofitable for most traders (Personal interview, August 29, 2015). Multiple handling and paper work have led to higher transaction costs, compounded by moves towards centralization. For instance, trade permits are no longer issued in Dharchula but are instead sent to Dehradun, the state capital, entailing a delay of several weeks (Personal interview, August 29, 2015).

Far from being marginal, the trans-Himalayan trader was in fact the central protagonist, as a reading of the social and economic history of the trans-Himalayan borderlands reveals. Interestingly, the transborder trader was not necessarily the quintessential big merchant; rather it was often the petty trader who played a big role in border economies and in the subregion. It was as Janet Rizvi notes "an economy made self-sufficient" due to the "enormous input of time and effort" by these peasant-traders (Rizvi 1985, 14–15). An illustrative example of this is the crucial linking role that Ladakh's "peasant-traders" played in creating webs of interdependence within the region. These peasant-traders bartered grain from their fields to the Chang-pa nomads of southeast Ladakh and western Tibet to exchange for *pashm*, wool and salt.[7] The trader performed important intermediary roles as well. For instance, the Lhasa Newars, influential expatriate traders from Kathmandu with historic trade links with Tibet, forged important links with South and Central Asia.[8] High-value commercial relationships controlled and managed by powerful merchant groups co-existed with the more subsistence-based barter trade in essential commodities traded by border villages on either side. For instance, a 92-year old small-time trader from Munsiari in Uttarakhand, who was a regular on the Indo-Tibetan trade route, recounted that he would often use the wool for his personal use to make woolen blankets or quilts called *chutkas* and *thulmas* (Personal Interview, Dharchula, August 30, 2015). In sharp contrast, Moti Ram Kharakhwal, a very influential big trader procured wool from Tibet and supplied it to big Indian companies Lal Imli, Raymonds and Dhariwals who in turn sold it in European markets (Personal interview, Dharchula, August 30, 2015).

## "Interrelated Territorialities"

Transnational social networks based on ancestral and kinship ties and interpersonal trust networks constitute a form of social capital that was integral to a transborder subregion, resting on a highly place-centric sense of self and community identity (Tilly 2007; Chen 2000). These also served a crucial economic function by helping to reduce transaction costs given the arduous challenges involved in conducting long-distance trans-Himalayan trade. For instance, the Dolpos, who traded rock salt from Tibet to the lower parts of Nepal maintained *netsang* ("nesting place") relationships with their Tibetan counterparts. Trade ties were underwritten by trust-based agreement such as *gamgya and netsang*. Such personalized trust-based contracts, which included preferential terms of barter, food and shelter, were so durable that they often lasted for several generations being passed on from trader to the next of kin.

A distinctive aspect of trans-Himalayan trade flows was that these were neither based on territorial assumptions nor did they emerge from a political center. These typically operated at multiple scales accommodating subsistence, localized trade with the wider globalized networks with consummate ease. This arrangement of trans-Himalayan trade serves as a fine example of juxtaposing as Wim van Spengen notes the "localised imperatives for subsistence" with "the wider economic network of exchange of surplus good between regions … " (Spengen 2013). Social histories underline the intrinsic synergies between the formal and the informal domains. For instance, inter-state trade relations relied on obligatory transport labor for success. Obligatory transport labor was an integral part of hill societies in Ladakh, Tibet and Kashmir, which included *inter alia* carriage of goods for officials and other important figures. For instance, there was an inter-state agreement between Ladakh and Tibet to provide transport labor to assist trade missions during their travels to each other's territories (Bray and Gongkatsang 2009, 43). Transport labor was fundamental to the effectiveness of trade networks that crisscrossed the region between Kashmir, Tibet and Central Asia. In fact, the key export item of central and western Ladakh was the labor of its porters. The obligatory transport arrangements between Ladakh and Tibet were crucial in ensuring the success and profitability of missions and their commercial functions such as the triennial *lo-phyag* mission (Lopchak) from Leh to Lhasa and the Cha-pa (Chaba) from Lhasa to Leh (Bray and Gongkatsang 2009, 47). At the village fairs of Gartok in Tibet and Patseo in the Indian montane state of Himachal Pradesh, for instance, nomadic herders exchanged wool, meat, and dairy produce for food grains and other commodities (Arora 2007). In these exchanges, the figure of the nomad was a significant one, providing a crucial linkage function bringing "peripheral civilizations to come into contact with one another. Like a chemical solution, the nomads allowed 'reactions' to take place, but were not themselves the main agents" (Cosmo 1999, 3). The pastoral nomad brought "peripheral civilizations to come into contact with one another" (Cosmo 1999, 3). Good relations with the pastoralist communities often was critical for the Silk Road since caravans bearing riches needed access to safe passage through the steppes. The Silk Roads also connected South Asia's agrarian worlds with Inner Eurasia's pastoral steppes Elaborate (Christian 2000).

Today, economic forces are in fact building on the very same complex histories of transnational social and cultural exchanges that have operated above and below the national level. As Darryl Crawford notes in this context that "social relationships have always been transnational in nature, but today their economic activities have come to match the transnationalism of their social connections and now constitute a series of coordinated socioeconomic networks" (Crawford 2000, 80). Rich narratives can be pieced together from a multiplicity of sources, not all of which come to us in the written form. There were for instance iconographic accounts that itinerant traders, pilgrims and monks carried in their heads and relayed orally to enrich a common knowledge base. We know for instance of the religious, cultural, and economic links Bhutan had with Cooch Bihar and Kamrup (Assam) during the 17th-19th centuries. Though Bhutan followed a policy of isolation towards much of the world during this period, historical accounts point to unbroken exchanges with its immediate neighbors. Hajo in Assam emerged as a pilgrimage hub for Tibetans in the late seventeenth to early eighteenth centuries, its popularity was aided no less by the ease of access via the oldest and only road then connecting India and Tibet, subverting the Monyul corridor east of Bhutan and directly through Bumthang and Devangiri (Huber 2008). Commercial trade was often woven around quasi-religious missions, motivating long-distance trade between Tibet and Ladakh. The Treaty of Tingmosgang of 1684, signed between Ladakh and Tibet, established the Lopchak, a biannual mission to offer tribute to the Dalai Lama as well as the Chaba, with annual caravan trade from Leh to Lhasa (Bray and Gongkatsang 2009).

The trade in silk brocades from Benaras to Leh commanded a religious value in monasteries reflected in the Dalai Lama's reference to it as the "fabric of our religion" (Ahmed 2002). Though trade marts and fairs were initially associated with religious and spiritual activity, Tibet's "theoretical openness to all trade and traders, irrespective of their provenance" transformed them into commercial gatherings (Spengen 2013). Trade marts were important centers of business in the trans-Himalayas with Gartok in western Tibet and Leh in Ladakh being the most prominent sites. These markets were situated on the trade routes to Tibet, Yarkand, Kashmir, and Central Asia in the north and the Indian plains to the south. The annual fair at Gartok in western Tibet brought traders from Ladakh, Kashmir, Tartary, Yarkhand, central Tibet and China.

## Re-engaging the "International"

While this is not an attempt to read back into history a larger-than-life role for the border actor, it is a cue to recall that the trans-Himalayan trader contributed in no small measure to dynamic processes of subregional integration from below. If engaged well, India's subregional discourse can creatively draw upon the rich form of social capital that the transborder trader represents. Shining a light on the agency that border sites and actors wielded in shaping the course of inter-Asian interactions, can also help fill a critical gap in India's subregional imaginary. It can also be a serendipitous moment to understand how quotidian processes can contribute to a bottom-up vision of India's subregional narrative by problematizing the Westphalian idea in imaginative ways. These flows also provide a much-needed caveat to the dangers of totalizing narratives and alert us to be mindful of recognizing the historical agency of the actors other than the state. Historically, there were limits to the sovereign control that the state could achieve over the frontiers and it often had to acknowledge and accommodate actors whose compliance was often valuable for the imperial state to its political agenda at the frontiers. These formed a honeycomb of institutional actors comprising merchants, officials, lamas and rulers that represented a powerful collusion of economic and political power (Giersch 2010, 218).

Historicizing the notions of the international can fundamentally call into question the trope of a domestic-external binary. Such an a priori assumption only "exaggerates the differences between the two realms" and "obscures the theoretically relevant similarities" (Whytock 2004, 27–8). The preoccupation with systemic battles has meant that IR often has little, or at any rate, little useful to say about micro-governance challenges at the borders. By doing so IR forsakes, almost unthinkingly, how quotidian IR engages with and fashions norms of territoriality. Reminding ourselves of these cultural crossings assumes greater relevance and can be useful counter-currents to much of mainstream scholarship on the region that remain hived into the cubbyholes of area studies. Asian histories, as Sanjay Subrahmanyam reminds us, are essentially "connected histories" and the tendency to compartmentalize regions to absurd levels are props for the "intellectually slothful," who accept them as givens and caricaturise these as closed systems (Subrahmanyam 1997, 742). These networks and flows also remind us that "it would be a mistake to assume that only the elite is capable of cosmopolitan practice" (Kahn cited in Harper and Amrith 2012, 257).

A critical re-engagement with the notion of the international has to be the first step to realize the potential of the subregional turn in Indian IR. This can help situate India's international relations within a larger historical template of social, economic and cultural flows that had little if any relevance to territory. Subregionalism defined as process (and not as project) can help situate Indian IR within a larger historical template of social, economic and cultural flows that had little if any relevance to territory. Across the fixed line, human geographies have reconstituted social and symbolic practice, transforming landscapes into multiple sites of interaction. Border ethnographies seldom obey easy categorization and border-spanning networks reveal the paucity of "methodological territorialism," in that it tries to trap complex social phenomena within territorial containers (Schendel 2005). These reconstructions by "nations from below" offer contraworldviews to the state on territoriality, history and sovereignty, taking their cue from ethnic boundaries as against state-drawn political boundaries.[9] The social reality of the borderlands also means that identity and citizenship defy easy categorization and get constantly transformed almost on a daily basis. The consonance of this shared social reality results in a consequent dissonance with their respective state strategies. It is this that transforms the border into a site of contestations and mires it in the binaries of illicit versus licit and the formal versus informal labels (Schendel and Abraham 2005). Lowering the research and policy gaze can throw up interesting instances of a growing bottom-up engagement by India's border states with its subregional neighborhood. These constitute subterranean subregionalism(s), a form of integration that mainstream research and policy has so far chosen to ignore. There are three reasons why research and policy needs to engage with these quotidian processes. Firstly, there is growing evidence that border regions are beginning to effectively engage the Indian state to deepen subregional integration processes.[10] Secondly, they are on occasion bypassing the state and directly forging cross-border issue-based linkages.[11] Thirdly, these processes have the capacity to socialize national policy makers towards a decentered approach to problem solving and thereby build subregional governance capacity.[12] These counter-narratives reinforce the reality that there is a multiplicity of ways a border can be read and imagined.

Paradoxically, for borderlanders the border is both an invisible as well as an integral aspect of their social existence. Its invisibility stems from the fact that much of the transactions not "authorised" by the state take place anyway, despite it (Kurian 2014). In a typically transnational frame, the border becomes not quite the "margin" but the center of a vast and bustling network of social and cultural flows. It is this traffic that is so vital to and an integral part of the everyday existence of border communities and which operate despite the exclusionary nature of territorial mapping. The border, while being "ubiquitous" in the consciousness of borderlanders through ties of trade, commerce and matrimony, no longer remains "an institution of exclusion" for them (Scott 2008). The politico-military understanding of borders as being mere geographical markers thus masks the enormous complexity that a border region encompasses. When the state seeks to "close" its borders through formal measures, informal processes go on to "open" the same border. While the logic of the former seeks to exclude, the latter is premised on a mutually constitutive relationship that spans the very same markers. There is a constant "manipulation of legal boundaries" by people on both sides who move "back and forth" and subvert procedures to their benefit (Cusick 2000, 48). Through such "open defiance of state border control" the border is thus "overcome" in visible and telling ways (Ghosh 2011, 54). Such processes also point to what Eilenberg and Wadley refer to as "interrelated territorialities," underwritten by a highly complex ethno-geographical mapping of resources and places (Eilenberg and Wadley 2009, 60). There is a distinctive perception of the border as being "natural" with residents of Dharchula on the Indian side and Darchula on the Nepal side of the border referring to bonds of *"roti, beti ka nata"* (Personal interviews, Dharchula and Darchula, 28 August 2015).

The paper has argued that a privileging of the formal and intergovernmental scales coupled with a capital-centric notion of space has left India's subregional narrative virtually incapable of acknowledging the quotidian dynamism that characterizes the borderlands. It is this shortcoming that renders it intellectually inept at dealing with nascent subregional policy networks with its own distinctive local governance particularities and set of stakeholders. Subregional policy networks can play the role of bridge-builders in transborder governance and their innate capacity to jump scales and blur traditional jurisdictional boundaries needs to be acknowledged. Mainstream research and policy also needs to systematize the diversity of this growing regional engagement by border regions in terms of its nature (formal or informal); activities (social, economic, cultural, political); duration (sustained or episodic) and actors (public or private). If it is willing to do so, the subregional turn in India's foreign policy can bring a long-overdue attention to the borderlands both as a missing level of analysis as well as a governance actor in its own right besides nudging Indian IR towards innovative intellectual pathways. Thus, at the very least, India's evolving border imaginary has to self-consciously be an eclectic imaginary that attempts an interface between the geopolitical and sociological notions of the international. Such discursive cross-fertilizations should be the first step towards recognizing the borderlands as the agentive sites that they are. But if it chooses to remain coy about this fundamental linkage, India's research and policy engagement with its borderlands at multiple levels- cognitive, territorial and disciplinary is likely to remain both cosmetic and unimaginative.

## Notes

1. For instance, there is a strong emphasis on positioning Northeast India as a gateway to the wider dynamic Asian neighbourhood. Sub-regional initiatives like the BIMSTEC (Bay of Bengal Multi-Sectoral Initiative for Technical and Economic Cooperation), the Mekong Ganga Economic Cooperation (MGC), and the BCIM Forum (Bangladesh China India Myanmar) formed in 1999 aim at integrating the entire eastern region of India with the fast growing economies of Southeast Asia and beyond.
2. Several growth triangles or quadrangles are already in operation in Asia, namely the Singapore-southern Johore-Batam Island, Greater Mekong Subregion, the Southern China Growth Triangle and the Yellow Sea Economic Zone.
3. This was the mandate the British Committee of the theory of international politics set for itself back in 1959 (Vigezzi 2005, 53).
4. As part of the Neighbourhood First policy, India's Prime Minister visited Bhutan, Nepal, Myanmar and Nepal in 2014 and Mauritius, Sri Lanka, China, Bangladesh, Afghanistan and Pakistan in 2015.
5. This at a time when the neighbouring Greater Mekong Subregion (GMS) has been moving towards a single-window clearance system. The GMS Cross-Border Transport Agreement (CBTA) adopted in the late 1990s, covers all trade transit facilitation measures within the region in a single document. These include single-stop, single-window customs inspection, visa regimes, eligibility criteria for cross-border traffic, exchange of commercial traffic rights and standardisation of road and bridge design, signs and signals (Srivastava and Kumar 2012).

SOUTH ASIA                                                                         19

6.  For instance, the Shipki La pass, which opened for border barter trade and trade on convertible currency basis in 1994 has seen woefully meagre levels of trade. The only motorable road on the Indian side is at Namgia Dogri in Himachal Pradesh, which is 14 kms from the border. This has meant that only the most intrepid of traders will make the trudge with goods carried on mule back (Dogra 2005).
7.  Ladakh was till 1947 a major hub of a trade network that included Skardu, Srinagar, Hoshiarpur, Kulu and radiated outward to Lhasa and Yarkand. Leh and Kargil traders would travel to the September market at Gartok in western Tibet to sell coral and gold from Yarkand for the Lhasa nobility (Rizvi 1985, 14).
8.  The control that valley merchants wielded over the two-way caravan trade with Tibet was also a lucrative source of tax revenue for the Newar kings (Lewis 2011).
9.  For instance, the collective imaginations of the Zos, the greater Naga homeland or the Tai-Ahoms conceptualises the nation as including those whom the state excludes (Roy 2005, 8).
10. The effects of this lobbying can be seen in India's decision to open 70 border haats along its border with Bangladesh, with 35 along the border with West Bengal; 22 at the Meghalaya border; five in Tripura and four in Assam (Chakrabarty 2015).
11. What is likely to be bookmarked as one of the first instances of subregional problem solving is the Palatana thermal power project. Given the challenges in transporting heavy equipment to Tripura due to the difficult terrain, Bangladesh allowed transhipment of heavy turbines and machinery through its territory. Bangladesh's decision to allow transhipment became a critical factor in the successful completion of the project (Kurian 2016).
12. The key organising principle here is that of subsidiarity, the idea that each issue or task is performed most effectively at the local or immediate level. There are successful international instances of local substate actors exercising effective functional autonomy with the role of central authority being a subsidiary one (Kurian 2017).

## Acknowledgements

The author wishes to gratefully acknowledge the financial support received from the India China Institute, The New School, New York for the fieldwork conducted in India and Nepal.

## Disclosure Statement

No potential conflict of interest was reported by the author.

## References

Agnew, John. 1994. The Territorial Trap: The Geographical Assumptions in International Relations Theory'. *Review of International Political Economy* 1, no. 1: 53–80.

Ahmed, Monisha. 2002. From Benaras to Leh – The Trade and Use of Silk-Brocade. *Textile Society of America Symposium Proceedings*, 498. http://digitalcommons.unl.edu/tsaconf/498.

Appadurai, Arjun. 2006. *Fear of Small Numbers: An Essay on the Geography of Anger*. Durham, NC: Duke University Press.

Arora, Anil. 2007. *International Trade: Theories and Current Trends in the Globalised World*. New Delhi: Deep and Deep Publication.

Ashley, Richard, and R.B.J. Walker. 1990. Introduction – Speaking the Language of Exile Dissident Thought in International Relations. *International Studies Quarterly* XXXIV, no. 3: 259–68.

Bilgin, Pinar. 2012. The Continuing Appeal of Critical Security Studies. In *Critical Theory in International Relations and Security Studies: Interviews and Reflections*, ed. Shannon Brincat, Shannon Lima, and Joao Nunes, 159–72. Abingdon: Routledge.

Blatter, Joachim. 2003. Beyond Hierarchies and Networks: Institutional Logics and Change in Trans-boundary Political Spaces During the 20th Century. *Governance* 16, no. 4: 503–26.

Booth, Ken, ed. 2005. *Critical Security Studies and World Politics*. Boulder, CO: Lynne Rienner Publishers.

Bray, John, and Tsering D. Gongkatsang. 2009. Three 19th Century Documents from Tibet and the Lo Phyag Mission from Leh to Lhasa. In *Mountains, Monasteries and Mosques. Recent Research on Ladakh and the Western Himalaya*, Supplement No. 2 to Rivista degli Studi Orientali 80 (New Series), ed. John Bray and Elena De Rossi Filibeck. Pisa: Sapienza, Università di Roma, Dipartimento di Studi Orientali.

Brubaker, R., and F. Cooper. 2000. Beyond 'Identity'. *Theory and Society* 29: 1–47.

Brunet-Jailly, Emmanuel. 2010. The State of Borders and Borderlands Studies in 2009: A Historical View and a View from the Journal of Borderlands Studies. *Eurasian Border Review* 1 (Spring), no. 1: 1–16.

Butler, J. 2004. *Precarious Life: The Powers of Mourning and Violence*. London: Verso.

Carney, Scott, Jason Miklian, and Kristian Hoelscher. 2011. Fortress India. *Foreign Policy*, July–August.

Chakrabarty, Arpita. 2015. Indo-China Border Trade Yet to Kick Off in Dharchula. *Times of India*, June 7.

Chen, X. 2000. Both Glue and Lubricant: Transnational Ethnic Social Capital as a Source of Asia-Pacific Subregionalism. *Policy Sciences* 33: 269–87.

Christian, D. 2000. Silk Roads or Steppe Roads? The Silk Roads in World History. *Journal of World History* 11, no. 1: 1–26.

Cosmo, N.D. 1999. State Formation and Periodization in Inner Asian History. *Journal of World History* 10, no. 1: 1–40.

Crawford, Darryl. 2000. Chinese Capitalism: Cultures, the Southeast Asian Region and Economic Globalisation. *Third World Quarterly* 21, no. 1: 69–86.

Cusick, J.G. 2000. Creolisation and the Borderlands. *Historical Archaeology* 34, no. 3: 46–55.

De, Prabir, and Buddhadeb Ghosh. 2008. Reassessing Transaction Costs of Trade at the India-Bangladesh Border. *Economic and Political Weekly* 43, no. 29: 69–79.

Dogra, Chander Suta. 2005. Barter on the Mount. *Outlook*, 28 February. https://www.outlookindia.com/magazine/story/barter-on-the-mount/226616.

Eilenberg, Michael, and R.L. Wadley. 2009. Borderland Livelihood Strategies: The Socio-economic Significance of Ethnicity in Cross-Border Labour Migration, West Kalimantan, Indonesia. *Asia Pacific Viewpoint* 50, no. 1: 58–73.

Ghosh, S. 2011. Cross-border Activities in Everyday Life: The Bengal Borderlan. *Contemporary South Asia* 19, no. 1: 49–60.

Giersch, C.P. 2010. Across Zomia with Merchants, Monks, and Musk: Process Geographies, Trade Networks, and the Inner-East–Southeast Asian Borderlands. *Journal of Global History* 5: 215–39.

Harper, T., and S.S. Amrith. 2012. Sites of Asian Interaction: An Introduction. *Modern Asian Studies* 46: 249–57.

Huber, T. 2008. *The Holy Land Reborn: Pilgrimage and the Tibetan Reinvention of Buddhist India*. Chicago, IL: University of Chicago Press.

Jackson, P. 1989. *Maps of Meaning: An Introduction to Cultural Geography*. London: Unwin Hyman.

Johnston, R. 2001. Out of the 'Moribund Backwater': Territory and Territoriality in Political Geography. *Political Geography* 20, no. 6: 677–93.

Jones, Reece. 2011. Dreaming of a Golden Bengal: Discontinuities of Place and Identity in South Asia. *Asian Studies Review* XXXV: 373–95.

Krishna, Sankaran. 1994. Cartographic Anxiety: Mapping the Body Politic in India. *Alternatives: Global, Local, Political* 19, no. 4: 507–21.

Kurian, Nimmi. 2010. Transnational Neighbourhoods, Subnational Futures: Reimagining North East India. In *Shaping India's Foreign Policy: People, Politics and Places*, ed. Amitabh Matoo, and Happymon Jacob, 235–54. New Delhi: Har Anand.

Kurian, Nimmi. 2014. *India China Borderlands: Conversations Beyond the Centre*. Atlanta, GA: Sage.

Kurian, Nimmi. 2015. *Indian IR's Subregional Moment: Between a Rock and a Hard Place?* CPR Policy Brief, November.

Kurian, Nimmi. 2016. Subregionalising IR: Bringing the Borderlands Back In. In *India and China: Rethinking Borders and Security*, ed. L.H.M. Ling, Adriana Erthal Abdenur, Payal Banerjee, Nimmi Kurian, Mahendra P. Lama, and Li Bo, 60–79. Ann Arbor: Michigan University Press.

Kurian, Nimmi. 2017. The Peripheral Protagonist: The Curious Case of the Missing Trans-Himalayan Trader. CPR Policy Brief, March.

Lewis, Todd T. 2011. Buddhism, Himalayan Trade and Newar Merchants. http://buddhim.20 m. com/8-4.htm/.

Lynch, Kathleen. 1999. Equality Studies, the Academy and the Role of Research in Emancipatory Social Change. *The Economic and Social Review* 30, no. 1: 41–69.

Middleton, Townsend. 2013. States of Difference: Refiguring Ethnicity and Its 'Crisis' at India's Borders. *Political Geography* XXXV: 14–24.

Mitchell, Don. 2000. *Cultural Geography – A Critical Introduction*. Malden, MA: Blackwell.

Ó Tuathail, Gearóid. 2000. Borderless Worlds? Problematizing Discourses of Deterritorialization. *Geopolitics* 4, no. 2: 139–54.

Ó Tuathail, G., and S. Dalby. 1998. *Rethinking Geopolitics*. London: Routledge.

Perkmann, M., and N.L. Sum. 2000. *Globalization, Regionalization and Cross-border Regions: Scales, Discourses and Governance*. London: Palgrave Macmillan.

Press Information Bureau. 2018. Intra-regional Trade Potential of South Asia Needs to be Tapped: Suresh Prabhu. September 28. http://pib.nic.in/newsite/PrintRelease.aspx?relid=183802.

Rangan, H. 1996. From Chipko to Uttaranchal: Development, Environment and Social Protest in the Garhwal Himalayas, India. In *Liberation Ecologies: Environment, Development, Social Movements*, ed. R. Peet, and M.J. Watts. London: Routledge.

Rizvi, Janet. 1985. Peasant-Traders of Ladakh: A Study in Oral History. *India International Centre Quarterly* 12, no. 1: 13–27.

Roy, Sanjay K. 2005. Conflicting Nations in North-East India. *Economic and Political Weekly* 40, no. 21: 2176–82.

Schendel, W.V. 2005. *The Bengal Borderland: Beyond State and Nation in South Asia*. London: Anthem Press.

Schendel, W., and I. Abraham, eds. 2005. *Illicit Flows and Criminal Things: States, Borders, and the Other Side of Globalisation*. Bloomington: Indiana University Press.

Scott, James. 2008. *The Art of Being Not Governed: An Anarchist History of Upland Southeast Asia*. New Haven, CT: Yale University Press.

Sohn, Christophe, Bernard Reitel, and Olivier Walther. 2009. Cross-border Metropolitan Integration in Europe: The Case of Luxembourg, Basel, and Geneva. *Environment and Planning C: Government and Policy* 27, no. 5: 922–39.

Spengen, Wim van. 2013. The Geo-History of Long-Distance Trade in Tibet 1850-1950. In *The Tibetan History Reader*, ed. Gray Tuttle, and Kurtis R. Schaeffer, 491–522. New York: Columbia University Press.

Srivastava, Pradeep, and Kumar Utsav. 2012. *Trade and Trade Facilitation in the Greater Mekong Subregion*. Mandaluyong: Asian Development Bank.

Subrahmanyam, S. 1997. Connected Histories: Notes Towards a Reconfiguration of Early Modern Eurasia. *Modern Asian Studies* 31, no. 3: 735–62. Special Issue: The Eurasian Context of the Early Modern History of Mainland South East Asia, 1400–1800. July.

Taylor, Peter J. 1994. The State as Container: Territoriality in the Modern World-system. *Progress in Human Geography* 18, no. 2: 151–62.

Tilly, Charles. 2007. History of and in Sociology. *The American Sociologist* 38, no. 4: 326–9.

Varadarajan, Latha. 2010. Reimagined Nations and Restructured States: Explaining the Domestic Abroad. In *The Domestic Abroad: Diasporas in International Relations*, ed. Latha Varadarajan, 22–50. New York: Oxford University Press.

Vigezzi, Brunello. 2005. *The British Committee on the Theory of International Politics (1954-1985): The Rediscovery of History*. Trans. Ian Harvey. Milan: Edizioni Unicopli.

Weldes, Jutta, Mark Laffey, Hugh Gusterson, and Raymond Duvall. 1999. *Cultures of Insecurity: States, Communities and the Production of Danger*. Minneapolis: University of Minnesota Press.

Whytock, C.A. 2004. Thinking Beyond the Domestic-International Divide: Toward a Unified Concept of Public Law. *Georgetown Journal of International Law* 36, no. 1 (Fall): 155–93.

# Borders and Bordering Practices: A Case Study of Jaisalmer District on India–Pakistan Border

Krishnendra Meena

**ABSTRACT**
Borders facilitate interactions of various kinds. The nature of these interactions can be friendly or outright hostile. The adjacent states employ bordering practices commensurate to the relationship they have. In a scenario where the relationship happens to be benign, the borders and bordering practices may hardly exist and where there is hostility, the borders are very heavily guarded and the bordering practices severe. In both the scenarios however, the impact of the sheer presence of two different spheres of sovereignty impacts the lives of the people inhabiting the border zone. The line demarcates, if not cultures, traditions and economies, but the conscious of the people and leaves a deep imprint. The paper explores narratives from the border and the prevalent bordering practices at the Indo-Pak border. In the exercise, the paper evokes Chris Rumford's formulation of Seeing like a State vs. Seeing like a Border (Rumford, Chris. 2011. "Seeing like a Border," in "Interventions on rethinking the 'border' in border studies" by Johnson et al. *Political Geography* 30: 61–9) to evaluate both perspectives from the State and the Border. The methodology is discursive wherein the narratives and stories from inhabitants of the border villages are juxtaposed with the perspective of the state and its apparatus at the border. The Case Study is located in Jaisalmer district of Rajasthan, a province at India's border with Pakistan on its western expanse.

## Introduction

Borders in South Asia, especially between India and Pakistan, are beset with exercise of sovereignty and territoriality with severe control and surveillance. This border, abruptly created and superimposed in 1947, intended to divide the larger Indian nation into two states (India and Pakistan), led to divisions of historically established communities of people. The settled cultural ecology of the subcontinent was fragmented over one midnight without consultations with the huge population. The partition of India led to the creation of two large states, which were based on totally different ideologies. These partitions, and borders, created especially in South Asia, partly to preserve the façade of British imperial power (Chester 2008 cited in Cons and Sanyal 2013) were based on the premise that religious communities are fundamentally incompatible (Cons and Sanyal 2013, 6). Decades after the transitions, these partitions and borders have left lasting and often deleterious impacts on various communities, particularly minorities in these new nation-states (Cons and Sanyal 2013, 6).

Pakistan was created as a nation of those following the religion of Islam whereas the idea of India was meant to be a secular one. For a large number of people, it meant displacement as they chose on which side of the artificial and arbitrary divide they wished to live. An important negative consequence of partition was religious riots in the western region of India. Acrimony borne out of partition still pervades the geopolitical reality of South Asia where India and Pakistan have emerged to be the fiercest geopolitical rivals in the subcontinent and with a number of unresolved border and territorial issues. This rivalry and geopolitical competition have led to four major wars since independence of India from the British rule in 1947. Violent manifestations of the rivalry are regularly displayed at the long western border between India and Pakistan in many forms including skirmishes at the border and frequent and heavy exchange of fire in some sectors and also as theatrical performances at certain locations at the border.

> Anxiety over the creation and maintenance of borders is at the heart of discussions of violence, social conflict, and contemporary politics in South Asia. Such anxieties exist not only at the physical borders between countries, but play out in the internal spaces of nation-states. (Cons and Sanyal 2013, 6)

The paper is concerned with a very specific part of the Indian border, which is generally perceived to be peaceful and the bordering practices seem to be performed at the border. It seeks to analyze and interpret everyday and mundane lives of the people at the border in the desert state of Rajasthan. More specifically the lives of people in the Jaisalmer district of Rajasthan where the density of population is very low and the entire border between the two nations is fenced on the Indian side. Borrowing from the framework provided by Chris Rumford (2011), the paper approaches the issue of creation of borders and the incumbent bordering practices from two diverging viewpoints i.e. of the state and the people inhabiting the border. If the focus in the view from the border is about narratives of the borderlanders, the statist viewpoint is highlighted through the hard bordering practices inside the border zone and at the actual border. In addition, the article also looks at non-state actors involved in border work, which, are in this case the local population, whose services are regularly employed with the provision of some benefits from the state to keep track of activities related to the border in their neighborhood and localities. Furthermore, Jason Cons and Ramola Sanyal make the case for locally grounded studies on borders in South Asia with an emphasis because:

> it is a space that is veritably bursting both with borders, margins, and bordering/marginalizing practices. It is a space that is rich with new postcolonial scholarship in which the connected problematics of borders and margins are being explored and worked out. And it is a space that articulates with broader debates about borders and marginalization, though not in ways that can be reduced to modular understandings of border practices. As such, detailed, grounded, and regionally located ethnographic engagements with geographies at the margins of South Asia. (Cons and Sanyal 2013, 10)

For the purposes of this research, the author surveyed two border villages Kishangarh, and Kuriya Bheri in Jaisalmer district of Rajasthan. These two villages are located respectively at 8 and 16 kilometers from the international border. However, more important than the location itself is the narratives and stories about the impact of the border in the everyday sphere. The paper also invokes the narrative from the state and examines the viewpoint of the most important political actor in the international system.

## I: Conceptual Background

Chris Rumford's (2011 and 2012) significant work related to the borders deals with the multi-disciplinarity or multi-perspectivism in border studies and the explication of two contending and converging viewpoints about the border i.e. *Seeing like a State* Vs. *Seeing like a Border*. In the work titled "Interventions on rethinking of 'the border' in border studies" (2011) published in the journal *Political Geography* as a collective effort to examine the state of border studies, Rumford emphasizes three key dimensions of borders and bordering. The first dimension, he argues, relates to borders being "engines of connectivity." He identifies various checkpoints, transport hubs (airports, maritime ports and railway ports) and border crossings that facilitate mobility and interaction (Rumford 2011, 67) around the world. The second dimension, relevant to the paper is "bordering is not always business of the state" (Rumford 2011, 67). He further explains that border work is not solely the domain of the state and increasingly various other actors (citizens, entrepreneurs and NGOs) perform border work (Rumford 2011, 67). Moreover, as Parker and Nissen emphasize the need to clarify what borders are and surmise they are "a more formalized and territorialized sub-category of 'boundaries', a term which can be used indifferently about various kinds of entity besides states: territorial, social, personal, etc. both collective and individual" (Parker and Nissen 2012, 775). This aspect of border work assumes significance in the context of the paper as the narratives encountered in the field attested to the border work conducted by many non-state actors like the villagers residing in close proximity to the international boundary.

The narratives here indicate that the vigilance of the borderlanders to any abnormal activity at the border and its reportage to the local government authorities or the Border Security Force (BSF) was prompt. The third dimension makes for a careful reading and application as it focuses on "the opportunities, which the border provides for claims-making" (Rumford 2011, 67). It refers to the claims made by the citizens about either their forward presence at the border or their contribution to the nation. The national borders are then supposed to be imposed by the locals who inhabit the border. Narratives in this research, elaborated in the next section, testify to such an approach in international studies. The paper foregrounds such border work and claims made by inhabitants of the border to understand the intricate network of bordering and bordering practices conducted by both state and non-state actors.

Rumford explains the constituent performance of "seeing like a border" shifts the focus of border studies in three important ways and each of them relates to the fieldwork conducted under this study. First, following Balibar (2002 cited in Rumford 2011) he suggests that "borders are found wherever selective controls are found" and indicates to the omnipresence of borders (Rumford 2011, 68). "Bordering processes permeate everyday life well captured in Urry's (2007 cited in Rumford 2011) notion of 'frisk society' in which passing through public spaces is akin to the experience of airport security" (Rumford 2011, 68). Such frisking is a common feature of public spaces across the state-space in India due to security and terrorism threats that are frequent. The threats remain acute at the border with Pakistan, India's archrival and therefore, the presence of border in everyday life of the citizens living in the border zone.

Second, Rumford argues that borders are not always working in the service of the state (Rumford 2011, 68). In a desire to shore up what may be perceived as the ineffectual borders of the nation-state border workers may engage in a local bordering activity designed to enhance status or regulate mobility; gated communities, respect zones, "resilient" communities of CCTV watching citizens (Rumford 2011, 68). Such a focus, related to the first formulation, provides a clue to the disparities and boundaries existing within the society and not only at the border. The broad suggestion is that bordering practices are spread throughout society and it is not only the state, which benefits from these practices, and at many occasions, the beneficiaries are privileged members of the citizen public.

The third focus in this perspective is that the

> seeing like a border does not necessarily mean identifying with the subaltern, the dispossessed, the downtrodden, the marginal. The border, and the border work which has led to its construction, may be the project of those seeking to gain further advantage in society: entrepreneurs or affluent citizens. (Rumford 2011, 68)

This echoes Sahlins' (1989) classic work on the French-Spanish boundary in the Pyrenees, which, underlines the duality of the national identity in the periphery of the modern state. To quote Sahlins'

> It appeared less as a result of state intentions than from the local process of adopting and appropriating the nation without abandoning local interests, a local sense of place, or a local identity. At once opposing and using the state for its own ends, local society brought the nation into the village. (Sahlins 1989, 9)

Such instances are relevant for the present study as the state provides incentives to the residents of the border zone, which aid it in the border work. Certain actors of the border region may be geared towards extracting incentives and benefits from the state. The district administration and the BSF run benefit programs for the borderlanders "to keep them pacified and to establish that they work for the benefit of the Indian state" explained a BSF official.

The paper also invokes the impact of the border and bordering practices upon the everyday lives of people at the border. Prevailing literature (Jones and Johnson 2014; Cooper, Perkins, and Rumford 2014; Coleman and Stuesse 2014; Paasi 1996; Newman and Paasi 1998; Paasi 1999; Paasi 2013; Anderson and O'Dowd 1999; Konrad et al. 2019; Cassidy, Yuval Davis, and Wemyss 2018) provides substantial evidence that the daily and mundane lives of the borderlanders are deeply affected by the border and related practices.

A brief survey of the literature impressing upon the same follows. Newman and Paasi (1998) argue

> For people living in border areas, boundaries are an essential part of the activities and discourses of daily life, which are not necessarily translated into the collective and historical meanings that manifest themselves in the more general socio-spatial consciousness and its concrete manifestations, such as national literature, monuments, curricula, etc. (Newman and Paasi 1998, 198)

On the other hand, specific details of border regions come to the fore within wider theoretical/ conceptual frameworks. Anderson and O'Dowd assert, "Local particularities, whether political, economic, social or cultural, can only be understood in terms of wider conceptualizations" (Anderson and O'Dowd 1999, 594). While underlining the presence of borders at various scales, Paasi (1999) impress upon the relationship between scale and boundaries, "Boundaries exist and gain meanings on different spatial scales, not merely at the state level, and these meanings are ultimately reproduced in local everyday life" (1999, 670). Further he relates

> Boundaries are rarely produced in the border areas themselves, however, since these are usually national peripheries in an economic sense and their essential meanings as far as foreign policy, the national economy and politics are concerned are typically produced in centres. This means that many competing discourses usually exist on the roles of boundaries. (Paasi 1999, 670)

Such formulation readily applies to the boundary in question in the paper as Sir Cyril Radcliffe carved the India-Pakistan boundary out in New Delhi in 1947 without adequate maps and even today, those historical meanings of this boundary find an echo in the narratives of the borderlanders. Cartographic lacunae have often been cited for the existing problems of the border between India and Pakistan. "These maps certainly did not represent terrain as it was at that moment, but this failure was due to other shortfalls in raj cartography"(Chester 2009, 83). The boundary in context reflects the statist narratives more than the local ones as the heavily militarized nature of the border region attests.

The border if it facilitates, it also restricts. "Borders facilitate or obstruct interactions" (Ramuntsindela 2013, 45). Borders have a duality about them.

> They appear inherently contradictory, problematical and multifaceted. They are at once gateways and barriers to the "outside world", protective and imprisoning, areas of opportunity and/or insecurity, zones of contact and/or conflict, of co-operation and/or competition, of ambivalent identities and/or the aggressive assertion of difference. (Anderson and O'Dowd 1999, 595)

The fence here in the context of the India-Pakistan plays a rather restricting role as there are no border crossing points in the desert state of Rajasthan, where the length of the border is more than a 1000 kilometers.

In an insightful introduction to an edited volume *Placing the Border in Everyday Life* (2014), Reece Jones and Corey Johnson argue "For every dramatic, hair-raising scramble across a wall or a fence, there are multiple, mundane encounters with the border and its agents"(Jones and Johnson 2014, 3). The context for the statement is Europe and its borders, these "mundane encounters" are a feature of every border around the planet. Moreover, the borders in South Asia are hard, militarized borders which are extremely difficult to cross, but their presence is reflected in the daily interactions with either the fence itself or the border paraphernalia. The degree of interactions with the border increases with encounters with border forces and more so with the border work, the borderlanders carry out on behalf of the state.

While being involved in the border work and the interactions/ restrictions effected by the border fence, the language of borders takes shape. Cooper, Perkins, and Rumford (2014) term this as the vernacularization of borders as the language at the borders is informed by the local particularities and is diffused throughout the society. "A border studies which embraces the vernacularization of borders allows for a shift of emphasis from state bordering, securitization, and the regulation of mobilities to a concern both with the role of borders in 'the politics of everyday fear'" (Cooper, Perkins, and Rumford 2014, 16). The borderlanders while speaking to the author expressed such fears. Carrying out the daily and mundane activities, for example, the movement with the livestock for grazing in this typically arid zone of the Thar Desert, brings attention of the border personnel, which meant that they had to be informed regularly of their movements.

In the case of South Asia, the restrictions are more prominent and significant than the facilitation function of the borders, as the colonial imprint of territorial demarcation has left severe geopolitical rivalries in its wake. The restrictions are reflected in the daily lives of the people, which have been divided owing to the demarcation of the territory and in the paper take the form of narratives. Borrowing from Rumford's work the paper attends to the statist perspective, seeped in deep geopolitical rivalry with Pakistan and juxtaposes against the narratives from the border residents in the following sections.

## II: Seeing like a Border (Narratives/Stories from Border Residents)

### Location 1: Eight Kilometers from the International Boundary between India and Pakistan, the Village of Kishangarh.

Bhai Khan close to 90 years of age and his daughter Sumri Devi (70) sit in the small courtyard of their house and speak about the border and its meaning for them. The border for them means a restriction of trade and exchange of goods, which used to take place prior to the construction of the fence from 1989-93. The fence, the old man argued, has meant a loss of ancestral business of dealing in dry fruits, cattle and livestock (sheeps, goats and camels). Speaking in almost incomprehensible (due to his old age) Rajasthani, the colloquial language of the area interspersed with words from Urdu (the national language of Pakistan), Hindi and Sindhi as the Sindh province of Pakistan abuts Jaisalmer district, he explains

> … that prior to the erection of the fence, the geopolitical rivalry between India was only played out in statements by politicians and governments from both sides and in the borders at the state of Jammu and Kashmir. The border in Rajasthan, in general, were peaceful with hardly any interference from the state and the business and economic linkages were the almost the same as prior to Independence in 1947. (As told to the author during the field visit in Feb, 2017)

The BSF, he remembers is a force, formed only in the 1960s. It is only after the 1971 War with Pakistan, that the BSF and the Indian Army has moved into the area. He elaborated further,

> … even that did not deter me from conducting the business and contacting my family members on the other side. It is the fence, which has made the difference and has caused much difficulty for people on both sides. My extended family, my cousins and relatives live on the other side and I have not had any contact with them since the fence has come up. Even though currently there is no cellular connection in the area, before severe acrimony and geopolitical rivalry between the two countries set in, border inhabitants were allowed to contact their relatives in Pakistan through basic

telephone lines. I have had no contact in Pakistan for years, but anyone with contacts from other side are looked at with suspicion by the security forces. (In conversation with the author during Feb, 2017)

Sumri Devi, his daughter, who nods in agreement with her father and explains whenever he suddenly lapses into silence, supports the narration from Bhai Khan. The daughter clarifies and agrees with his father on most of the aspects and then adds her bit that both of them believe that the conditions on the Indian side are better in terms of economic and social opportunities. She tells very emphatically that her sister, who lives in Pakistan, not very far from the International Boundary only has tales of lack of economic opportunities and restriction of mobility from the authorities and very strict surveillance. The border makes it presence felt on both the sides, but it can be less restricting for one side and can mark the division for a life with more opportunities, she argued.

The village being located so very close to a very sensitive border between two geopolitical archrivals does play an important role in the calculus of the state. Vernacularization of the border, as defined by Cooper, Perkins, and Rumford 2014 "the activity of ordinary people in contributing to the processes of bordering" (Cooper, Perkins, and Rumford 2014, 18). The narrative from this small family, is incomplete without the mention of their own role in border work. The family claims its allegiance to India in spite of the fact that most of the 35 residents do not display much enthusiasm for the Indian state and the nation.

The father explained that

When I was active i.e. prior to the fencing, I regularly went to the other side and did inform the BSF and Army, if there was any event or person of interest was either seen or if I came across any other information. Similarly, if there was any person of interest or suspicious activity was seen in the village or its surroundings, I would inform the military and paramilitary forces. (As told to the author during the field visit in Feb, 2017)

He was therefore, engaged in the border work for the Indian state. As he grew old, the daughter took over the mantle from her father and started sharing, if she had any significant information with the forces. Her mobility due to the shepherding of her livestock in the area allowed her to keep track of any suspicious activity. A diverging feature of the conversation was about the animals wandering very close to the border fence and during such occasions, she has to be very vigilant and careful of the forces even on the Indian side. The environment, the wildlife and the livestock, she suggested are not immune from the impact of the fence.

Apart from the father-daughter duo, siblings of Sumri Devi, other residents of the village were not very forthcoming in their conversations about the border and they shared very close bonds with people across the border. Bhai Khan's son Noor Mohammed reminded us of his inability to meet his wife who is from across the border and lives in a village not very far from the International Boundary. He argued that he has not seen his wife for the last seven years, as the geopolitical relationship between the countries has not been permitting. "Borders enclose, separate, and bring spaces into relation. they are relational rather than substantive objects, which generate different sorts of relations within and between communities around them" (Piliavsky 2013, 27). He has been applying for visa to travel to Pakistan every year without success. On the other hand, the authorities on the Indian side look at him with suspicion and he has to update either the BSF or the district administration about his travel plans, whenever he moves out of the village, in advance.

On the other hand, the village being close to the border witnesses much of the military activity of the forces and is constantly under the watch of the armed forces (military and paramilitary). The local administration also maintains surveillance on the activities of the village population, as Kishangarh is the first village at such proximity with the border. In December 2016, the police for supplying sensitive information to Pakistan, arrested two village residents. The discovery was made through a surveillance of the bank accounts of these two residents, which received a substantial amount of money from the Middle East and the phone details revealed that they were supplying information to their contacts in Pakistan. Thus, the act of bordering in this case of espionage was carried out not at the border but at a location far removed from the border, wherein the surveillance was technological rather than physical. However, the threat itself was present at the edge of the territory of the nation-state. The dislocation of the border away from the border and into various computer programs and data matrices provides evidence that "borders are everywhere" (Balibar 2002) or as Walters argues "today we are witnessing a 'delocalization' of the border. If policing and control were previously concentrated in this special place, currently there is a disaggregation of border functions away from the border" (Walters 2006, 191). The border besides from being present as the fence is also spread over state territory.

### Location 2: Village Kuriya Bheri, 16 Kilometers from the International Boundary between India and Pakistan.

The village of Kuriya Bheri has a very interesting history as the original residents of the village vacated the area and their respective houses during the 1971 War between India and Pakistan. The war was fought along this border for almost its entire duration. The current residents of the village moved in after the war as the area, they suggested is suitable for livestock rearing. Livestock rearing remains the main source of livelihood for people in the region as the desert soil is not suitable for agriculture and the sources of water are limited. With a population of only 100 people in 30 households, Jagge Khan heads the village. The village is a non-revenue village and is counted under Netsi Panchayat, from where the residents migrated into the village. In his late 70s, Jagge Khan is a wealthy man by all standards as the owner of a herd of goats and sheeps numbering over 4000.

However, Jagge Khan's calm demeanor and wealth belies his experience of war and its consequences. He constantly evokes the memory of displacement during the war and the continuing experience of marginality. His most marginal experience, he argues is the fact of having an elementary school in the village which does not function because the sole teacher deputed to the school appears only once in a month to mark his attendance for the whole month. The district headquarter of Jaisalmer itself is a marginal location in the context of the province of Rajasthan. Moreover, the village is further marginal with reference to its location to the border and its status as a non-revenue village. On the other hand, it is useful to be reminded that "Borders as margins of the state and nation, places at once removed from and central to debates about identity, security, risk, and survival" (Cons and Sanyal 2013, 6). Nonetheless, they are manifest themselves in many ways in the society.

Jagge Khan, though undeterred by the non-availability of a government-appointed teacher has himself recruited one for the 20 odd children of the village. The children however, ranging from 4 to 12 years of age have no clue that they live very close to the border of two very antagonistic states of India and Pakistan. After a little more prodding it appeared that the children do not even know that they are citizens of India. Furthermore, they did not have a clue what India is and they lived at one of the most militarized borders in the world and why there are a large number of uniformed men in the area.

Jagge Khan narrated further:

> The BSF has been helpful and we as citizens aware of our critical location at the border, in the context of India-Pakistan relations support the forces and pass on any "information" available to us and if we see any suspicious movement. Since we know the area well owing to our movements for livestock rearing, we also help the BSF with their lost camels and the BSF in turn helps us with matters related to the basic amenities in the village and building infrastructure for the village in collaboration with the local administration. (As told to the author during Field Trip, 2017)

Chris Rumford's formulation that border residents contribute to the border work and the bordering activity is used for claims making is evident in the narratives from the perspective of the borderlanders who extract benefits from the local administration and the Border Security Force. The local administration and the BSF on the other hand run the monthly Civic Administration Programme to facilitate the everyday life and catering to limitations faced by border residents.

Common to both the villages was the incidents of the temporary displacements during the events of Kargil War (1999), Operation Parakram (2001) in the wake of attacks on Indian Parliament and during 2008 after Mumbai terrorist attacks. The residents of these two villages had to vacate their respective houses and move to locations in either temporary shelters away from the border or to relatives' houses. The mobilization of the armed forces along the expanse of the Western Border and subsequent planting of mines in the area required the villagers to be moved away to safer locations.

## III: Seeing Like a State (Classifying Residents at the Border)

The state apparatus is present in the area surveyed, in two main forms; the Border Security Force, the Indian Army and the district administration, which included the local elected representatives and the bureaucracy. "The two arms of the state have to function in coordination in the border area" emphasized one of the BSF officers, as sharing of the information is crucial to understand and identify any threat to the sovereignty of the nation. The visits to the two villages were also crucial to understand the statist perspective as the BSF officers identification/classification of the villagers as leaning towards India and that of an orientation which belied the expectation of the forces, indicated towards a process of bordering within the territory. The hard bordering practices were clearly visible at the border fence and at the Border Outposts (BOPs) but the segregation of the populace on the basis of perceived nationalism or lack of it is being underlined within the territory. Significant here is the state agencies use mechanisms to identify defaulters/ threats to security not only on the basis of evidence or any existing record but also the perceptions linked to the familial connections individuals have across the border. The BSF and the army, however, on their part base their perception on certain incidents of the past. For example, the recent arrest of two individuals from the village of Kishangarh who were allegedly supplying sensitive information to the Pakistani forces weighed upon the minds of the BSF personnel.

The daily newspapers published from the main cities in the area, Jaisalmer, Jodhpur and Bikaner frequently carry news about smuggling activities and illegal border crossing across the fence. The recurring theme in such stories is that of the smuggling of illicit drugs and narcotic substances. The BSF and the Army constantly monitors the border zone for such activities.

The militarization of the area seems to be complete, even within the territory, and geographically, the border appears to be a zone rather than a boundary line. The route from the district headquarter of Jaisalmer to the boundary line is dotted with camps and garrisons of the BSF and the Indian Army. A very significant institution is a War Museum constructed on the outskirts of Jaisalmer city. The Indian Army runs the museum and the exhibits include tanks and armored vehicles captured during the Indo-Pak war of 1971. The museum's most important indoor displays include a history of war since ancient time. The exhibits include different types of hand-held and artillery guns and their utilization during different wars by the Indian forces. One section is dedicated to the recipients of India's highest gallantry award, the Param Veer Chakra. The museum sells memorabilia and runs a film show, which depicts the courage and bravery of Indian Armed forces. The Audio-Visual gallery of the museum is dedicated to a general history of War.

On the other hand, the BSF, Indian Army and the local administration run the monthly Civic Action programs in the border zones as an extension of the border work. The information collected from the borderlanders is crucial for the forces to effectively manage the border. The villagers enhance the capabilities of these forces through their watch on activities in the region. The forces on their part supply them with groceries and the weekly commute to the nearby towns for purchasing household items is also facilitated by the BSF. Moreover, one very essential commodity, in this arid region is water and the BSF and the local administration ensure that water supply in these villages is regular either through water tankers or through digging bore wells. Most of the elementary schools in the area have been constructed with the involvement of the BSF.

## Conclusion

The case study of the two villages following the narrative method from both the perspectives i.e. of the border residents and the security forces deployed at the border substantially indicates that borders are present not only at the border but also within the larger society. The impacts of the presence of the international boundary without a fence and with a fence are clearly felt in the everyday lives of the border residents. Chris Rumford's (2011) conceptualizations hold value in the context of the surveyed area as the fence built by the Indian state is a status enhancer signifying not only India's economic status vis-à-vis Pakistan, but also indicating technological and military superiority. The boundary and the fence restrict mobility as well as the socio-cultural milieu and historically evolved bonds within society. However, the border residents are involved in the border work for the state to presumably extract benefits from the state and to remain on the right side of the law. Rumford (2011) becomes relevant when the border residents with their border work intend to remain in the good books of Indian armed forces present in the area and thereby obviating the downtrodden and the subaltern image of the border-landers. They frequently extract benefits from the state-run Border Area Development Programmes in terms of provision of ration and stores. The border work may involve from passing sensitive information to helping out the forces in searching for camels, which are extensively used in border work. The vision of the state for this particular border cannot be overstated, as it is omnipresent in the area with different arms of the military. Further, the forces in consultation with the local administration work hard to keep the border residents involved various bordering practices and border work. The impact of the events in the "Centre" is evident at the border as the mobilization of the forces takes place in the border zone.

## Disclosure Statement

No potential conflict of interest was reported by the author.

## Funding

The research work was possible through a grant from the Jawaharlal Nehru University under a University with Potential for Excellence II (UPE II) project. The title of the project is "Border Theory and Globalization: Perspectives from the South." Project ID: 205

## References

Anderson, James, and Liam O'Dowd. 1999. Borders, Border Regions and Territoriality: Contradictory Meanings, Changing Significance. *Regional Studies* 33, no. 7: 693–704.

Balibar, Etienne. 2002. *Politics and the Other Scene*. London: Verso.

Cassidy, Kathryn, Nira Yuval Davis, and Georgie Wemyss. 2018. Intersectional Border(ing)s. 139–41.

Chester, L. 2008. Boundary Commissions as Tools to Safeguard British Interests at the End of Empire. *Journal of Historical Geography* 34: 494–515.

Chester, Lucy P. 2009. *Borders and Conflict in South Asia: The Radcliffe Boundary Commission and the Partition of Punjab*. Manchester: Manchester University Press.

Coleman, M., and Angela Stuesse. 2014. Policing Borders, Policing Bodies: The Territorial and Biopolitical Roots of US Immigration Control. In *Placing the Border in Everyday Life*, ed. Reece Jones and Corey Johnson, 33–63. Surrey: Ashgate pp.

Cons, Jason, and Ramola Sanyal. 2013. Geographies at the Margins: Borders in South Asia – an Introduction. *Political Geography* 35: 5–13.

Cooper, A., Chris Perkins, and Chris Rumford. 2014. The Vernacularization of Borders. In *Placing the Border in Everyday Life*, ed. Reece Jones and Corey Johnson, 15–32. Surrey: Ashgate.

Johnson, C., Reece Jones, Anssi Paasi, Louise Amoore, Alison Mountz, Mark Salter, and Chris Rumford. 2011. Interventions on Rethinking the "Border" in Border Studies. *Political Geography* 30: 61–9.

Jones, Reece, and Corey Johnson., eds. 2014. *Placing the Border in Everyday Life*. Surrey: Ashgate.

Konrad, V., J.P. Laine, I. Liikanen, J.W. Scott, and R. Widdis. 2019. The Language of Borders. In *Handbook of the Changing World Language Map*, ed. S. Brunn and R Kehrein. Cham: Springer.

Newman, D., and Anssi Paasi. 1998. Fences and Neighbours in the Postmodern World: Boundary Narratives in Political Geography. *Progress in Human Geography* 22, no. 2: 186–207.

Paasi, Anssi. 1996. *Territories, Boundaries and Consciousness: The Changing Geographies of the Finnish Russian Border*. Chichester: Wiley.

Paasi, Anssi. 1999. Boundaries as Social Practice and Discourse: The Finnish Russian Border. *Regional Studies* 33, no. 7: 669–80.

Paasi, Anssi. 2013. Borders. In *The Ashgate Research Companion to Critical Geopolitics*, ed. Klaus Dodds, Meje Kuus, and Joanne Sharp, 213–230. Farnham: Ashgate.

Parker, Noel, and Rebecca-Adler Nissen. 2012. Picking and Choosing the "Sovereign" Border: A Theory of Changing State Bordering Practices. *Geopolitics* 17, no. 4: 773–96.

Piliavasky, Anastasia. 2013. Borders Without Borderlands: On the Social Reproduction of State Demarcation in Rajasthan. In *Borderland Lives in Northern South Asia*, ed. David N Gellner, 24–46. New Delhi: Orient Blackswan.

Ramuntsindela, Maano. 2013. Experienced Regions and Borders: The Challenge for Transnational Approaches. *Regional Studies* 47, no. 1: 43–54.

Rumford, Chris. 2011. "Seeing Like a Border", in "Interventions on Rethinking the 'Border' in Border Studies" by Johnson et al. *Political Geography* 30: 61–9.

Rumford, Chris. 2012. Towards a Muliperspectival Study of Borders. *Geopolitics* 17, no. 4: 887–902.

Sahlins, Peter. 1989. *Boundaries: The Making of France and Spain in the Pyrenees.* Berkeley: University of California Press.

Urry, J. 2007. *Mobilities.* Oxford: Polity Press.

Walters, W. 2006. Border/Control. *European Journal of Social Theory* 9, no. 2: 187–203.

# Portraying the "Other" in Textbooks and Movies: The Mental Borders and Their Implications for India–Pakistan Relations

Dhananjay Tripathi ⓘ and Vaishali Raghuvanshi ⓘ

**ABSTRACT**

Borders have been traditionally known just as physical cartographic boundaries on maps. However, the epistemological and ontological underpinnings of Border Studies have witnessed constant evolution in the past century. This has brought to the fore the importance of mental borders along with the physical borders. When it comes to a region like South Asia, the lack of regional integration is conspicuous. One of the reasons for this is the existence of mental borders along with rigid physical borders. The paper seeks to understand the process of creation of mental borders between the two South Asian neighbours by probing it from the point of view of school textbooks and cinematic narrative. School textbooks are the most fundamental building blocks of knowledge in any society. Analysis of these texts brings forward the metaphysical construction of mental borders at a very early stage. Subsequently, cinema as a mode of popular culture is an effective tool in order to understand social phenomena from people's perspective. Here, the process of meaning creation is largely embedded in linguistics and is derived from people's experiences. The deconstruction of these data sources leads to the understanding of the process of mental border formation.

## I. Introduction

South Asia is one of the least integrated regions of the world and it implies that it is a region with different and difficult borders and boundaries. In other words, borders and boundaries define much of the regional politics in South Asia. To highlight just a few, the India–Pakistan tension over borders of Kashmir, the Pakistan–Afghanistan dispute over the Durand line and unsettled border questions between India and Bangladesh. Along with these hard state borders there are other socio-political boundaries like religious divides, caste divisions, oppressive patriarchal social orders and rampant poverty in almost every South Asian country. Thus in South Asia, for an individual, it is a daily encounter with hard borders of the state and boundaries of the society. In a way borders and boundaries are part of normal life in South Asia and there is a resistance to any transformation in the present system both from the top (state) and the bottom (society). Unsurprisingly, with few exceptions, most of the state borders in South Asia are highly militarized. Likewise, old social structures in South Asia make it difficult for common people to go beyond certain defined parameters of societal freedom. Looking from the perspective of regionalism and societal development, these borders and boundaries are a matter of perennial concern in South Asia. In this paper, we will approach South Asian borders and boundaries from a regional perspective trying to understand the reasons for the lack of regional integration in South Asia. The story of South Asian integration has a number of factors—some helping and others dampening the process. But all of these stop at the gateway of India–Pakistan relations. Two big developing countries of South Asia—India and Pakistan are in possession of nuclear weapons and among the largest importers of weapons. Ignoring the low positions on the Human Development Index (HDI) there is a general acceptability in the political establishment of these two countries, to maintain a large army by diverting funds from the national coffer (Cohen 1975). All these are indications of conflicting relations between these two neighbors reflected in terms of securitized borders between the two.

In fact, if we study South Asia with respect to borders and boundaries, a pessimistic view will emerge. Rifts, unsettled claims and counter-claims on territories, strict border control, and tough visa regimes are some of the glaring facts of this region. Not wrong to say that borders are one of the most critical issues in South Asia. In the words of Paula Banerjee, "[I]n South Asia, bilateral relations do not construct the border, on the contrary, it is the borders which shape relations" (Banerjee 1998, 181). Borders are the cause of prevalent security anxiety in the region. They are meant to be defended, without permitting any dilution in the border security. South Asian states inherited the idea of secure and hard borders from the British who colonialized the region and created borders to safeguard their political interest (Mishra 2008). The Durand Line between Afghanistan and Pakistan, the MacMahon line between India and China, borders between India and Nepal, all were created by the British precisely to maintain their political control over colonial India. Many South Asian borders in this respect were drawn and shaped by the British.

One could understand the security dilemma of the British in India—they wanted to keep a check on the expansionist ambition of Russia and others. The borders were to safeguard British colonial interest in India. The British left the region in 1947 but thereafter the post-colonial states (primarily India and Pakistan) remain hesitant to make it a soft and porous border in South Asia. Although conversion from hard to soft border should be easy in South Asia because of the shared cultural, historical and social linkages between states, still governments are disinterested in this progressive transition of borders and are comfortable with highly guarded hard borders. To defend such a stand, there are official policies to convince the common citizenry about the significance of hard borders in South Asia. The mainstay of such policies is to create mental borders to justify hard securitized borders in South Asia. Thus there are persistent efforts to create and subsequently maintain the mental borders in South Asia. This phenomena is discussed in this paper by taking the case of India and Pakistan.

Borders are not sacrosanct and in many regions they have changed with the objective of promoting peace and regional prosperity. The success of European integration is an inspiration for other regions. Notably in the European integration process border issues were resolved amicably making them "contact zones" rather than the old version of "lines of division." "Today Europe is marked by a patch work of cross-border regions" (Wastl-Walter and Kofler 2000, 90). Regional integration tacitly endorses relaxed border regimes for promotion of trade and movement of people. While the rest of the world made attempts and slowly moved towards reaping the benefits of regionalism, South Asia remained economically the least integrated and politically divided. According to the World Bank analysis for South Asia, even today India's trade with Brazil is 20% cheaper compared to its trade with next-door neighbor Pakistan. The intra-regional trade in South Asia is abysmally low and less than 5% of its total trade (World Bank 2016). The states in South Asia have never remained open to the free movement of people. There are mass migratory phases in South Asia but they only occurred during the times of crises like the India–Pakistan partition (1947), the Bangladesh liberation war (1971), and the Sri-Lanka civil war. These were forced movements which were a consequence of the erection of more borders and boundaries in South Asia. According to Myron these were "rejected peoples and unwanted migrants in South Asia" (Weiner 1993, 1737). Generally, a stringent visa control is the natural preference of the states in South Asia.

The question is why there is no big challenge to these borders in South Asia. In this paper we have made an attempt to understand how mental borders are created in South Asia and how at times these borders help the state policy to maintain hard borders. We will be discussing the case of India and Pakistan and using textbooks and movies for our analysis. Border Studies open prospects to analyze borders both physical and mental by using different epistemological and ontological mediums. Textbooks and movies are two such mediums that can give a very concrete idea of borders and how they are perceived by the people. These two mediums, if engaged properly, could possibly add to large and expanding canvass of Border Studies (Staudt 2018). In this respect, this article is also a part of the effort to study India–Pakistan borders from a varied perspective, departing from the established lens of Security Studies.

## II. India–Pakistan Relations and Mental Borders

One should not get confused on the basis of prevailing regional distrust in South Asia. In South Asia, interestingly, countries are more globalized and less regionalized. As a matter of fact, South Asian countries are presently highly integrated with the global economy. India is acclaimed as an economic giant of the region and one of the fastest growing economies of the world. Opting for liberal economic policies in the 1990s India swiftly integrated herself with the international capitalist system without much hesitation (Friedman 2007). A section in India is immensely benefitted by this international integration and presently has strong stakes in an interconnected and borderless world. India has its substantial contribution to the group of "global citizens" who are on the move for professional needs and demands. "Indians make up the largest diaspora: 16 million Indians are scattered across the world, which partly reflects the country's demographic size (1.2 billion) and youth (median age is around 26)" (Sengupta 2016). The statistics from other South Asian countries too is encouraging in terms of the diaspora community. Similarly, Pakistan also remained quite an integrated country with the West even during the period of the Cold War. Pakistan as a western ally was the member of the Central Treaty Organization (CENTO), and the Southeast Asia Treaty

Organization (SEATO). Pakistan was a formidable partner of the West after the Soviet Union invaded Afghanistan in 1979. These all are examples indicating Pakistan as contented with international alliances.

Simple reading of these facts raises certain questions as to what explains regional borders and boundaries if South Asian countries are unhesitant to be part of global political and economic processes? This paper deals with India–Pakistan relations so we limit the discussion to these two neighbors. India–Pakistan relations are very complex and could be a perfect case study for a number of disciplines. India and Pakistan have a common historical past and social-cultural affinity, still the political relations are marked by three wars and countless border conflicts. Is this a "partition syndrome?"

> [b]y one account, over 8 million refugees poured across borders to regions completely foreign to them, while other accounts state that 7 million people migrated to Pakistan from India and vice-versa. By another estimate, Partition resulted in the forced movement of 20 million people (Hindus and Sikhs to India and Muslims to Pakistan).[1]

Mindless violence, brutalities, atrocities on women and children and complete chaos were the defining features of the Indian partition of 1947 (Menon and Bhasin 2000; Pandey 2002). This is certainly a bitter part of India–Pakistan history. Still there has been no effort for reconciliation and its bitterness is retained by the political elites on both sides for a purpose. It is to justify the partition more in the case of Pakistan but India too avoids an objective engagement with this part of her problematic past (Tripathi 2016a). The miserable accounts of partition are retained in national memories, not allowed to diminish in the people's discourse by maintaining different mediums. The normal practice is to blame the other side without any general sense of remorse. Although, at the time of partition even the political leadership of India and Pakistan had not expected the scale of violence that was later witnessed (Naqvi 2010).

Thus, the "partition wound" is still unattended. There is a permanent scar of partition, revisited at times of war and whenever the two sides indulge in warmongering. This is like a mental border that the majority of people in India and Pakistan live with. The image of enemy is in the minds of the people; there is a feeling of "other." This mental border helps the cause of belligerent state actors and different mediums are used to fortify it. The "partition scar" on the borders of India and Pakistan can be discerned easily (Staudt 2018). Textbooks are one such state-owned medium giving the official version of events and movies are part of popular culture and probably could justify the state's narratives. In this paper, we will draw references from textbooks and movies to analyze how these two helped in strengthening the mental borders in the case of India and Pakistan.

According to David Newman, "[A]ll borders share a common function to the extent that they include some and exclude many others." He further argues that:

> [B]y creating "otherness," we create separate identities through the maintenance of the border. The location of the boundary may change through time, as some groups or territories expand and others decline, but they will always demarcate the parameters within which identities are conceived, perceived, perpetuated and reshaped. (Newman 2003, 15)

Border Studies scholars therefore give equal relevance to mental borders. According to Houtum "[P]hysical borders can be removed relatively easily as compared to mental borders, which can be rather sticky" (as cited in Nemeth 2015). The mental boundaries stays with people, "the boundary of human community inevitably exists within the consciousness of its members, and hence to some extent is subjected to mental processes and patterns" (Kuznetsov 2015, 81).

Border in a way is not a natural phenomenon, it is created by powerful political actors to maintain control. It is to create division—political, economic and social between humans and a border is immaterial if such divisions are blurred. It is important to ensure legitimacy of borders and many a time only securitization is not of much help. Mental borders only brace physical borders of division thus we retain some lines in our minds. To be frank, "[A] border is not a military defence alone. To create a border is essentially the creation of an Innerspace of reflection, a narcissian centripetal orientation, a truth in which one can find pleasure and ease" (Houtum 2011, 50).

Borders remains with us, in our imagination and daily practices, making it highly difficult to overcome.

> We may not necessarily see the lines, but they order our daily life practices, strengthening our belonging to, and identity with, places and groups, while at one and the same time perpetuating notion of difference and othering. (Newman 2006, 143)

Thus one can conclude that borders are "not just hard territorial lines—they are the institution that results from bordering policies—they are thus about people" (Brunet-Jailly 2011). Coming to South Asia, states have a preference for securitized borders. South Asian states consciously use methods to justify these securitized borders (Tripathi 2015). The unquestioned support from the people to the state for such a security centric approach towards the neighborhood is only possible by mental borders. Cognitive confinement of citizens is the basis of mental borders.

## III. The Case of Textbooks

Textbooks are used to train young minds and they are an excellent medium for the State to create a favorable knowledge systems. Thus, "[I]t is naïve to think of the school curriculum as neutral knowledge. Rather what counts as legitimate knowledge is a result of complex power relations and struggles among identifiable class, race, gender, and religious groups" (Apple 1990, 18). At the elementary stage almost 80% of knowledge for the student comes from textbooks. This extra dependence on the single knowledge source is not beneficial. Critical thinking is inhibited and powerful sections use textbooks for disseminating their values in the name of objective information (English 1980). There are states that use textbooks to even misinform citizens and this is the case we are highlighting in this paper.

In Pakistani school textbooks facts are often distorted and at times selectively presented for political purposes. It is to generate support for official statist discourse. This is the reason why K.K Aziz termed Pakistani textbooks as the "death of history."

> History as a subject was abolished by the government of Field Marshal Ayub Khan. Its place has been taken by a subject called "Mu'ashrati Ulum" or "Social Studies" for classes 1–8 and by another subject called "Mutala'a-i-Pakistan" or "Pakistan Studies" for classes 9–12. Both are amalgams of bits of geography, history, economics, civics, Islamic Studies and international relations. (Aziz 1993, 2)

This was not the case in Pakistan from the beginning and textbooks shared information on the common cultural past with India. Much of these politically motivated changes occurred after the 1960s. This is when the military regime under the Ayub Khan started creating a distinct Islamic identity in Pakistan (Zaidi 2009). Muhammad Ali Jinnah, the founder of Pakistan indeed wanted to have a Muslim majority secular Pakistan with nothing to do with what is presently represented as "Islamic identity" (Hoodboy 2007). This secular side of Jinnah's political perspective was concealed from the general public during the Zia-ul-Haq regime where "truth was the immediate casualty" (Hoodboy 2007). Much had changed in the textbooks of Pakistan after the political control of military dictators Ayub Khan (1958–1969) to Zia-ul-Haq (1978–1988).

"What is Pakistan all about? For decades, Pakistani school children have grown up learning a linguistically flawed (but catchy) rhetorical question sung together with answer: *Pakistan ka matlab kya? La illaha illala*! (What it the meaning of Pakistan? There is no God but Allah!)" (Hoodboy 2007, 3300). This is to teach the school children that Pakistan is a unique nation and Islam is the inherent part of its national identity. "In case of Pakistan, as we will see, reshaping the past through curricular reform has responded to the government's desire to prevent ethnic fragmentation, appease conservative groups, and pursue foreign policy goals" (Giunchi 2007, 376). There are several reasons but, ultimately, the goal of distorting knowledge is to create an image of Pakistan in the minds of students that it is different from India. The Pakistani school curriculum is prepared to relinquish association with the common past of a united India. Nation building was the main task of the new country Pakistan and in the process it widened the gap with India in turn, creating a border in young minds. The task was to prove that the idea of Pakistan is a *sui-generis* and it is closer to Muslim civilization (Tripathi 2018). In Pakistan, historians were assigned duties to write textbooks "enchanted with glories of Damascus, Baghdad, Cairo, and Cordoba than with the Indian counterparts of Delhi, Agra or Fatehpursikri" (Ali 2002, 4530).

In Pakistani textbooks, India is painted as a Hindu country and not as a secular country. This is denying the constitutional position of India as a secular country. There are a number of wrong examples in the Pakistani textbooks to present India as a Hindu country but the most shocking is the portraying of M.K Gandhi in the Pakistani textbooks. M.K Gandhi all over the world is a respected figure for his virtuous non-violent anti-colonial struggle. In India he is known as *Mahatama* (Saint) Gandhi and officially accepted as the "father of the nation." Gandhi was a religious person, respected by all religious groups, played a significant role in consoling the communal riot victims during the partition and was murdered by a Hindu fundamentalist. The secular credential of Gandhi was never doubted (Xaxa and Mahakul 2009). To term such a person as a "Hindu leader" is a gross misrepresentation and cannot be assumed as an innocent act. The distortion becomes more evident when we look at the representation of Gandhi in textbooks of two different periods. In the old Pakistani textbooks Gandhi was referred to as "Mahatama Gandhi Who Died for Peace" (Haye 1973, 207). The same book by the same author and similar text changed the introduction of Mahatama Gandhi. In the revised textbook it is "Mahatama Gandhi – A Great Hindu Leader" (Haye 1990, 38). This alteration in representations of Gandhi is not without a purpose and obviously it is to equate him with Jinnah. Notably, Muhammad Ali Jinnah was the leader of the All India Muslim League, the party that raised the demand of a separate homeland for Muslims. During partition, Jinnah was accepted as the representative of the Muslim community that demanded Pakistan. To justify Jinnah and his politics, Gandhi was termed as the Hindu leader.

Moreover, India is presented as a divided society. Through the textbooks, an impression is created that India is a fragmented country whereas Pakistan is a homogenous community. The following text from the Social Studies textbook of class VI will illustrate it in a clear way.

(Page 53) "Children of Pakistan - The children of different regions of Pakistan are quite similar. All these children know the national language Urdu and can read and write it ... .... (Pages 53–54) "Children of India - In India, the Muslim children generally wear Shalwar Kameez or Kurta Pyjama. While Hindu children war Dhotee. Children in North India like Chapati whereas the children of Southern India like to eat rice. Muslim children like eating meat while Hindu children eat pulses and vegetables." (Balal 2014)

It is also a communal representation of Indian children where Muslim children are shown to be different from Hindu children. Similarly in the textbook *Pakistan Studies for classes IX–X* there is an extensive exposure of political speeches of leaders who advocated the creation of Pakistan. The content of these speeches to an extent are provocative and this gives us a reason to question its familiarization to the young minds. The following are a few examples.

Page 10: Statements of Allama Iqbal.

India is a subcontinent and not a country, where people belonging to different religions and speaking different languages are inhabited. Muslim nation has its unique religious and cultural identity.

Page 10 and 11: Statements of Quaid-i-Azam Mohammad Ali Jinnah

Hinduism and Islam are not merely two religions but they are two separate social systems ....Pakistan had come into being the day the first non-Muslim was converted into a Muslim in India. (Khokhar 2014, 10–11)

This anti-Hindu narration becomes vitriolic in the class VII textbooks. Here are a few excerpts.

The Muslims had to face brutalities, hardships and insult as a reward for their kindness, generosity and equal treatment to non-Muslims when the British usurped power from them and encouraged Hindus to support them to crush the erstwhile ruling Muslims. This they gladly did ... It is a fact of history that had Muslims been intolerant and cruel, there would have been not a Single Hindu or non-Muslim who could have survived ... Hindus hated Muslims as unclean and Muslims treated them as non-believers. (Shah 2016, 49)

These impressions about India mostly remain with ordinary people of Pakistan for their lifetime unless they first "de-learn" and afterwards "re-learn" the lessons taught in childhood (Tripathi 2016b). The general picture of India represented in Pakistani textbooks is not positive. From the perspective of Border Studies, we can easily locate this as a kind of border—the mental border. This is difficult to overcome even when an individual gets an opportunity to cross borders.

There is resistance in Pakistan about the misrepresentation of history in school textbooks. An influential section of Pakistan's civil society is opposed to these texts of hate introduced in schools. There are reports by Pakistan-based organizations criticizing the school textbooks as "the subtle subversion—the state of curricula and textbooks in

Pakistan" (Nayyar and Salim 2005). Another strong report that created intense debate both within and outside Pakistan about textbooks is "Curriculum of Hate" from the Centre for Research and Security Studies. There is no dearth of reports and commentaries demanding a revision of these textbooks in Pakistan. Still, these rational voices are ignored to create and maintain a mental border in Pakistan.

The case of Indian textbooks is better in comparative terms but there is scope of improvement. The unbiased education system is a reflection of the secular constitution of India that prohibits the state from promoting religious values and views of any community. Also significant is the composition of Indian society, which is multi-religious and the state's patronage to one particular section will have constitutional and political ramifications. In this respect, creation of mental borders might be problematic in an Indian context because it will subsequently have repercussions in domestic politics. Thus, primary responsibility as envisaged by Indian political elites for the education system, was to attain unity in diversity. The Education Commission of 1964–1966 directed school towards the end, "to bring about social and national integration, cultivation of social, moral and spiritual values and acceleration of the process of modernization" (Gottlob 2007). Also important to note that being a federal country, education is a subject in the federal list and central government cannot impose all its policies. Although there are certain basic guidelines decided by the central government for the school education. The National Council Educational Research and Training (NCERT), is the responsible public organization in India for preparing indicative syllabus for the school education.

The legal political structure of India is as such where deviation from secular ethos might be a problem. Still there are sections in India who time and again expressed their dissatisfaction from what they call the "western influence on Indian education." The "Hindu nationalists" in India have their own distinct agenda for the school education. The primary objective of these Right Wing political outfits is to "Indianize" the school education. This was a long-standing demand of Hindu political outfits that Hindu texts—like Upnishad, Geeta, Ramayana and Mahabharat should be part of the school textbooks (Gottlob 2007). Previously and even in the present time, Hindu political parties have demanded change in the school curriculum and textbooks. In 1977, when a political coalition formed the government in India, it made an attempt to bring substantial changes in the textbooks. Likewise after the election of 1999, the National Democratic Alliance (NDA) led by the Bhartiya Janta Party (BJP) gained the majority and took an interest in "Indianizing" the school textbooks, in other words to bring more of a "Hindu" bias (Thapar 2009). "As the Hindu right consolidated from the mid-1970s, books became a target of persistent attacks. The secular condemned as anti-Hindu, keen on sanitizing Muslim their misdeeds" (Bhattacharya 2009, 104). Even at present with a Hindu Right party in absolute majority, there are efforts to change the content of Indian textbooks. Although changes in Indian textbooks will not have an immediate impact on India–Pakistan relations. Only the long-term and persistent alterations will be detrimental because "Hinduization" of textbooks is susceptible to the idea of the "two-nation theory" (Sundar 2004).

What revisions there will be in textbooks is still a matter of speculation, but there is a bit of disappointment in regard to the contemporary India textbooks, if we read it in terms of engaging with India–Pakistan relations. The other critical point is that Indian textbooks were more perceptible for debate on difficult socio-political issues that includes communal violence during the India–Pakistan partition. While several progressive themes like caste and racial discrimination, gender justice etc, are well highlighted and discussed in the textbooks, there is a kind of shyness in dealing with the violence during the partition in the Indian textbooks.

We will now bring some examples from the Indian textbooks. There is a discussion on partition in class X in the textbook *Democratic Politics – II* under the heading of communalism that is part of chapter 4. The horrors of communal politics is explained in this chapter. The example of India–Pakistan suffering due to sectarian politics at the time of partition is referred to in this textbook. Apart from this, other themes of political science are discussed in the book without any mention of Pakistan. Only in the chapter that is on democracy, is there a remark on Pakistan but it is not so relevant and clubbed with examples of countries witnessing a coup against democracy. This little teaching on partition and Pakistan might be defended as avoidance of an acrimonious past. Nevertheless it will be good if we first discuss some critical issues before students start creating a picture of Pakistan by following many other mediums. The classroom could be an ideal place for sensitive debates rather than exposing the young mind to a belligerent rhetoric of the outside world that is quite visible in the case of India–Pakistan. Thus, the Indian textbooks just failed to capitalize on an initial progressive base.

School is the first place of learning and it could be used by the ruling elites for specific purposes. According to Gramsci, "[S]chool is the instrument through which intellectuals of various levels are elaborated" (Gramsci 2009, 10). This is what we can see in Pakistan where textbooks are used to defend the political posture of the state. This is an impediment for India–Pakistan relations and is a mental border. A change in the Pakistani textbooks in terms of representation of India will help to minimize the mental borders. Likewise, a proper engagement with the partition violence could help Indian young minds to view things differently.

## IV. The Case of Cinema

There are various epistemological tools and processes related to the production of knowledge, ideas, and perceptions. Textbooks are discussed in the above section. Likewise cinema is also one such tool that has played a very important role in disseminating ideas and influencing perceptions.

Images have slowly become an important medium for studying and highlighting social and political processes. Texts and verbal sources provide meaning to phenomena but they are not the only tools for provision of meaning. Images are also an important tool for communication and providing meaning. For any context meanings are as effectively produced by non-verbal sources as they are done by verbal or textual ones. The importance of visual media has increased multifold in the current age of information revolution when creation, transmission and reception of images has become extremely convenient. The importance of images in conveying meanings has led to an aesthetic turn in the discipline of International Relations (IR). Aesthetic turn has come in two waves which have altered the epistemological understanding and processes of IR. While the first wave came in the 1980s when post modernism began to redefine the theoretical underpinnings of IR, the second wave is more recent where an increasing reliance on tools such as cinema, theater, music, and arts has opened newer ways to analyze global political affairs. This new turn in the IR scholarship also open ways to engage with other subjects. Border Studies is one of the potential subjects for IR scholars where variety of images could be studied as contributing factors to the creation of mental borders.

Roland Bleiker has explained the use of aesthetics by comparing them with "mimetic" forms of representation. Mimetic forms of representation have been a mainstream tool in the discipline of IR. The focus of mimetic is on a depiction of events which captures the true essence of it without any gap in representation.

> An aesthetic approach, by contrast, assumes that there is always a gap between a form of representation and what is represented therewith. Rather than ignoring or seeking to narrow this gap, as mimetic approaches do, aesthetic insight recognizes that the inevitable difference between the represented and its representation is the very location of politics. (Bleiker 2001, 510)

The aesthetic turn has enhanced the use of images and visual media in order to provide a different perspective to epistemological enquiries. The memetic approaches lead to narrowing the scope of discipline by being unidimensional. Aesthetic approach brings a newer way of analysis that leads to broadening of the discipline. In this regard aesthetic approach has several commonalities with post-structuralism such as repudiation of traditional approaches, use of power, representation and interpretation (Aháll 2009). The importance of aesthetic approach is further highlighted in the studies of emotions. It is important to note that emotions are an important part of global political developments. Aesthetic approach is appropriate in the study emotion which collectively shapes sociopolitical processes. Use of visual representations such as cinema brings forward the manifestation of aesthetic turn in IR and is also a useful tool for Border Studies.

Cinematic representations play a definitive role in constructing popular imagination regarding the issues of identity, refugee crisis and notions of cultural and psychic frontiers. The effect on collective imagination is through engaging narratives and powerful images that cinema is capable of presenting to viewers. This in turn helps construct and deconstruct the popular notions by altering dialectics of cognitive mapping. Manifestation of this effect can be seen in the way that it has impacted mental borders with regard to India and Pakistan.

Such influence of cinema situates perfectly in the Gramscian framework of intellectual hegemony. According to Gramsci the process of hegemony is actualized with the help of "intellectual and moral leadership." These tools are able to present a lopsided view of reality and are instrumental in repetitively reinforcing that view. In this way, ideas and practices that are in consonance with the dominant class are presented in a way that the subordinate class accepts them to be of its own. This leads to "a society in which subordinate groups and classes appear to actively support and subscribe to values, ideals, objectives, cultural and political meanings, which bind them to, and 'incorporate' them into, the prevailing structures of power" (Storey 2006, 80).

This section elaborates the various depictions of the India–Pakistan border in the movies and analyzes the way in which they have reinforced mental borders. Two Bollywood movies (Indian Hindi Movies) namely *LoC Kargil* and *Sarfarosh* and two Lollywood movies (Pakistani movies) namely *Ramchand Pakistani* and *Waar* have been selected for a proper discussion in this section.

The movie *LoC Kargil* (Bollywood) was made in 2003 and presents a fictionalized account of the Kargil war between India and Pakistan. As the name itself suggests, the movie is predicated on the India–Pakistan border in Kashmir. While the film centers around the valor of the Indian armed forces and the strategic depth of the military operations, it is also filled with references to India–Pakistan relation in general and the border between the two countries in particular. Such references in the movie have portrayed the India–Pakistan relations to be marred by conflict and hostility even before the commencement of war. The thematic developments and the dialogues in the movie represent border not only as highly securitized and non-porous but also as a dividing line which needs to be protected from any kind of infiltration, in turn providing impetus to a mental image of border that is rigid and hostile. Such a depiction finds manifestations in dialogues when in the beginning of the movie an army commander orders one of his lieutenants to conduct a recce for lost petrol. He says that "information is received that certain rats have crossed the LoC!" "We will trample those rats and push them to the other side of the LoC" replies the lieutenant (Here LoC refers to the Line of Control between India and Pakistan). The movie also presents the strategic planning of the Indian army. During this sequence an officer suggests crossing the LoC and cutting the enemy supplies from behind. However, the general replies that "The orders are very clear, we will be going by the book. At no point of time, we will cross the line of control."

These dialogues which are made with regards to physical borders are also capable of constructing mental borders by the process of "othering" the neighboring country. Such powerful dialogues coupled by the finesse of the actors are pertinent tools that draw up an imagery that hostility lies across the border. This also creates an impression that people beyond the border are significant "others" who are antagonistic to "us." Such imagination of physical borders and military strategy leads to development of a mental border that is universalized and persists even during peace times. The contention that the Indian army will not cross the LoC even during the war, gives a moral high ground to India as a nation, thus consolidating and glorifying the oneness of a group against the other.

*Sarfarosh* (Bollywood) released in 1999 is a more complex tale, which not only focuses on Pakistan as an enemy state but also touches upon the psychological outcomes from the wounds of partition. Ajay Singh Rathore a police officer, is on a trail of the terrorists responsible for attacks on civilians in the south of India. As he conducts his investigation, he traces the weapons to Pakistan, their agent in India being a singer, Gulfam Hasan who represents the archetypical manifestation of the trauma of dislocation experienced by Indian Muslims who were forced to go to Pakistan after partition. As the movie starts, a Pakistan army officer reports to his general about gun violence in India executed by weapons sent from Pakistan. The officer reports "look at this, India's newspapers are full of news about our success." The general further instructs the officer to carry on the good work and reminds him that "this is war and we have to win this war." The memories of partition are revisited when *Gulfam Hasan* says that "we were forced out of our homes for no reasons." Such depictions showcase and reinforce the psychological pains related with bilateral relations between the countries. Imagery is made that creates a mental border.

The movie *Ramchand Pakistani* (Lollywood) was released in 2008. It is set around the India–Pakistan border at a time when the friction between the two countries was high due to the terrorist attack on the Indian parliament. The movie presents the story of a father (Shankar) and a son (Ramchand) who are Hindu Dalit and live in Pakistan. They inadvertently cross the border and are caught by the security forces on the Indian side. Even a kid is not spared by the security forces and arrested on the suspicion of him being a spy. Ramchand and Shankar are kept in a jail in Bhuj without officially registering them as prisoners. In the end, as the Indo-Pak ties begin to improve, Ramchand and his father were released and sent to Pakistan via Wagha border in Punjab. The dialogues and the sequences in the movie show the nature of India–Pakistan relations which indicate the existence of mental borders.

As Ramchand is caught by the Border Security Force (BSF) the suspicion and mistrust of the BSF officer is evident when he finds a slingshot with the boy and says – "he has brought a weapon with him to free Kashmir." The general rigidity of the India–Pakistan border is understood when Ramchand's mother eagerly runs towards the border but other villagers stop her and chatter in chorus saying that "one cannot go that side." While emphasizing the rigidity of the physical border, the dialogue also develops a feeling of a mental border as the people on the other side of the border are seen as different from people from this side and no means of communication exists among them.

As Ramchand's mother goes to the authorities she was told by the officer that "had it been earlier, I would have asked. At this juncture the countries are ready to fight. I can't ask for any favor at this time." This dialogue shows that what little communication used to exist between the two sides before the parliament attack, was now over. The later part of the movie indicates the rigid nature of the mental border when a jail officer tells Ramchand that it is not even possible to send letters across the border. The movie also touches upon the role played by borders in giving identity to people. Despite Shankar and Ramchand being minority Hindus in Pakistan, they are not dealt with any sympathy in India as their identity of being Pakistani comes from belonging to the other side of the border. They are treated as any other Pakistani in the jail. It is shown that even religious identity is side-lined when it comes to identity provided by the virtue of them being Pakistani. Portrayal of such deep divide strengthens the mental border and feeling of otherness.

One of the dialogues narrates the role of border in giving identity to people when an inmate in the jail says "had there been no border, you wouldn't have been Bengali, he wouldn't have been Indian and I wouldn't have been Pakistani." Such a border is more mental than physical.

Waar (2013) (Lollywood) is a blockbuster Pakistani movie that has a patriotic tone and presents Indian as an enemy. The movie is based on an imminent terrorist attack on Pakistani soil which is planned with help coming from across the border. The movie shows the presence of a RAW operative (Indian intelligence agency), named Laxmi, in Pakistan who is working on destabilizing Pakistan by planning the biggest attack on the country. The attack is ultimately thwarted by the Pakistani security agencies and the Indian agent is killed by her own agency as punishment. The movie has also presented the issue of tribal community of Northern Pakistan who are shown as up in arms against Pakistani government and receiving help from India.

The movie does the job of building mental borders by portraying India as a country that is only interested in destroying Pakistan. In one of the sequences, the Indian spy and the terrorist are shown to be passionately enjoying the moment of a fatal attack on the police academy in Pakistan. The India spy informs her boss of the success of the attack smilingly and triumphantly: "turn on the TV and all you see is chaos" to which the boss replies "you have kept my confidence, I am proud of you." Such depiction is likely to build a mental border by sending a message that destruction in Pakistan is the subject of amusement in India and Indian agencies take pride in this. In another sequence, the Indian spy is killed by her own agency as a punishment for failure to succeed in conducting an attack on Pakistan. Her boss says that "I am sorry it has come down to this. You know in our game failure is not an option."

Such non-democratic and unjust punishment represents an extraordinary degree of commitment to destroy Pakistan. Thus India's image of a hostile other is created which encourages the formation of mental borders among the people.

To conclude, these are blockbuster movies from two neighboring countries portraying each other as archrivals. While movies are a medium of entertainment, such jingoistic presentations make it political and create a sense of hate. Although, there are excellent movies on the theme of India–Pakistan advocating peace and also mocking the obsession that political establishment of both sides have with each other. Some of these movies are *Bajarangi Bhaijaan, Filmistan,* and *Total Siyappa.*

*Bajrangi Bhaijan* was released in 2015 and is based on the emotional bond between a Pakistani child and a devout religious Indian man. The movie is a beautiful depiction of the similarities and shared historical and religious beliefs of both the countries. It is shown that despite the fact that the political establishments of both the countries are obsessed with the ongoing friction, people are inclined towards each other and appreciate the shared history of both the nations.

The movie *Filmistaan,* released in 2012 is an interesting tale of an Indian who is mistakenly kidnapped to Pakistan from Rajasthan border. It is a tapestry that takes the viewer close to the day-to-day living of an average Pakistani and presents the commonalities between the two nations which are supposed to be enemies. The movie is a representation of how the shared love for Bollywood and Cricket is a virtual link between the people of the two countries.

*Total Siyapaa* is a romantic comedy movie released in 2014. It is based on a love story between an Indian girl named Asha and a Pakistani boy named Aman who are based in London. It is shown how the family of Asha has preconceived notions about Pakistanis but as they come to know more about Aman they realize that their attitude is ill founded. The movie advocates peace between Indian and Pakistan and sends a message that people are not entirely defined by nationalities or religion and that people of both the nations must see beyond the statist agenda in order to appreciate the similarities between the two nations.

## V. Conclusion

To conclude, South Asia has all the potential to deal with the contemporary socio-economic challenges. The requirement is that states understand the futility of regional political discords and sincerely work to address the question of rigid borders and boundaries in the region. Moreover, there is a need for a long-term peace between India and Pakistan.

Recently Jacob, in his book that is based on personal experience of traveling to India–Pakistan borders highlighted how the larger political narratives on both sides are not much different (Jacob 2018). The securitized borders of India and Pakistan have specific meaning and only a study of physical borders may not be of much help to understand why things between the two neighbors have not improved in the last seven decades. Therefore, it is important that we study other factors that consolidate borders between India and Pakistan. This is what we have attempted in this paper. The paper has analyzed how textbooks and movies could be important mediums for creating perceptions. In the case of India and Pakistan, already there are ample political problems reflected in terms of a bitter relationship between the two. This animosity between the two immediate neighbors has its cost in terms of low trade between the two, wasting a huge amount of money on security and also has a repercussion for the regional integration process of South Asia. There is a need to bridge the division, reduce the hard security borders and to bring down the mental borders between India and Pakistan. The article has discussed how textbooks and movies are also adding to the existing political antagonism between the two countries.

## Note

1. Partition, August 1947, [Online: web] Accessed on February 29, 2012, URL: http://www.globalsecurity.org/military/world/war/indo-pak-partition2.htm

## Disclosure statement

No potential conflict of interest was reported by the authors.

## ORCID

*Dhananjay Tripathi* ⓘ http://orcid.org/0000-0003-3984-270X
*Vaishali Raghuvanshi* ⓘ http://orcid.org/0000-0002-3572-3685

## References

Aháll, L. 2009. Images, Popular Culture, Aesthetics, Emotions: The Future of International Politics? *Political Perspectives* 3, no. 1: 1–44.
Ali, M. 2002. History, Ideology and Curriculum. *Economic and Political Weekly* 37, no. 44: 4530–1.
Apple, M.W. 1990. The Text and Cultural Politics. *The Journal of Educational Thought* 24, no. 3A: 17–33.
Aziz, K.K. 1993. *The Murder of History: A Critique of History Textbooks Used in Pakistan*. Lahore: Vanguard Books Pvt. Ltd.
Balal, Q. 2014. *Social Studies for Class VI*. Jamshoro: Sindh Textbook Board.
Banerjee, P. 1998. Borders as Unsettled Markers in South Asia: A Case Study of the Sino-Indian Border. *International Studies* 35, no. 2: 179–91.
Bhattacharya, N. 2009. Teaching History in Schools: The Politics of Textbooks in India. *History Workshop Journal* 67: 99–110.
Bleiker, R. 2001. The Aesthetic Turn in International Political Theory. *Millennium: Journal of International Studies* 30, no. 3: 509–33.

Brunet-Jailly, E. 2011. Special Section: Borders, Borderlands and Theory: An Introduction. *Geopolitics* 16, no. 1: 1–6.

Cohen, S.P. 1975. Security Issues in South Asia. *Asian Survey* 15, no. 3: 202–14.

English, R. 1980. The Politics of Textbook Adoption. *The Phi Delta Kappan* 62, no. 4: 275–8.

*Filmistaan.* 2012. Film. Directed by Nitin Kakkar. India: Satellite Pictures Private.

Friedman, T.L. 2007. *The World is Flat: the Globalized World in the Twenty First Century.* London: Penguin Publisher.

Giunchi, E. 2007. Rewriting the Past: Political Imperatives and Curricular Reform in Pakistan. *Internationale Schulbuchforschung* 29, no. 4: 375–88.

Gottlob, M. 2007. Changing Concept of Identity in the Indian Textbook Controversy. *Internationale Schulbuchforschung* 29, no. 4: 341–353.

Gramsci, A. 2009. *Selections from the Prison Notebooks.* Hyderabad: Orient BlackSwan.

Haye, K.A. 1973. *First Steps in Our History.* Lahore: Ferozsons Ltd.

Haye, K.A. 1990. *First Steps in Our History.* Lahore: Ferozsons Pvt Ltd.

Hoodboy, P. 2007. Jinnah and the Islamic State: Setting the Record Straight. *Economic and Political Weekly* 42, no. 32: 3300–3.

Houtum, H.V. 2011. The Mask of Border. In *The Ashgate Research Companion to Border Studies,* ed. D.W Walter, 49–62. Surrey: Ashgate Publishing Limited.

Jacob, H. 2018. *The Line of Control Travelling With the Indian and Pakistani Armies.* Gurgaon: Penguin Rando House India.

Khokhar, F.H. 2014. *Pakistan studies for classes IX-X.* Jhamshoro: Sindh Textbook Board.

Kuznetsov, A.M. 2015. Symbolic Boundaries of Social Systems. In *Introduction to Border Studies,* eds. S.V. Sevastianov, J.P. Laine, and A.A. Kireev, 80–97. Vladivostok: Dalnauka.

*LoC Kargil.* 2003. Film. Directed by J.P. Dutta. India: J P Films.

Menon, R., and K. Bhasin. 2000. *Borders and Boundaries: Women in India's Partition.* New Delhi: Kali for Women.

Mishra, A. 2008. Boundaries and Territoriality in South Asia: From Historical Comparisons to Theoretical Consideration. *International Studies* 45, no. 2: 105–32.

Naqvi, T.H. 2010. The Politics of Commensuration: The Violence of Partition and the Making of Pakistani State. In *Beyond Crisis: Re-Evaluating Pakistan,* ed. N. Khan, 61–88. New Delhi: Routledge Publication.

Nayyar, A.H., and A. Salim. 2005. *The Subtle Subversion the State of Curricula and Textbooks in Pakistan.* Retrieved March 20, 2017, from http://unesco.org.pk/education/teachereducation/reports/rp22.pdf.

Nemeth, A. 2015. Watching the Other Across the Border: Representations of Russia and Estonia on Finnish National Television. *Journal of Borderlands Studies* 30, no. 1: 37–52.

Newman, D. 2003. On Borders and Power: A Theoretical Framework. *Journal of Borderlands Studies* 18, no. 1: 13–25.

Newman, D. 2006. The Lines That Continue to Separate Us: Borders in Our Borderless World. *Progress in Human Geography* 30, no. 2: 143–61.

Pandey, G. 2002. India and Pakistan, 1947–2002. *Economic and Political Weekly* 37, no. 11: 1027–33.

*Ramchand Pakistani.* 2008. Film. Directed by Mehreen Jabbar. Pakistan: Geo Films.

*Sarfarosh.* 1999. Film. Directed by John Matthew Matthan. India: Cinematt Pictures.

Sengupta, S. 2016. *Indian Diaspora is World's Largest at 16m: UN.* January 14, from The Times of India: http://timesofindia.indiatimes.com/world/us/Indian-diaspora-is-worlds-largest-at-16m-UN/articleshow/50569762.cms (accessed June 1, 2017).

Shah, S.Z. 2016. *Social studies for Class VII.* Jhamshoro: Sindh Textbook Board.

Staudt, K. 2018. *Border Politics in a Global Era Comparative Perspectives.* Lanham: Rowman and Littlefield.

Storey, John. 2006. *Cultural Theory and Popular Culture: A Reader.* Athens: University of Georgia Press.

Sundar, N. 2004. Teaching of Hate: RSS' Pedagogical Programme. *Economic and Political Weekly* 39, no. 16: 1605–12.

Thapar, R. 2009. The History Debate and School Textbooks in India: A Personal Memoir. *History Workshop Journal* 67: 87–98.

*Total Siyaapa*. 2014. Film. Directed by Eeshwar Nivas. India: Reliance Entertainment.

Tripathi, D. 2015. Interrogating Linkages Between Borders, Regions, and Border Studies. *Journal of Borderlands Studies* 30, no. 2: 189–201.

Tripathi, D. 2016a. Sustainable Peace Between India and Pakistan: A Case for Restructuring the School Education System. In *History can Bite*, eds. B. Denise, M.S. Karina, and V. Korostelina, 125–38. Gottingen: V & R Unipress.

Tripathi, D. 2016b. Creating Borders in Young Minds: A Case Study of Indian and Pakistani School Textbooks. *Regions and Cohesion* 6, no. 1: 52–71.

Tripathi, D. 2018. Manufacturing Enemy: The Presentation of Indian in Pakistani Textbooks. In *Cultural and Educational Exchanges Between Rival Societies Cooperation Competition in an Interdependent World*, eds. C.P. Chou, and J. Spangler, 99–114. Singapore: Springer Publication.

*Waar*. 2013. Film. Directed by Bilal Lashari. Pakistan:ARY Films.

Wastl-Walter, D., and A.C. Kofler. 2000. European Integration and Border-Related Institutions: A Practical Guide. *Journal of Borderlands Studies* 15, no. 1: 85–106.

Weiner, M. 1993. Rejected Peoples and Unwanted Migrants in South Asia. *Economic and Political Weekly* 28, no. 34: 1737–46.

World Bank. 2016. *The Potential of Intra-Regional Trade for South Asia*. May 24. http://www.worldbank.org/en/news/infographic/2016/05/24/the-potential-of-intra-regional-trade-for-south-asia (accessed April 17, 2017).

Xaxa, J., and B.K. Mahakul. 2009. Contemporary Relevance of Gandhism. *The Indian Journal of Political Science* 70, no. 1: 41–54.

Zaidi, A.S. 2009. A Conspicuous Absence: Teaching and Research on India in Pakistan. *Economic & Political Weekly* 44, no. 38: 57–61.

# Pakistan's Border Policies and Security Dynamics along the Pakistan–Afghanistan Border

Lacin Idil Oztig

**ABSTRACT**

After the US-backed international military alliance toppled the Taliban in Afghanistan in 2001, most Afghan militants took shelter in neighboring Pakistan, blending into Pakistan's tribal groups. Even though Pakistan took a variety of measures to control its border, the Pakistan–Afghanistan border has become a safe haven for Afghan and Pakistani militant groups. Despite mounting militancy along the border, especially after the fall of the Taliban, the Pakistani government opted for a defensive border strategy and started erecting a border fence. Left with few options, in 2017, the Pakistani government switched to an offensive border strategy by giving a shoot-to-kill order against anyone who illegally crosses the border. This article examines the rationale behind Pakistan's different border strategies by analyzing the security dynamics along the Pakistan–Afghanistan border.

## Introduction

Border control is traditionally linked to a state's sovereign authority over its people and territory. At most borders, state authority is manifested through the presence of passport control points and customs checks that control the movement of people and goods across state boundaries. By checking the legality of border crossers through the verification of identity documents and visas, passport control points serve the purpose of differentiating those with proper documentation from unauthorized border crossers. Once unauthorized border crossers are detected, they are sent to detention centers and/or deported. Hence, unauthorized border crossers attempt to enter the territory of a state in a manner that allows no official citizenship inquiry to take place.

Thus, when states opt to reinforce their borders against unauthorized border crossers, they take extra security measures between and/or beyond passport control points. Border reinforcement strategies might have deadly consequences for unauthorized border crossers by compelling them to take less desirable, and often more dangerous routes. For instance, fences constructed along the US-Mexican border from 1993 onwards forced Mexican unauthorized immigrants to go through rivers, deserts, and mountains in attempts to circumnavigate the fences. As a consequence, after the erection of the border fences, migrant deaths at the border rose considerably (Eschbach et al. 1999).

While some states build physical barriers to deter illegal border crossing activities, other states prefer to adopt "push-back" policies at their maritime borders. For example, in 2009, Italy pushed boats full of asylum seekers to Libya, a common launching point for unauthorized border crossers in Africa (Vogt 2012). Italy continued this policy during the height of the migrant crisis that affected Europe in 2015. Furthermore, in July 2018, Italy's refusal to disembark the ship *Aquarius*, which was carrying more than 600 migrants rescued at sea, caused an international outrage (Euronews 2018).

Similar to Italy, Australia systematically intercepts and turns back asylum boats. This policy set an example for neighboring Thailand, Indonesia, and Malaysia (Doherty and Wahlquist 2016). Usually, asylum boats are filled over capacity with people and, as a result, are at risk of sinking. Even if asylum seekers survive the arduous journey after being sent back to their home countries, they would then face the risk of being tortured, killed or being tried unlawfully.

While fences can be seen as a passive and defensive strategy, pushback policies are rather pro-active in nature. Even though states that adopt both passive and pro-active approaches do not intend to kill unauthorized border crossers, these strategies have unintended consequences, as they create enabling conditions that may lead to the deaths of unauthorized border crossers. At the extreme end of the spectrum, states may adopt "shoot-to-kill" policies at their borders as a measure of border control. A shoot-to-kill policy is an offensive strategy that has directly lethal consequences for unauthorized border crossers. Put differently, while a shoot to kill policy is a border reinforcement strategy, it differs from other border reinforcement strategies by being based on violent physical force to deter unauthorized flows of people.

A cost–benefit calculation could be a determining factor with respect to which border reinforcement strategy that states effectively choose. Building fences might be expensive for impoverished states. A shoot-to-kill policy might not technically be expensive, but could be politically costly, in terms of causing condemnation at both domestic and international levels. However, states that have poor human rights records might feel less restrained in killing unauthorized border crossers. Oztig (2013) finds that advanced democracies eschew shoot-to-kill policies and often implement other border reinforcement strategies such as fencing, militarization, etc. On the other hand, states that shoot unauthorized border crossers are characterized by having a weak rule of law system.

Indeed, between 2007 and 2010, Egypt killed dozens of African migrants who tried to cross its border to reach Israel (Human Rights Watch 2008; Lynch 2010). Similarly, since the beginnings of 2000s, India adopted a shoot-to-kill policy against unarmed Bangladeshi unauthorized immigrants (Human Rights Watch 2010). Egypt and India both justified their shoot-to-kill policies by portraying illegal immigration as a threat to their national security (Human Rights Watch 2008; Human Rights Watch 2010; Lynch 2010).

Interestingly, while India and Egypt adopted shoot-to-kill policies against unauthorized immigrants who were unarmed, Pakistan initially adopted a defensive border strategy against militants who were moving freely along its border with Afghanistan. Put it more specifically, in order to prevent the flows of militants at the border, it opted for militarizing and fencing its border, rather than a shoot-to-kill policy. Pakistan chose defensive border policies despite multifaceted security problems experienced especially after the toppling of the Taliban in 2001 (BBC News 2002; Eurasia Net 2003; Al Jazeera 2005).

Strikingly, in 2017, Pakistan reversed its passive security approach and gave a shoot-to-kill order against anyone who crosses the Afghanistan border illegally (Pakistan Today 2017). Why did Pakistan follow a defensive strategy, despite increasing threats at its border with Afghanistan since 2001? More interestingly, why did it adopt an offensive border policy in 2017? This article argues that it is the very security dynamics that induced Pakistani policymakers to both refrain from and later adopt a shoot-to-kill policy at its border with Afghanistan.

While considerable attention is given to state-to-state violence at borders (Mandel 1980; Diehl and Goertz 1988; Diehl 1999; Huth 2000), scarce interest has been devoted to the implications of border practices on unauthorized border crossers. The study of Karl Eschbach et al. (1999) that analyzes the impact of the increased US border control enforcement on Mexican unauthorized border crossers stands out as a notable exception. Furthermore, Oztig (2013) analyzes the question of why some states adopt shoot-to-kill policies as a measure of border control, while other states do not. This study makes a novel contribution to the literature by analyzing the dynamics that induce a state to change its strategies towards unauthorized border crossers. In particular, it asks the question of why Pakistan changed its defensive border strategy to an offensive strategy against militants on its Afghanistan border.

The article proceeds as follows. The first section explains what shoot-to-kill policies are and provides insight into how and why these policies are implemented. The second section sheds light on Pakistan's border policy towards Afghanistan. The third section looks at Pakistani policymakers' discourses on border reinforcement strategies. The fourth section explains the research query by delving into the security dynamics along the Pakistan–Afghanistan border. The final section discusses the implications of these security dynamics for Pakistan's border strategies.

## Shoot-to-Kill Policies at Borders

Shoot-to-kill policies are systematic shooting practices employed by border guards against unauthorized border crossers as an official state policy. These policies differ from self-defence cases in which border guards use force to protect themselves from armed attacks. International law does not prevent border guards from relying on force when their life is threatened. Article 4 of the United Nations Basic Principles on the Use of Force and Firearms by Law Enforcement Officials, which was adopted by the Eighth United Nations Congress on the Prevention of Crime and the Treatment of Offenders in Havana in 1990, states that

> Law enforcement officials, in carrying out their duty, shall, as far as possible, apply non-violent means before resorting to the use of force and firearms. They may use force and firearms only if other means remain ineffective or without any promise of achieving the intended result (OHCR 1990).

Shoot-to-kill policies are not isolated events. Rather, they are systematic shooting practices targeting unauthorized border crossers. A shoot-to-kill policy might develop from a shoot-to-kill order given by state authorities to border guards to kill any unauthorized border

SOUTH ASIA

crosser detected at the border. A shoot-to-kill policy might also start at the local level with arbitrary practices carried out by border guards. In such cases, if state authorities do not try to prevent these practices (and even justify them), then these arbitrary border practices develop into an official state policy

In addition to militants and drug traffickers, unauthorized immigrants might be targets of shoot-to-kill policies. For example, since the beginning of 2000s, more than 1.000 unarmed Bangladeshis were killed by Indian border guards. Most of them were Bangladeshi cattle rustlers who were attempting to enter India for economic purposes (Human Rights Watch 2010). Similarly, between 2007 and 2010, Egypt systematically killed African immigrants who tried to cross its borders to reach Israel (Human Rights Watch 2008; Lynch 2010). Shoot-to-kill policies might also differ in terms of implementation. Some states (as in the case of India) might adopt shoot-to-kill policies against unauthorized border crossers who try to enter into their territory. Other states, however, might implement shoot-to-kill policies against people who try to leave their territory (as in the case of Egypt).

India and Egypt policymakers justified their respective shoot-to-kill policies at their borders by presenting unauthorized immigration as a security threat. For example, in a parliamentary meeting in 2003, then Indian President A.P.J. Abdul Kalam said that "the problem of illegal migration from Bangladesh has assumed serious proportions and affects many states. The government is determined to take all necessary steps to check [on] this problem" (Pathania 2003). In the same year, Shri Mukhtar Abbas Naqvi, the Bharatiya Janata Party General Secretary, explicitly supported the country's shoot-to-kill policy at the Bangladeshi border by stating that:

> ... The socio-economic and political manifestations of illegal immigration are seriously affecting the fabric of the country. Given the implications of continuing illegal infiltration into India, the BJP supports every move and effort including use of force, if the deemed fit, by the Government. No stone should be left unturned in solving the problem of illegal immigration for once and all (Bharatiya Janata Party 2003).

Along similar lines, India's West Bengal Chief Minister Buddhadeb Bhattacharjee, from the Communist Party, stated "our government can no longer tolerate *infiltration* across the border, that has reached alarming proportions. Enough is enough; this can't go on any longer" (quoted in Ramachandran 2005, 14). By placing special emphasis on "no toleration," the Minister implied that any method is considered legitimate in an attempt to deter unauthorized flows.

The Egyptian shoot-to-kill policy on its Israeli border began shortly after a meeting between the Israeli Prime Minister Ehud Olmert and the Egyptian President Hosni Mubarak in 2007. Ehud Olmert demanded that Egypt take more steps to prevent unauthorized flows into Israeli territory. Both states reached a consensus after Egypt agreed to take back unauthorized border crossers detected by Israeli authorities on their shared border (Irin Humanitarian News and Analysis 2007). Olmert also demanded that Mubarak protect the lives of deported unauthorized immigrants from Israel to Egypt (Yacobi 2011). Strikingly, Egypt started to adopt a shoot-to-kill policy against unauthorized immigrants escaping the country to Israel. From 2007 to 2010, more than 80 African unauthorized immigrants were murdered by Egyptian border guards (Lynch 2010). Egypt justified its violent border practices on the grounds that it is battling against smuggling activities along the border (Human Rights Watch 2008). In 2007, the report of the Ministry of Foreign Affairs noted that:

> The number of people trespassing to Israel through the Egyptian-Israeli borders has increased exponentially over the last couple of years. Both countries [should prevent] illegal activities such as trespassing across the borders or smuggling ... after the outrageous terrorist attacks on Sinai. Egyptian authorities are combating this growing phenomenon since it jeopardizes security and should be firmly dealt with, especially now there are organized networks that facilitate illegal trespassing (Arab Republic of Egypt Ministry of Foreign Affairs 2007).

As seen above, India and Egypt legitimized killing of unarmed unauthorized border crossers by presenting them as threats to their national security despite the fact that those who were targeted did not carry out attacks against the border guards. Interestingly, while India and Egypt adopted offensive border strategies against unauthorized immigrants who were unarmed, Pakistan implemented a defensive border strategy against armed militants at its border with Afghanistan since the fall of the Taliban in 2001 (BBC News 2002; Eurasia Net 2003; Al Jazeera 2005). Furthermore, in 2017, Pakistani authorities reversed this strategy by giving a shoot-to-kill order to security officials (Pakistan Today 2017). The following sections explain the rationale of Pakistan's different border strategies.

## Pakistan's Border Policy Towards Afghanistan

Historically, the border between British India and the Emirate of Afghanistan was open, allowing the population on both sides to interact frequently (Mirza 2010). After the creation of Pakistan in 1947, Afghan and Pakistani people continued to interact for trade and employment purposes across the border (Mirza 2010). The Soviet occupation of Afghanistan in 1979 caused a massive number of Afghans to cross the Pakistan border. Initially, Pakistan followed an accommodationist policy towards Afghan refugees (Safri 2011). Pakistani authorities employed religious discourse to legitimize Pakistan's policy. As the then Pakistani President Zia ul-Hak stated: "Pakistan was carved out of the Indian subcontinent as a homeland for Muslims anywhere in the world. If 3 million refugees have come from Afghanistan, we feel it is our moral, religious, and national duty to look after them" (quoted in Stedman and Tanner 2003, 69).

As part of the U.S. policy to push the Soviets out of Afghanistan during its Soviet occupation period (Gibbs 2006), the Pakistani government trained Afghan Islamists (mujahedeen) and sent them back to Afghanistan to fight Soviet troops (Hussain 2005; Gul 2009). As of 1989, 20,000 militants received training in Pakistani camps per year (Kapur and Ganguly 2012). Pakistan also used the Pashtun card to gain influence in Afghanistan. Pakistan aided Afghanistan's the ruling Gulbuddin Hekmatyar Pashtun-dominated Hezb-i-Islami Party ruled by Gulbuddin Hekmatyar in the 1990s (Goodson 2001).

The withdrawal of Soviet troops from Afghanistan in 1989 did not lead to stability in the region as the militant groups, which were initially trained to fight the Soviet troops, started to clash with one other (Brunet-Jailly 2015). In the 1990s, Pakistan was condemned by the international community due to its harboring of militant groups on its soil. In order to prevent international sanctions, Pakistan moved the training camps of militants to Afghanistan. That move gave the Taliban an upper hand in the country and created an enabling condition for its capture of Kabul in 1996 (Brunet-Jailly 2015).

When the Pashtun-dominated Taliban came to power in Afghanistan in 1996, Pakistan, along with the United Arab Emirates and Saudi Arabia, were the only countries to have officially recognized the Taliban government (Bajoria and Kaplan 2011). Despite the Taliban's extremely repressive policies that appalled the international community, Pakistan maintained formidable relations with the Taliban government (Goodson 2001). In 2000, when the President of the United States, Bill Clinton, criticized Pakistan's relationship with the Taliban, Pakistan's then Chief Executive Pervez Musharraf stated that "Afghanistan's majority ethnic Pashtuns have to be on our side ... This is our national security interest ... The Taliban cannot be alienated by Pakistan. We have a national security interest there" (quoted in Rashid 2009, 50).

After the Taliban was toppled by the U.S. led invasion in 2001, the tribal areas along the Pakistan–Afghanistan border became a safe haven for the Taliban and al Qaeda militants. While U.S. forces focused on tackling al Qaeda in Pakistan's northwestern frontier province, Pakistan's southwestern province of Balochistan (where the Taliban was based) was largely glossed over. Consequently, Taliban militants moved freely between Balochistan and southern Afghanistan (Rashid 2009). Furthermore, Taliban militants from Afghanistan were welcomed by Pakistan militants in Waziristan, one of the tribal agencies of Pakistan (Grare 2006).

Immediately after the fall of Taliban, Pakistan sent extra troops to the border to prevent the flows of Taliban militants into its territory (Pakistan beefs up border security 2001). In 2002, in a televised speech to the nation, the President Musharraf expressed Pakistan's determination of not allowing terrorists to take shelter in the country (BBC News 2002). In 2003, Pakistani and Afghan authorities agreed to cooperate to prevent the incursions of Taliban militants who took shelter in Pakistan into Afghanistan (Eurasia Net 2003). Pakistan again militarized the Afghanistan border in 2005 (Al Jazeera 2005). Furthermore, in order to prevent the militarization of refugee camps by Afghan militants, it closed all refugee camps near its Afghanistan border (Ghufran 2008). Nevertheless, Pakistan's border security measures were unsuccessful as Afghan militants were still able to still cross the border with ease.[1]

When the Afghan President Hamid Karzai visited Pakistan in 2006, even though the two countries stressed their good diplomatic relations, Karzai voiced Afghanistan's concern over the presence of Al-Qaeda and the Taliban in Pakistan. Karzai complained that Pakistani authorities were not taking concrete steps to oust these groups from their territory (Zeb 2006). In 2007, the then Pakistani President General Pervez Musharraf openly admitted that some Pakistani border guards turned a blind eye to the flows of Taliban militants crossing the border (BBC News 2007).

In order to tackle the border porosity problem more efficiently, Pakistan sent 80,000 troops to its Afghanistan border in 2006 (Zeb 2006). Even though Afghanistan objected to the fencing of the border, due its non-recognition of the Pakistan–Afghanistan border line (Firstpost 2018), Pakistan subsequently fenced 37 km of its border with Afghanistan between 2007 and 2009 (The Nation 2011). Despite Pakistan's attempts to secure the border, the porosity of the border against militant flows fueled clashes between border guards on both sides of the border and caused a diplomatic rift (Saikal 2014; Khan and Nordland 2016).

The Afghanistan–Pakistan Transit Trade Agreement mediated by the U.S. in 2010 did not contribute to the amelioration of bilateral relations (Brunet-Jailly 2015). The diplomatic relations plunged to the lowest level when, after border skirmishes, Pakistani forces intruded into the Afghan side of the border in both 2012 and 2013 (Saikal 2014). In response, the Afghan President Karzai accused Pakistan of harboring the Taliban militants (Saikal 2014). In 2014, Afghan and Pakistani authorities agreed to cooperate in order to thwart the flows of militants across their borders (Raza 2014). In 2016, a 1,100-kilometre-long trench along its Afghanistan border was completed in the Balochistan province (Butt 2016). Nevertheless, despite the unilateral, bilateral initiatives, and even the US economic assistance to Afghanistan in providing border security, the border has remained porous (U.S. Department of State 2010).

In 2017, a shoot-to-kill order was officially announced by Pakistani policymakers to prevent illegal flows at its Afghanistan border (Pakistan Today 2017). As noted previously, shoot-to-kill policies differ with respect to the way they are adopted. The Pakistani shoot-to-kill policy is different from Indian and Egyptian shoot-to-kill policies. There are no reports that indicate that Indian and Egyptian policymakers gave shoot-to-kill orders to their border guards. However, as Indian and Egyptian policymakers justified their border guards' shoot-to-kill practices at their borders, these violent incidents managed to transform and ultimately merge into an official shoot-to-kill border policy. In such cases, systematic and arbitrary shooting practices at the local level eventually became a state policy. On the other hand, the Pakistani shoot-to-kill policy was set in place by state officials, authorizing border guards to shoot unauthorized border crossers on sight. In other words, unlike the cases of India and Egypt, Pakistan's offensive strategy was designed by policymakers as a border control method.

## Pakistan's Border Discourse

As noted previously, after the Soviet occupation of Afghanistan, Pakistan hosted a massive number of Afghan refugees. Following the Soviet withdrawal from Afghanistan, Pakistani policymakers started to see Afghan refugees as economic and social burden to the country. In 1992, 1.5 million Afghan refugees were repatriated, yet 2 million Afghan refugees remained (Ghufran 2008). In 1994, when the Afghan civil war (1992–1996) intensified, Pakistan temporarily closed its border to prevent the influx of refugees (Goodson 2001). In 2000, Pakistan again closed its border when another refugee influx was prompted by a drought in Afghanistan (Goodson 2001). In order to tackle the militancy problem at its Afghanistan border, Pakistan started to build a fence in 2005. Nevertheless, before fencing the border, Pakistan considered various border reinforcement strategies. For instance, Pakistan considered (but eventually ruled out) placing land mines along the border as an alternative measure to provide border security. In 2007, the Pakistani Foreign Minister Khurshid Kasuri explained this land mining rationale as the following:

> In fact, we wanted to mine the border so that there would no movement across the border. But as a mark of respect to the sensitivity of our European colleagues, we have decided that we will not mine the border for the time being. We will only fence it in certain areas (Pakistan Today 2017).

In 2008, the Foreign Minister of Pakistan, Makhdoom Shah Mahmood Qureshi, stressed the importance of the stability of the Pakistan–Afghanistan border for Pakistan's national security. He went on to say that "Pakistan believes that there is an intrinsic link between peace and development. Peace on our borders can strengthen stability and bring economic development as well as the much needed improvement in the quality of life of our people" (Ministry of Foreign Affairs, Government of Pakistan 2008b). With respect to the strengthening of the border, the Minister emphasized the importance of cooperation with Afghanistan:

> There should be a matching response on the Afghanistan side to the border control measures we have instituted. We have some 1,100 posts along the border. There are about a hundred or so on the Afghan side. These posts and measures should act as a double net. Those that manage to evade one should be ensnared in the other (Ministry of Foreign Affairs, Government of Pakistan 2008b).

In an interview with BBC in 2014, Sartaj Aziz, Pakistan's national security and foreign affairs adviser to the prime minister, made a similar point by stressing the importance of operational and intelligence cooperation between Pakistan and Afghanistan for border security (Khalil 2014). The Foreign Minister Hina Rabbani Khar, in an extensive speech concerning Pakistan's Afghan border in 2012, placed emphasis on peace and stability in Afghanistan. She went on to say that:

> Pakistan today fears for instability in Afghanistan because instability from Afghanistan permeates through the 2,000-plus kilometer border that we have with Afghanistan directly into Pakistan's territory, as it has for the last three decades. There are 53,000 people that cross the Pakistan-Afghan border every day. So you can imagine the permeation and the instantaneous effects of any instability in Afghanistan.
>
> Because we know from history that until and unless there is peace and stability in Afghanistan, we will not be able to find our peace and stability. And we will not be able to grow economically the way we wish. We will not be able to achieve the social goals for our children that we wish to achieve. So it is -- we consider it to be in our core national interest to have a peaceful, stable Afghanistan and it is time that we put all our energy together to be able to achieve those ends.
>
> The other area that I want you to concentrate on is what Pakistan is trying to achieve within the region, what type of relations it is pursuing within the region. Because one thing that is clear to us is that we will not be able to see peace within if we do not find peace on our boundaries, on our borders with our neighbors.
>
> And as far as the bigger question of Afghan presence -- or presence of Afghan nationals in Pakistan is concerned, I think we need to find serious answers to that, because we will be very happy to look for border controls, for biometric system, for ensuring that as 53,000 people cross the border in and out (Council on Foreign Relations 2012).

Taken all together, in their statements on border security, Pakistani policymakers were concerned about not only Pakistan's international image and welfare, but also Afghanistan's overall stability which had direct implications for Pakistan's national security. Mining, fencing and cooperation with Afghan authorities were discussed as border security measures. As noted previously, Afghanistan did not want the Pakistan–Afghanistan border to be fenced, as it did not recognize the current border line between the two countries. Despite Afghanistan's objections, Pakistan took measures to fence the border. While Afghanistan evaluated the border fence through the legality of the border, Pakistan saw it as a measure of national security.

In contrast to Indian and Egyptian policymakers, Pakistani policymakers did not openly suggest "indiscriminate killing" in order to thwart unauthorized flows along the border. Nevertheless, this does not translate into Pakistan's concern for human security at borders. As the following section shows, Pakistani policymakers were rather concerned for the side-effects of violent border practices for Pakistan's domestic security and stability.

## Security Dynamics along the Pakistan–Afghanistan Border

Pashtuns are the largest ethnic group in Afghanistan and the second largest ethnic group in Pakistan after Punjabi. Pashtuns in Afghanistan and Pakistan are mostly concentrated along the Pakistan–Afghanistan border. Pashtuns were divided with the Durand Line established with the Durand Agreement signed between the British Empire and the Afghan Emirate in 1896. The Durand line was also recognized in a peace agreement (Rawalpindi agreement) signed between Great Britain and Afghanistan following the 1919 Anglo-Afghan war and the 1921 Kabul agreement signed between the two countries for the purpose of establishing friendly commercial relations (Qassem 2008).

However, after British India collapsed in 1947, Afghanistan refused to recognize the Durand line as an international border between Afghanistan and Pakistan (Qassem 2008). Even though the Durand Line is recognized by the United Nations (UN), Afghanistan disputes the legality of it (Qassem 2008). While the newly created Pakistan justified the validity of the Durand Line by arguing that she inherited British India's rights, Afghanistan argued that a new border should be drawn up as Pakistan emerged due to the partition of India (Brunet-Jailly 2015). Afghanistan's unwillingness to recognize the border has become a contentious issue in its relations with Pakistan (Saikal 2014).

Furthermore, from 1947 until the Soviet occupation of Afghanistan, the Afghan governments demanded that Pashtuns that straddle the border should become either independent or integrated into Afghanistan (Rais 1994). Pakistan's repression of Pashtun nationalist movements and its bombardments of Pashtun tribes situated near the Pakistan–Afghanistan border paved the way for border skirmishes (Brunet-Jailly 2015). In 1950, Pakistan closed its border with Afghanistan for three months due to strained diplomatic relations (Brunet-Jailly 2015). In 1955, both countries went so far as to withdraw their diplomatic representatives (Adamec 2003).

When the Taliban came to power in Afghanistan in 1996, it continued the previous Afghan governments' policy of not recognizing the Durand Line. Even though this caused acrimony in Pakistan, the relationship between the two sides did not deteriorate, as the Taliban avoided playing the Pashtun card in order to meddle in Pakistan's affairs (Saikal 2014). However, as mentioned previously, Pakistan used Pashtuns to have more influence in Afghanistan.

During the Soviet occupation of Afghanistan, the Islamist Jamaat-e-Ulema-Islam Party established *madrasas* (religious schools) in Pashtun areas of Khyber Pakhtunkhwa (formerly known as the North Western Frontier Province), Federally Administered Tribal Areas (FATA), and Balochistan. These madrasas created favorable conditions for the breed of radical Islam. The Taliban emerged out of Afghan refugees and veterans trained in these madrasas in 1994 (Goodson 2001; Kapur and Ganguly 2012). After the Taliban came to power in Afghanistan, it continued to recruit *madrasa*-educated young Pakistanis (Goodson 2001). The *madrasas* also contributed to the radicalization on the Pakistani side of the border.

As mentioned previously, after the fall of the Taliban in 2001, many Taliban militants who operated in Afghanistan moved to Pakistan (Grare 2006). In his address to the Foreign Affairs Committee of the European Parliament in Brussels in 2006, the then Pakistani President Pervez Musharraf stated that the Taliban poses a greater threat than Al-Qaeda. He noted that even though most Pashtuns are moderate, they face the risk of "Talibanization" (RFE/RL 2006).

Until 2007, most militant groups in Pakistan's FATA region operated independently. In 2007, they were gathered under Tehrik-i-Taliban Pakistan (TTP) under Baitullah Mahsud. The TTP which is also referred to as the Pakistani Taliban is an umbrella group which also includes militants from North-West Frontier Province of Afghanistan (later named Khyber Pakhtunkhwa province) (Gunaratna and Bukhari 2009). The main objective of the TTP is to attack Pakistan along with the U.S. and NATO forces in Afghanistan (Fishman 2013). Yet, the TTP's main target has been Pakistan. TTP's first attack against Pakistan was carried out in 2007 (Global Terrorism Database).

The TTP's and the Taliban are interconnected. After the TTP's establishment, Mullah Omar, head of the Taliban, was declared as the supreme leader (Mir 2009). The TTP's agenda is, in turn, supported by the Taliban militants (Fishman 2013). The TTP also receives the support of Pashtun tribes in Pakistan, such as the Mehsud tribe (Abbas and Qazi 2013). All in all, the TTP, the Taliban, and Pashtun tribes in Afghanistan are merged together (Ghufran 2009). For example, the Mehsud tribe has increased its support to the Afghan Taliban by building training camps after the Taliban was overthrown in Afghanistan. The TTP also have close linkages with the Haqqani network, an Afghan militant group located in Pakistan that fights against the Afghan government along with the Afghan Taliban (Fantz 2012; Laub 2013). After the majority of Taliban groups were relocated to Pakistan, the Taliban and Pakistani Taliban have become more integrated (Fishman 2013).

In the aftermath of September 11th 2001, Pakistan joined the US's War on Terror (Ghufran 2009). After the US intervention in Afghanistan, while Pakistan closely collaborated with the US to root out al Qaeda affiliates in Pakistan, it turned a blind eye to the activities of Taliban militants in its territory (Bajoria and Kaplan 2011). In 2004, with US pressure, Pakistan conducted operations to root out the Taliban located in the tribal areas along the Pakistan–Afghanistan border. 80,000 Pakistani soldiers were deployed in North and South Waziristan. However, Pakistani soldiers of Pashtun descent showed reluctance to fight against Taliban militants with whom they shared ethnic affinities and the operation failed as a result (Zissis and Bajoria 2007).

Between 2004 and 2014, Pakistan followed a "peace through dialogue" strategy towards the militants. President Musharraf legitimized this strategy by arguing that military operations would alienate the local population and contribute to the strengthening of the Taliban (Ghufran 2009). Peace deals were signed with the Ahmadzai (Wazir) clan; Nek Muhammad who led Taliban militants in South Waziristan; Baitullah Mehsud, the leader of the TTP; Hafiz Gulbahadur, the leader of the TTP faction in North Waziristan and Mullah Nazir, leader of the TTP faction in South Waziristan (FATA: Beyond military operation 2015). Through these peace deals, the Pakistani government attempted to maintain a ceasefire and persuade Pashtun tribes to withdraw their support from Afghan militants and cease their cross-border illegal activities (Ghufran 2009).

The peace process between the Pakistani government and Pashtun tribes did not go smoothly, as it was shattered by the attacks of Afghan militants. After these attacks, the

Pakistani army retaliated by launching operations along Pakistan's border areas with Afghanistan. Even though the peace process was interrupted with the attacks launched by both sides, the Pakistani government maintained its policy of dialogue with the militant groups. During this period, Pakistani policymakers warned against the consequences of indiscriminate state violence in tackling the militancy problem. For example, in 2008, the then Pakistan's Foreign Minister Makhdoom Shah Mahmood Quereshi stated that:

> ... We, in Pakistan, have been the victims of terrorism and extremism, and we have paid a heavy price, and more than 1,000 of our brave soldiers have made the ultimate sacrifice while confronting this menace. But the fight against terrorism is a multifaceted fight, not just a military one. Our comprehensive strategy seeks to isolate and marginalize the extremists and combines political engagement, economic development and social reforms (Ministry of Foreign Affairs, Government of Pakistan 2008a).

In another speech, the Foreign Minister went on to say that:

> Force is certainly the most important ingredient in fighting any insurgency in the short term. However, force alone will never be sufficient. The terrorism we see in FATA is a toxic brew of many elements - Taliban and Al Qaeda presence, ideology, ignorance, lack of economic, social and political opportunities, governmental neglect, marginalization and an insular way of life. The strategy to combat it must be equally comprehensive. The objective is to win the hearts and minds of the populace so that the Taliban and Al Qaeda find it difficult to hide in the population. Single minded reliance on force will however result in further alienation of the populace ... Force must be complemented by political, economic and social engagement. We must not undertake any action that hardens the resolve of those already committed to violence or to sway the hostile neutrals to join them (Ministry of Foreign Affairs, Government of Pakistan 2008b).

As the above statements show, Pakistani policymakers were concerned about the consequences of violent border practices for tackling Pakistan's militant problem. Therefore, Pakistan, due to fears of inciting future terrorists attacks at home, followed a defensive policy towards the militants. After the TTP broke the ceasefire, the Pakistani military launched military operations against the TTP in Swat Valley and South Waziristan in 2009 (Ghufran 2009; Saikal 2014). Nevertheless, despite these military operations, the Pakistani government maintained its interest in persuading the TTP into a ceasefire. After the 2013 general elections, Pakistan's Muslim League leader Nawaz Sharif became the Prime Minister. Despite the new government's attempts to reinvigorate the peace process with the TTP, the peace process eventually collapsed (FATA: Beyond military operation 2015).

There are a number of reasons for the failure of the process. First, the peace process inadvertently led to the TTP's consolidation of power in Pakistan's tribal areas (Ghufran 2009). Ceasefires gave the TTP an opportunity to recruit more militants and re-arm (Shah 2014). Second, since 2004, the US attacked militant bases in the FATA through drone strikes. The Pakistani Human Rights Commission reported that the drone attacks killed a significant number of civilians along with militants (Nebehay 2012). Pakistani authorities officially condemned the attacks. The Foreign Ministry of Pakistan stressed that these attacks are illegal and violate Pakistan's territorial sovereignty (Nauman 2012). Despite the official condemnations, the attacks ignited resentment among the local population in the tribal areas and fed into escalated militancy (Ghufran 2009).

In 2014, terrorists, disguised as policemen, attacked Jinnah International Airport. The TTP claimed responsibility for the attack, announcing it as a revenge for the killing of its leader (Hakimullah Mehsud) by a U.S. drone attack in 2013 (Gul 2014). Following this attack, Pakistan reversed its policy of dialogue with the TTP. The Pakistani government organized an operation (Operation Zarb-e-Azb) in North Waziristan with 30,000 ground troops (Mujtaba 2014). In the operation, in addition to the TTP, the Islamic Movement of Uzbekistan (IMU), the East Turkestan Islamic Movement (ETIM), Al-Qaeda, that are active within Pakistani territory, were also targeted.

Strikingly, differing from previous military operations, the Zarb-e-Azb signals the end of the peace process. In a speech at the National Assembly in 2014, the Prime Minister Nawaz Sharif expressed the end of the peace process and the commencement of the offensive policy against the militants with a poignant clarity:

> We gave peace a chance despite the sacrifice of thousands of lives by the army and others ... The PM regretted that the offer of initiating the peace talks was made in all sincerity but was not reciprocated in the same coin. On the one hand, the peace negotiations were in the process, while on the other, the bloodshed of our women and children also continued ... So much so that our places of worship, educational institutions, army installations, airports and residences became unsafe (quoted in FATA: Beyond military operation 2015, 94–5).

Taken all together, Pakistan adopted different strategies (defensive and offensive) to prevent militant flows at its Afghanistan border. In both strategies, "national security" has been the central concern of Pakistani state authorities. Security dynamics played a major role in Pakistan's reluctance to adopt an offensive border strategy at the initial stage of the Taliban threat. Pakistani authorities calculated that adopting a shoot-to-kill policy against unarmed Pashtuns along its border with Afghanistan would destroy the negotiations with Pashtun militants and tribes and trigger domestic instability. Nevertheless, Jinnah International Airport attack in 2014 became the breaking point that broke the camel's back for Pakistan. After peace negotiations failed, Pakistan started to cracking down on militants. Consistent with a shift from a policy of negotiating with militants towards cracking down on militants, Pakistan shifted its defensive border strategy towards a subsequently offensive strategy.

## Discussion and Conclusion

In summary, between 2004 and 2014, Pakistan was engaged in a policy of dialogue with militant groups such as the TTP and Pashtun tribes located in the tribal regions that runs along the Afghanistan border. During this period, even though the Pakistani army conducted military operations against the TTP, rather than rooting out the militant groups, the Pakistani government was interested in persuading them to disarm through peace talks. Pakistan's eschewal of a shoot-to-kill policy at its Afghan border can be evaluated in terms of its defensive policy towards the militant groups that operate on its soil. Pakistani authorities refrained from giving a shoot-to-kill order against Afghan Pashtuns at the border as it would alienate the local Pashtun population and instigate more social support towards the TTP and other militant groups. Furthermore, it would cause the Pashtun militants and tribes to carry out retaliation attacks.

After the TTP attacked Jinnah International Airport in 2014, the Pakistani government dropped its policy of dialogue and launched an operation against the TTP and other militant groups. With respect to the Zarb-e-Azb operation, the Pakistani army stated that "Our valiant armed forces have been tasked to eliminate these terrorists regardless of hue and color, along with their sanctuaries" (quoted in Mujtaba 2014). It was further noted that "with the support of the entire nation, and in coordination with other state institutions and law enforcement agencies, these enemies of the state will be denied space anywhere across the country" (quoted in Mujtaba 2014).

In this respect, Pakistani authorities' shoot-to-kill order against Afghan unauthorized border crossers in 2017 can be evaluated as a continuation of Pakistan's policy of rooting out militant groups in Pakistan. In conclusion, this paper argues that Pakistan's defensive and offensive border strategies at its Afghanistan border are closely related the security dynamics in the region generally and its national security priorities and domestic policies against militant groups particularly.

## Note

1. It should be specified that it is extremely difficult to control the border between Pakistan and Afghanistan. The length of the border is 2,430 km. Furthermore, the border runs through deserts and mountains (Liwal 2010).

## Disclosure Statement

No potential conflict of interest was reported by the author.

## References

Abbas, H., and S.H. Qazi. 2013. Rebellion, Development and Security in Pakistan's Tribal Areas. *CTC Sentinel* 6, no. 6: 23–26.

Adamec, L.W. 2003. *Historical Dictionary of Afghanistan*. 3rd ed. Landham: The Scarecrow Press.

Al Jazeera. 2005. Pakistan Plans Afghan Border Fence. September 12. http://www.aljazeera.com/archive/2005/09/2008410151129552298.html (accessed September 12, 2016).

Arab Republic of Egypt Ministry of Foreign Affairs. 2007. Egyptian Efforts to Combat Trespassing Across the International Borders with Israel. http://www.mfa.gov.eg/Missions/canada/OTTAWA/Embassy/en- (accessed August 11, 2016).

Bajoria, J., and E. Kaplan. 2011. The ISI and Terrorism: Behind the Accusations, Council on Foreign Relations. http://www.cfr.org/pakistan/isi-terrorism-behind-accusations/p11644 (accessed April 3, 2017).

BBC News. 2002. Musharraf Speech Highlights. January 12. http://news.bbc.co.uk/2/hi/south_asia/1757251.stm (accessed January 12, 2012).

BBC News. 2007. Musharraf Admits Border Problems. February 2. http://news.bbc.co.uk/2/hi/south_asia/6323339.stm (accessed February 2, 2008).

Bharatiya Janata Party. 2003. Statement Issued by Shri Mukhtar Abbas Naqvi, BJP General Secretary & Spokesman. http://www.bjp.org/index.php?option=com_content&view=article&id=4760&catid=68:press-releases&Itemid=494 (accessed February 6, 2003).

Brunet-Jailly, E., *eds*. 2015. *Border Disputes: A Global Encyclopedia*. Santa Barbara: ABC-CLIO, LLC.

Butt, Q. 2016. 1,100 km Trench Built Alongside Pak-Afghan Border in Balochistan. *Tribune*, June 20. https://tribune.com.pk/story/1126353/1100km-trench-built-alongside-pak-afghan-border-balochistan/ (accessed June 20, 2016).

Council on Foreign Relations. 2012. Pakistan Relations Beyond National Security Concerns. http://www.cfr.org/pakistan/pakistan-relations-beyond-national-security-concerns/p29106 (accessed September 21, 2015).

Diehl, P.F., ed. 1999. *A Road Map to War: Territorial Dimensions of International Conflict.* Nashville: Vanderbilt University Press.

Diehl, P.F., and G. Goertz. 1988. Territorial Changes and Militarized Conflict. *Journal of Conflict Resolution* 32, no. 1: 103–22.

Doherty, B., and C. Wahlquist. 2016. Australia Among 30 Countries Illegally Forcing Return of Refugees, Amnesty Says. *The Guardian.* February 23. https://www.theguardian.com/law/2016/feb/24/australia-among-30-countries-illegally-forcing-return-of-refugees-amnesty-say. (accessed March 20, 2017).

Eschbach, K., J. Hagan, N. Rodriguez, R. Hernandez-Leon, and S. Bailey. 1999. Death at the Border. *The International Migration Review* 33, no. 2: 430–54.

Eurasia Net. 2003. Afghan-Pakistan Summit Yields Commitment to Improve Border Security. April 24. http://www.refworld.org/docid/46f257ddc.html (accessed March 23, 2016).

Euronews. 2018. Aquarius Migrant Ship Drifts in Med as Italy and Malta Close Doors. June 6. http://www.euronews.com/2018/06/11/aquarius-migrant-ship-drifts-in-med-as-italy-and-malta-close-doors (accessed July 9, 2018).

Fantz, A. 2012. The Haqqani Network, a Family and a Terror Group. *CNN.* September 7. http://edition.cnn.com/2012/09/07/world/who-is-haqqani/index.html (accessed September 8, 2016).

FATA: Beyond military operation. 2015. *Policy Perspectives* 12, no. 1: 93–107.

Firstpost. 2018. Pakistan Launches Military Operation Near Afghanistan Border to Combat Militants; Urges Kabul to Take Similar Steps. July 16. https://www.firstpost.com/world/pakistan-launches-military-operation-near-afghanistan-border-to-combat-militants-urges-kabul-to-take-similar-step-3820257.html (accessed June 4, 2018).

Fishman, B. 2013. The Taliban in Pakistan: An Overview. In *Talibanistan: Negotiating the Borders Between Terror, Politics, and Religion*, ed. P. Bergen, and K. Tiedemann, 336–388. Oxford: Oxford University Press.

Ghufran, N. 2008. Afghans in Pakistan: A 'Protracted Refugee Situation'. *Policy Perspectives* 5, no. 2: 117–29.

Ghufran, N. 2009. Pushtun Ethnonationalism and the Taliban Insurgency in the North West Frontier Province of Pakistan. *Asian Survey* 49, no. 6: 1092–1114.

Gibbs, D.N. 2006. Reassessing Soviet Motives for Invading Afghanistan: A Declassified History. *Critical Asian Studies* 38, no. 2: 239–263.

Global Terrorism Database. Tehrik-i-Taliban Pakistan (TTP). https://www.start.umd.edu/gtd/search/Results.aspx?expanded=no&casualties_type=&casualties_max=&success=yes&perpetrator=20442&ob=GTDID&od=desc&page=70&count=20#results-table (accessed 28 September 2018).

Goodson, L.P. 2001. *Afghanistan's Endless War: State Failure, Regional Politics, and the Rise of the Taliban.* Seattle and London: University of Washington Press.

Grare, F. 2006. Pakistan Afghanistan Relations in the Post-9/11 Era. *Carnegie Papers*, no. 72: 4–18.

Gul, I. 2009. *The Most Dangerous Place: Pakistan's Lawless Frontier.* New York: Viking.

Gul, I. 2014. What's BEHIND KARACHI AIRPORT ATTACK? *CNN.* https://edition.cnn.com/2014/06/09/opinion/pakistan-karachi-gul-explainer/index.html (accessed 7 March 2018).

Gunaratna, R., and S.A.A.S. Bukhari. 2009. Militant Organizations and Their Driving Forces. In *Pakistan-Consequences of Deteriorating Security in Afghanistan*, ed. K. Zetterlund. FOI Swedish Defence Research Agency.

Human Rights Watch. 2008. Sinai Perils: Risk to Migrants, Refugees, and Asylum Seekers in Egypt and Israel. http://www.hrw.org/sites/default/files/reports/egypt1108webwcover.pdf. (accessed September 12, 2016).

Human Rights Watch. 2010. Trigger Happy Excessive Use of Force by Indian Troops at the Bangladesh Border. http://www.hrw.org/reports/2010/12/09/triggerhappy-0. (accessed January 25, 2016).

Hussain, R. 2005. *Pakistan and the Emergence of Islamic Militancy in Afghanistan.* Aldershot, UK: Ashgate.

Huth, P.K. 2000. Territorial Disputes and International Conflict: Empirical Findings and Theoretical Explanations. In *Borderlands Under Stress*, ed. M. Pratt, and J.A. Brown, 97–141. The Hague: Kluwer.

Irin Humanitarian News and Analysis. 2007. Israel-Sudan: Government to Turn Back Refugees at Border. July 4. http://www.irinnews.org/Report.aspx?ReportId=73078 (accessed April 3, 2016).

Kapur, S.P., and S. Ganguly. 2012. The Jihad Paradox: Pakistan and Islamist Militancy in South Asia. *International Security* 37, no. 1: 111–41.

Khalil, S. 2014. Pakistan-Afghan Border Security a Major Challenge -Sartaj Aziz. *BBC News*, November 18. http://www.bbc.com/news/world-asia-30093261 (accessed November 18, 2016).

Khan, I., and R. Nordland. 2016. Afghanistan and Pakistan Exchange Heavy Gunfire along Border. *New York Times*, June 13. https://www.nytimes.com/2016/06/14/world/asia/afghanistan-pakistan-torkham-border-crossing.html?_r=0 (accessed April 1, 2017).

Laub, Z. 2013. "Pakistan's New Generation of Terrorists. *Council on Foreign Relations*. http://www.cfr.org/pakistan/pakistans-new-generation-terrorists/p15422 (accessed September 26, 2016).

Liwal, A.G. 2010. Areas Between Afghanistan and Pakistan and the Present Turmoil. *Eurosia Border Review* 1, no. 1: 75–86.

Lynch, C. 2010. They Shoot Migrants, Don't They? Foreign Policy, October 8. http://turtlebay.foreignpolicy.com/posts/2010/10/08/they_shoot_migrants_dont_they (accessed April 5, 2017).

Mandel, R. 1980. Roots of the Modern Interstate Border Dispute. *Journal of Conflict Resolution* 24, no. 3: 427–54.

Ministry of Foreign Affairs, Government of Pakistan. 2008a. The Foreign Minister of Pakistan, Speaking at the Brookings Institution; Washington, D.C., July 11. http://www.mofa.gov.pk/mfa/pages/article.aspx?id=763&type=3 (accessed July 11, 2016).

Ministry of Foreign Affairs, Government of Pakistan. 2008b. The Foreign Minister of Pakistan at Princeton University. October 2. http://www.mofa.gov.pk/mfa/pages/article.aspx?id=750&type=3 (accessed October 29, 2015).

Mir, A. 2009. Of Pakistani Jihadi Groups and their al-Qaeda and Intelligence Links. *The News*, March 24. (accessed March 13, 2017).

Mirza, N. 2010. Pakistan Border Security Problems vis-à-vis Afghanistan and Iran, eds. A. Neill Towards cross-border security, occasional paper. https://rusi.org/sites/default/files/201002_op_towards_cross-border_security_0.pdf (accessed February 16, 2011).

Mujtaba, H. 2014. Pakistan Army Launches Big Operation after Airport Attack. *Reuters*, June 15. http://www.reuters.com/article/us-pakistan-airstrikes-idUSKBN0EQ0F720140615 (accessed April 23, 2017).

The Nation. 2011. Pakistan to Mine, Fence Afghan Border. February 24. http://www.webcitation.org/6RKtRZlMP (accessed June 24, 2016).

Nauman, Q. 2012. Pakistan Condemns U.S. Drone Strikes. *Reuters*. June 4. http://www.reuters.com/article/2012/06/04/us-pakistan-usa-drones-idUSBRE8530MS20120604 (accessed June 4, 2013).

Nebehay, S. 2012. U.N. Investigator Decries U.S. Use Of Killer Drones. *Reuters*. June 19. http://uk.reuters.com/article/2012/06/19/uk-usa-un-drones-idUKBRE85I0FR20120619 (accessed June 19, 2013).

OHCR. 1990. Basic Principles on the Use of Force and Firearms by Law Enforcement Officials Adopted by the Eighth United Nations Congress on the Prevention of Crime and the Treatment of Offenders. Havana, Cuba, August 27 – September 7. *Criminal Law Forum* 1, no. 3: 513–548. https://www.ohchr.org/en/professionalinterest/pages/useofforceandfirearms.aspx (accessed 3 September 2016).

Oztig, L.I. 2013. Why Do Border Guards Shoot? An explanation of Shoot-to-Kill Policies that Target Unauthorized Border Crossers. PhD diss., University of Tuebingen. https://publikationen.unituebingen.de/xmlui/bitstream/handle/10900/48019/pdf/Diss_oztig.pdf;sequence=1.

Pakistan beefs up border security. 2001. *BBC News*, November 16. http://news.bbc.co.uk/2/hi/south_asia/1659639.stm (accessed November 16, 2016).

Pakistan Today. 2017. Shoot-on-Sight Orders Over Illegal Entry into Pakistan from Afghan Border. *Pakistan Today*. February 19. http://www.pakistantoday.com.pk/2017/02/19/shoot-on-sight-orders-over-illegal-entry-into-pakistan-from-afghan-border/ (accessed February 19, 2017).

Pathania, J.M. 2003. India & Bangladesh-Migration Matrix-Reactive and Not Proactive South Asia Analysis. Group Paper no. 632. http://www.southasiaanalysis.org/paper632 (accessed December 16, 2013).

Qassem, A.S. 2008. Pak-Afghan Relations: The Durand Line. *Policy Perspectives* 5, no. 2: 87–102.

Rais, R.B. 1994. *Wars Without Winners: Afghanistan's Uncertain Transition After the Cold war.* Karachi: Oxford University Press.

Ramachandran, S. 2005. Indifference, impotence, and intolerance: Transnational Bangladeshis in India. Global Migration Perspectives, no. 42. http://www.unhcr.org/refworld/docid/435f84da4.html (accessed September 29, 2015).

Rashid, A. 2009. *Descent Into Chaos: The U.S. and the Disaster in Pakistan, Afghanistan, and Central Asia.* New York: Penguin Publishing Group.

Raza, S.I. 2014. Pakistan, Afghanistan Agree to Thwart Cross-Border Movement. *Dawn.* July 4. https://www.dawn.com/news/1116939/pakistan-afghanistan-agree-to-thwart-cross-border-movement (accessed December 13, 2016).

RFE/RL. 2006. Afghanistan: Taliban Could Spark Pashtun 'National War.' September 12 (accessed 30 September 2018).

Safri, M. 2011. The Transformation of the Afghan Refugee: 1979–2009. *The Middle East Journal* 65, no. 4: 587–601.

Saikal, A. 2014. *Zone of Crisis: Afghanistan, Pakistan, Iraq and Iran.* New York: I. B. Tauris.

Shah, A. 2014. Pakistan Fights Back: Behind the operation in North Waziristan. *Foreign Affairs.* June 19. https://www.foreignaffairs.com/articles/pakistan/2014-06-19/pakistan-fights-back (accessed June 19, 2014).

Stedman, S.J., and F. Tanner. 2003. *Refugee Manipulation: War, Politics, and the Abuse of Human Suffering.* Washington, DC: Brookings Institution Press.

U.S. Department of State. 2010. Afghanistan and Pakistan Regional Stabilization Strategy. https://www.state.gov/documents/organization/135728.pdf (accessed March 19, 2017).

Vogt, A. 2012. Italy Violated Human Rights by Returning Migrants to Libya, Court Rules, the Guardian. February 23. https://www.theguardian.com/world/2012/feb/23/italy-human-rights-migrants-libya. (accessed April 15, 2017).

Yacobi, H. 2011. 'Let me go to the City': African Asylum Seekers, Racialization and the Politics of Space in Israel. *Journal of Refugee Studies* 24, no. 1: 47–68.

Zeb, R. 2006. Cross Border Terrorism Issues Plaguing Pakistan–Afghanistan Relations. *China and Eurasia Forum Quarterly* 4, no. 2: 69–74.

Zissis, C., and J. Bajoria. 2007. Pakistan's Tribal Areas. *Council on Foreign Relations.* October 26. http://www.cfr.org/pakistan/pakistans-tribal-areas/p11973 (accessed April 19, 2017).

# The Status of Durand Line under International Law: An International Law Approach to the Pakistan-Afghanistan Frontier Dispute

Fawad Poya

**ABSTRACT**

The Durand Agreement, which gave birth to the Durand Line-the border between Afghanistan and Pakistan, is one of the most controversial issues for Afghanistan. This Agreement resulted in the annexation of a part of the territory of Afghanistan to British-India (now in Pakistan). Although, the agreement was concluded by the direct participation of the ruler of Afghanistan, the consecutive governments of Afghanistan, in particular, those after partition of British-India, refused to accept Durand Line as an international border. They asserted that the territory of Afghanistan extends beyond the Durand Line, thereby giving rise to a dispute with the neighboring state of Pakistan. What course of action should be adopted by the government and the people of Afghanistan within the contours of international law in order to resolve the border dispute with Pakistan is always being pertinent. This necessarily entails two significant arguments- (1) whether the disagreement over the Durand Border between Afghanistan and Pakistan falls in a "dispute" situation and (2) if there exists a legal dispute, how it should be settled. The paper, therefore, tries to examine above-mentioned arguments and suggests legal/practical solutions within the international law framework to prevent further conflict, thus taking a momentous pace towards regionalism.

## I. Introduction

The Durand Line covering a distance of 1500 miles, starts from the Pamirs, the snow-capped mountains in the north, passing through the fertile mid-section, it touches the barren areas of the south near to the Arabian Sea (Kayathwal 1994, 37). It came into existence as a result of an agreement known as Durand Agreement which was signed in 1893 between King Abdur Rahman Khan, Amir of Afghanistan, and Sir H. Mortimer Durand, the British Foreign Secretary to India, after whom the line was named (Qassem 2007, 66). The Durand Line demarcated the boundary in a region whose people had claimed allegiance to neither of the two countries, British India and Afghanistan. Both countries had been competing for influence in this area but no one of them succeeded until the boundary was created by the 1893 agreement. Based on this Agreement, each of the signatories, the Amir and Durand, vowed not to "exercise interference" in the territories of each other- lying beyond the line, and both sides declared to respect the agreement (Qureshi 1966, 103).

However, it was expected that the Durand Agreement would put an end to uncertainty, mutual distrust and all misgivings but the boundary remained troublesome mainly because of arbitrary character of the boundary (Kayathwal 1994, 38). The issue became further complicated since the emergence of Pakistan in 1947 as an independent State (Hussain 1985, 255). While Pakistan recognizes the Durand Line as its official border with Afghanistan, consecutive Afghanistan governments have vigorously rejected to acknowledge the Durand Line as its official border with Pakistan (Brasseur 2011, 5). And so, the Durand Line issue locked both States in a durable confrontation (Blarel 2015, 1).

Thus, this paper critically examining the contentious views between Afghanistan and Pakistan and trying to answer whether there was duress when the Agreement was concluded? Shall the validity of the Agreement be questioned on the basis of Vienna Convention on the Law of Treaties 1969 (VCLT) and Vienna Convention on Succession of States in Respect of Treaties 1978 (VCSSRT)? Is Pakistan a successor State to British India under international law and how does recognition of Afghanistan affect the international status of Pakistan as a State? How all these assertions are tenable to challenge the validity of Durand Border? Does legally any dispute exist between the two countries in relation to the Durand Agreement, if there is a dispute, how it should be settled.

This paper is divided into three parts. The first part deals with the origin and historical evolution of the Durand Line. The Agreement and the arguments of both States are embraced in the second part. The last part outlines whether there is a dispute between the two States and in case there is a dispute, how it should be tackled. This paper is also followed by a conclusion.

## II. Geneses and Historical Evolvement of the Durand Line

By the late nineteenth century, the British had succeeded in confining Afghanistan, mainly, within its present eastern and southern boundaries by the two most famous treaties: the Treaty of *Gandamak*, signed in 1879; and the conclusion of the Durand Agreement (Saikal 2004, 28). The Amir (Amir Abdur Rahman Khan) and Durand (Sir H. M. Durand) signed two agreements on November 12 1893. One concerning the north-eastern region of Afghanistan, and the other relating the south-eastern region. The latter, came to be known as the Durand Agreement or the Kabul Convention of 1893 (Kakar 2006, 179). Indeed, it was the time that Russians were pressing on the river Oxus and advanced further to Afghanistan northern borders. On the other hand, the British had concluded that official borders needed to be established between Afghanistan and British India to hold off the Russian advance toward British India (Omrani 2009, 177). The boundary further secured British control over strategic passes and access routes to India and cut the Pashtun ethnic group in two (Blarel 2015, 3&6).

Nevertheless, Amir Abdur Rahman Khan was well-satisfied with the outcome of his tough negotiations with the British delegation headed by Sir H. M. Durand (Mahmood 2005, 19). In return, the Amir was to receive £60,000 a year and guarantees of assistance in case of foreign aggression (Rasanayagam 2003, 8). After signing of the documents, the Amir held a "durbar" on November 13 1893. In this gathering that his two of elder sons (including Habibullah Khan who later became Amir of Afghanistan), four hundred leading chiefs and high civil and military officers attended, he urged his people to be true friends to the British (Mahmood 2005, 19). In this regard, the Amir (1900 , 163) stated in his memoirs,

> Before the audience I made a speech to commence the proceedings, in which I gave an outline of all the understandings which had been agreed upon and provisions which had been signed for the information of my nation and my people, and all those who were present. I praised God for bringing about the friendly relations which now existed between the two Governments.

Further he (1900, 146) mentioned,

> At the time when I was occupied in breaking down the feudal system of Afghanistan and moulding the country into a strong consolidated kingdom, I was not unaware nor neglectful of the necessity of defining my boundaries with the neighbouring countries. I well knew that it was necessary to mark out the boundary lines between my dominions and those of my neighbours, for the safety and protection of my kingdom, and for purpose of putting a check on their advances and getting rid of misunderstandings and disputes

Almost a year later, the demarcation of the boundary started on the ground. Therefore, several boundary commissions were established to delimit the frontier between British India and Afghanistan as defined in the Durand Agreement. As an eminent author, G. P. Tate (1909, 26–27) claims,

> From the British side, Mc Mahon was entrusted the task of surveying and demarcating, jointly with an Afghan Commission. The work occupied altogether more than a couple of years, from April 1894 to 1896. During the first portion of the time Sir Henry Mc Mahon was accompanied by Capitan R. J. Mackenzie, R. E., as survey officer and four other British officers acting in various capacities. The total British following, including contingents from friendly tribes, amounted to little if anything short of a thousand men and six hundred camels, horses and ponies. On his side, the Afghan Commissioner, Sardar Gul Mahammad Khan, a near relative of the Amir, enjoyed the support of an equally numerous following.

On the other hand, there are arguments that the Amir who relinquished part of his claimed territory, was not much pleased. D. Loyn (2008, 146) argues that Amir at the same time, secretly spread propaganda against the British, saying that he was not happy and that it would be better to move the Line over towards the east. Amin Saikal (2004, 28), an Afghan historian, also claims that the Durand Line, drawn by the British, was the line arbitrarily determining Afghanistan's present eastern and southern borders and it demarcated British and Afghan responsibilities in the Pashtun area which later became the basis for what subsequently developed as a border dispute between Afghanistan and its southeast neighbor. On the contrary, Amir Abdur Rahman (1900, 164) was of the view that the misunderstandings and disputes which arose before the Durand Agreement, the border matters were put an end by then and after the boundary lines had been marked out according to the agreement.

## III. The Agreement and the Arguments

The Durand Agreement[1] comprises of seven short Articles which created the boundary line between two countries, Afghanistan and British India. The preamble of the Durand

Treaty expresses the purpose of treaty which both sides were desirous of settling questions regarding the boundaries by friendly understanding, and of fixing the limitation of their respective spheres of influence, so that for the future there may not be any difference of view on the subject between the allied Governments. In addition, the Amir (1900, 164) noted in his memoirs,

> Having settled my boundaries with all my other neighbours, I thought it necessary to set out the boundaries between my country and India, so that the boundary line should be definitely marked out around my dominions, as a strong wall for protection.

Under Article 2&6 of the Agreement, governments of both Afghanistan and India, have promised a friendly settlement of the boundary issues and laid down that at no time would exercise interference in the territories of each other, lying beyond the line. Furthermore, Article 1, 3, 4 and 5 of the Agreement, in detail, deal with the demarcation of the eastern and southern borders of Afghanistan, from Wakhan to the Persian border.

Since the emergence of Pakistan in 1947 as an independent State, Afghanistan has on a number of grounds challenged the validity of the Durand Agreement and so the boundary line which resulted from the agreement (Hussain 1985, 255). In addition, the Afghan government opposed Pakistan's application on September 30 1947 for the membership of the United Nations. Although agreed later (October 20 1947) to recognize the new State (Burke 1973, 71). Pakistan has also questioned the Afghan stand on Durand Line and has claimed the Agreement as a valid boundary treaty between the two countries (Hussain 1985, 255). Thus, many arguments have been raised from both sides. Although, there are ample of arguments regarding the status of Durand Line as a border. Some of these views are not dealt in this paper due to the dearth of a strong legal basis. However, the legal arguments relating to the validity of the agreement are highlighted as follows:

## A. Duress and Coercion

An argument put forward by some that the validity of Durand Agreement can be questioned on the ground that the Amir was forced by British India to accept the boundary demarcation (Giunchi 2013, 26). Hassan Kakar (2006, 182), a well-known Afghan historian, believes that the conditions under which the agreement was concluded were more fearsome than those treaties were concluded in the nineteenth century between the European and weaker Asian powers. It means that the real factor was the Amir's fear that made the agreement possible. Also M. G. M. Ghobar (1967, 692), another Afghan historian, stated that the Amir signed the treaty solely under the shadow of British threat and deception and accepted a historical responsibility forever. Afghanistan government invokes Article 51 of the VCLT 1969 to challenge the validity of the Durand Agreement. Article 51 can be read as follows-

> The expression of a State's consent to be bound by a treaty which has been procured by the coercion of its representative through acts or threats directed against him shall be without any legal effect.

Also Article 52 of the VCLT is invoked which provides-

> A treaty is void if its conclusion has been procured by the threat or use of force in violation of the principles of international law embodied in the Charter of the United Nations.

However, these assertions have been challenged by many others. They believe that the Amir in his memoirs does not support the view that the agreement was signed in fear of British threats (Qassem 2007, 65). Indeed, he held a *darbar* "of endorsement" after signing the agreement in which he praised the agreement as an achievement. Further legality of the Durand Line would have to reckon with the relevance of four other agreements signed consecutively in 1905, 1919, 1921 and 1930, where Afghanistan accepted the Durand Line as its international border (Qassem 2007, 69). Moreover, the Durand Agreement led to continued annual payments "subsidy" and shipment of weapons by British to the Amir (Brasseur 2011, 5). Although the latter view is claimed to be economic coercion and a kind of bribery to the Amir of Afghanistan. The payment of subsidy thence nullified the agreement due to the fact that caused corruption as laid down in Article 50 of the VCLT. Article 50 avows that-

> If the expression of a State's consent to be bound by a treaty has been procured through the corruption of its representative directly or indirectly by another negotiating State, the State may invoke such corruption as invalidating its consent to be bound by the treaty

It is noteworthy that the validity of the agreement cannot be contested on the basis of corruption as provided under Article 50 of the VCLT. Because, during the colonial period, the practice of subsidy was not viewed as bribery and the term subsidy was used as today's world economic aid and financial support of a rich State to developing countries. These aids can be an instrument to influence the policies of recipient States but their payment is not regarded as an act of bribery (Hussain 1985, 257).

On the other hand, the term coercion is restricted under Article 52 of VCLT merely to the threat or use of force which does not contain economic coercion. During the ILC discussions on Article 52, some countries tried to expand the scope of the Article by inclusion of the other forms of coercion, like; economic pressure. But the view was not favored by majority and the present formation was retained. Moreover, there is no consensus regarding the customary international law status of Article 52 of the VCLT. The ILC (1966 vol. II, 247, para 7–8) also has not confirmed the retroactive effect of Article 52 of the VCLT on the validity of treaties which were concluded before the formation of modern law.

### B. Unilateral Termination of the Agreement

On July 26 1949, Afghanistan convened a tribal assembly (Loya Jirga) that announced the unilateral cancelation of all the former treaties had been signed with the British India, including the Durand Agreement. Afghanistan thereby questioned the legality of Durand line as a border and unilaterally terminated the agreement and the stand remains unchanged till now (Biswas 2013). There is no similar view regarding the unilateral termination of treaties, which is used interchangeably with exit, denunciation and withdrawal to refer the act by which a state unilaterally quits its membership in a treaty pursuant to the terms of the treaty providing for such denunciation or withdrawal, among international jurists (Helfer 2005, 1579). L. H. Woolsey (1926, 348), a distinguished international jurist argues that treaties which duration is not fixed imply the clause *rebus sic stantibus*, in case there is a change in the circumstances which have given rise to the conclusion of a treaty may bring about its cancelation by one of the contracting parties, if it is not possible to cancel it by mutual agreement.

Unlike breach, withdrawal from a treaty, is an internationally lawful act. To denounce a treaty, a State must follow, usually procedural conditions that the treaty postulates. Specifically, a State that follows the procedures for withdrawal from a treaty is not to be counted as its failure to comply before a tribunal created by that treaty or to be targeted for treaty-authorized sanctions (Helfer 2005, 1589). But the two possible exceptions, which more or less have been reflected in Article 56 of the VCLT, must be taken into consideration. First, exit from a treaty that does not contain any provision for denunciation or particularly preclude the withdrawal. Second, exit from a treaty that overlaps with customary international law (Helfer 2005, 1589).

Furthermore, the plea of *rebus sic stantibus* or "change in the circumstances" which is one of the grounds to terminate the agreements, cannot be invoked in boundary agreements, particularly, in the context of Durand Treaty. Since Article 62 of the VCLT excludes the boundary treaties from the scope of the Article. It should also be borne in mind that the foundational principle of State consent, governs the design and operation of all treaty exit clauses (Helfer, Terminating Treaties 2012, 634). Moreover, under the *Pacta sunt servanda* principle- "Every treaty in force is binding upon the parties to it and must be performed by them in good faith" (Vienna Convention on the Law of Treaties 1969).

## C. Status of Pakistan as a Successor

Succession of States under the international law can be defined as the replacement of State's responsibility by a new State for its international relations (VCLT 1969, Art 2). This means that succession happens when a State fundamentally changes its structure of power and authority (Qerimi and Krasniqi 2013, 1648). Indeed, international law distinguishes between succession of States and changes of regime which the latter will not, as a rule, affect the rights and obligations of the State (Emanuelli 2003, 1279). Moreover, State succession may take different forms, in particular, a portion of the territory of a State may secede or separate and become the seat of a new State, like; Pakistan from India in 1947 and Bangladesh from Pakistan in 1971 (Emanuelli 2003, 1278). Pakistan, for the first time in 1947 unilaterally asserted that she is a successor state (to British India) and has derived full sovereignty over the area and its people and had all the rights and obligations of a successor State. Also she claimed that Durand Line is a valid international boundary recognized and confirmed by Afghanistan on several occasions "in 1905 and 1919" (Sykes 2002, 176).

On the other side, the status of Pakistan as a successor, was questioned on those initial days of which Pakistan was a new State carved out of the British dominion of India (Biswas 2013). Afghanistan Prime Minister, Shah Mahmood Khan, during a meeting with the British Secretary of Foreign Affairs on July 31 1947, declared that all agreements in respect of the Indo-Afghan border had been concluded with British Indian authorities would be null and void after British India ceased to exist and power was handed over to the new state of Pakistan. Later this viewpoint was officially announced before Pakistan after her independence (Qaseem 2008).

The ILC has tried to codify the rules governing the succession of States in three arenas: Succession of States with respect to treaties; succession of States with respect to public property, archives, and debts; and succession of States and nationality of natural persons. For the purpose of this paper, only the Vienna convention on succession of states with respect to treaties (VCSSRT) which was concluded in 1978 and entered into force in 1996, is taken into account. It prescribes the rules which govern the continuity or termination of a predecessor State's treaties upon the succession of a territory of that State (Cheng 2006, 4). Article 16 of the VCSSRT reads-

> A newly independent State is not bound to maintain in force, or to become a party to, any treaty by reason only of the fact that at the date of the succession of States the treaty was in force in respect of the territory to which the succession of State relates.

According to this Article which is based on *clean-slate doctrine* in Latin "Tabula Rasa",[2] the new States born out of the decolonization process, do not automatically inherit treaty rights and obligations previously concluded on their behalf by colonial powers (Emanuelli 2003, 1284). Though, these newly independent States, may unilaterally choose to succeed to those treaties to which the Predecessor State is party to them (VCSSRT 1978, Art.17). In addition, the VCSSRT has sought to balance the clean-slate doctrine through the incorporation of the *Continuity Principle* which is also known as doctrine of universal succession (O'Connell 1956). The latter principle which is mainly provided in Article 11 of VCSSRT recommends that, in certain treaty matters like; boundary regime, may remain unaffected by the occurrence of a succession of States. Article 11 of the VCSSRT can be read-

> A succession of States does not as such affect: (a) a boundary established by a treaty; or (b) obligations and rights established by a treaty and relating to the regime of a boundary.

Afghanistan has always invoked the clean-slate doctrine regarding the Durand boundary dispute with Pakistan. During the UN conference on Succession of States in respect of Treaties, Afghanistan opposed the inclusion of Article 11. On the contrary, Pakistan was of the view that the VCSSRT does not cover the validity of a treaty as per Article 14 and it covers mere fact of succession which does not contain validity issues and supported the inclusion of Article 11 (Hussain 1985, 271).

As far as the question whether Pakistan is the successor of British India is concerned, not only Pakistan claimed being a successor State to British India but also the British Government had clarified in many occasions,[3] particularly, in the Indian Independence Act (1947), that the "Rights and obligations under international agreements having an exclusive territorial application to an area comprised in the Dominion of Pakistan will devolve upon that Dominion". Furthermore, the application of the Convention depends to expressing the consent to be bound by the present Convention and applies only in respect of a succession of States which has occurred after the entry into force of the Convention except as may be otherwise agreed. The VCSSRT Article 7 (1) reads-

> Without prejudice to the application of any of the rules set forth in the present Convention to which the effects of a succession of States would be subject under international law independently of the Convention, the Convention applies only in respect of a succession of States which has occurred after the entry into force of the Convention except as may be otherwise agreed.

Pakistan and Afghanistan are both non-member parties` to the VCSSRT. It can only be applicable as rules of customary international law. Although some commentators suggest that the 1978 Vienna Convention codifies customary international law in the field, it is broadly accepted that the Convention does not in fact reflect customary international law (Qerimi and Krasniqi 2013, 1648).

## D. Recognition of Pakistan as a State

In September 1947 at the United Nations, the representative of Afghanistan, speaking on the question of Pakistan's request for the membership of the UN declared that

> We cannot recognize the North-West border as part of Pakistan so long as the people of the North-West border have not been given an opportunity, free from any kind of influence, to determine for themselves whether they wish to be independent or to become part of Pakistan. (Razvi 1971, 151)

Therefore, Afghanistan opposed Pakistan's membership to the United Nations on September 30 1947. However, she withdrew the negative vote within one month and established her diplomatic relations with Pakistan (Salim 2007).

According to the 1933 Montevideo Convention on the Rights and Duties of States, the recognition of a State merely signifies that the State which recognizes, indeed accepts the personality of the other with all the rights and duties determined by international law which is unconditional and irrevocable (Article 6). The Convention also provides that a State as a person of international law should possess- a permanent population; a defined territory; a government; and the capacity to enter into relations with the other States (Article 1). Thus, Afghanistan has already recognized the personality of Pakistan with all rights and duties and all the four qualifications of a State, including Pakistan's defined territory by the international law in 1947, which might be irrevocable.

On the other hand, admission of a State as a member of the UN assumes that the candidate is a State based on Article 4(1) of the UN Charter. Accordingly, the decision of the General Assembly for admission of a candidate as per Article 4(2) of the UN Charter, is binding on those States even they outvoted and the obligations contained in the Charter can no longer be contested by any member in their relations with the member that has been admitted (Gruber 1998, 496). Besides, Afghanistan is obliged by certain other treaties to have a defined territory to fulfill its international obligations. For instance, under the Marrakesh Agreement (1994), contracting parties should be a State or customs territory for being a member to WTO (Article XII.1). Therefore, under WTO regime, the MFN and National Treatment obligations can be fulfilled only when there is a defined territory and these principles shall be applicable at the moment goods enter to the territory of a contracting party.

## IV. The Durand dispute and the settlement obligation

Disputes are an unavoidable part of international relations as in domestic sphere. A renowned international jurist, J.G. Merrills (2011, 1) suggests that "a dispute may be defined as a specific disagreement concerning a matter of fact, law or policy in which a claim or assertion of one party is met with refusal, counter-claim or denial by another." Furthermore, the Permanent Court of International Justice (PCIJ) in the *Mavromattis Palestine Concessions* case (Greece v. U.K 1924, 11), defined the dispute as-

> A disagreement on a point of law or fact, a conflict of legal views or interests between two persons.

Essentially, the two elements must be embraced by parties, in a disagreement. First, the disagreement must be specific and well-defined in terms of its subject matter. Second, the disagreement must involve assertions and conflicting claims. Such claims and assertions may be through statements, diplomatic notes, specific actions or otherwise (Bilder 1986, 4). Moreover, among all types of dispute between States, territorial claims originating from agreements are most common claims (Sumner 2004, 1779). Looking at the divergent positons between Afghanistan and Pakistan with regard to the Durand boundary line, especially after emergence of Pakistan as an independent State, give us more space to call the latest contentions as dispute. In particular, Afghanistan Prime Minister, during a meeting on July 31, 1947, declared all agreements in respect of the Indo-Afghan border null and void (Qaseem 2008). Also, the representatives of both countries in the UN conferences like the UN Conference on the Law of Treaties and the UN Conference on Succession of States, carried different opinions regarding the territorial treaties, specifically Durand treaty which indicates not only a disagreement on a point of law but also disagreement on a point of fact. It can also be argued that the existence of a dispute in the technical sense, is rather more complex than these definitions would suggest (Schreuer 2008, 961). In some ICJ cases, the parties denied to accept the divergent legal views to be considered as evidence of the existence of a dispute. But the Court, for example, in *Certain Property case* (Liechtenstein v. Germany, para25) said-

> The Court thus finds that in the present proceedings complaints of fact and law formulated by Liechtenstein against Germany are denied by the latter. In conformity with well-established jurisprudence (…), the Court concludes that '[b]y virtue of this denial, there is a legal dispute between Liechtenstein and Germany.

As a result, it shows that the threshold for the existence of a dispute does not require a high degree of intensity between parties. Instead, the formulation of opposing positions by the parties can be a sufficient ground. In addition, the mere denial of parties to rebuff a dispute, shall not affect the existence of a dispute (Schreuer 2008, 961). In this case, as it is determined that there is dispute regarding the Durand Line between both States, this part elaborates further the question whether there is an obligation to resolve the disputes. If there is an international obligation, how these States should make it out. Therefore, this part ponders over the three key issues; the obligation for the pacific settlement, the obligation to settle disputes and the obligation to reach a pacific result.

### A. The Obligation for the Pacific Settlement of Disputes

At the end of the nineteenth century, endeavors were taken to restrain claims to sovereignty and governments have been conscious of the necessity to create, as an alternative, mechanisms for the peaceful settlement of disputes (Simma 2012, 183). In the international sphere, the Hague Convention for the Pacific Settlement of International Disputes of 1899, for the first time, proposed an obviation of recourse to force between States. Article 1 provided-

> With a view to obviating, as far as possible, recourse to force in the relations between States, the Signatory Powers agree to use their best efforts to insure the pacific settlement of international differences.

Further efforts were made in the Covenant of the League of Nations 1919, to develop a strong opinion to support resorting to peaceful means while dispute arrives. However, using of force was not absolutely prohibited by the Covenant. It was only the Kellogg-Briand Pact 1928 that banned wars of aggression and renounced war as an instrument of national policy. The principle of the peaceful settlement of disputes is a cornerstone of the contemporary world order, which has been profoundly marked by the United Nations charter 1945 and followed by other international instruments like; the Friendly Relations Declaration 1970 and the Manila Declaration 1982. Article 2(3) of the UN Charter states-

> All Members shall settle their international disputes by peaceful means in such a manner that international peace and security, and justice, are not endangered.

It is worth noting that the obligation arising from Article 2(3) is incumbent upon members of the UN and has reached to a customary status under International Law (Simma 2012, 188). In a view of that, Afghanistan and Pakistan both being UN members, are under an obligation to resolve their dispute over Durand Line in a pacific manner. Furthermore, the obligation that the settlement of disputes should be peaceful, is strengthened by the prohibition on the use of force contained in Article 2(4) of the Charter and by the authority of the Security Council under Chapter VII of the Charter to intervene when it determines that any situation or dispute involves a "threat to the peace, breach of the peace, or act of aggression" (Bilder 1986, 10).

## B. The Obligation to Settle Disputes

Article 2(3) of the UN Charter on pacific settlement is one of a series of principles which articulates the obligation of pacific settlement in positive terms. While there is some doubt whether the obligation includes all international disputes, specifically those which have no nexus to peace and security and do not endanger justice (Murphy 1974, 57). Likewise, elucidation is required whether the obligation embraces settlement of disputes or is restricted only to pacific settlement. The prevailing view is that, in the absence of special agreement, States are under no international legal obligation to settle, recourse to the third party, or even try to settle, their disputes (Bilder 1986, 7).

However, some commentators have maintained that, Article 2(3) does indeed require of disputants to take action to resolve their disputes (Hutchinson 1992, 2). Furthermore, the first seven words of Article 2(3) provides that "All Members shall settle their international disputes ... " at first sight, might appear to impose on States an obligation to take action to settle disputes arising between them. Also, the content of the obligation, in particular, its scope is defined with greater particularity in Article 33(1) of the UN Charter. Indeed, more accommodating of such an interpretation which predicates that it does impose an obligation of that type is clearly elaborated by Hutchinson (1992, 54), an eminent international jurist, as follows-

> Understood in this way, the main clause of the sentence constituting Article 2(3) gives expression to two obligations, rather than one. The first, and most fundamental, is an obligation to initiate and to engage in action for the purpose of settling disputes, the words "shall settle" directing disputing States to take action to resolve their differences ...

As a result, not only Afghanistan and Pakistan are obliged to resolve their disputes peacefully, but also they are under an obligation to engage in action for the purpose of settling of Durand dispute.

## C. Obligation to Reach a Specific Result

It is worth nothing that Article 2(3) obliges States only to struggle for the resolution of an existing dispute between them. Therefore, there is no legal obligation on Afghanistan and Pakistan to reach a specific result while engaging in settlement of disputes. As each international conflict has its parties, because of the principle of sovereignty, neither of them can impose will upon the other. Hence, a violation of the duty of "peaceful" settlement of disputes can be affirmed only if one side refuses, persistently, even to attempt to reach a settlement (Simma 2012, 191).

Consequently, the disagreement over Durand Line between Afghanistan and Pakistan can simply fall in a dispute situation. Although, one or both sides do not agree or recognize the situation as a dispute. As a result, both States are under two international obligations. First, to resolve and settle their dispute over the Durand Line. Second, to take into account the pacific settlement of disputes as per the UN Charter instructions. Also, there is no legal obligation on Afghanistan and Pakistan to reach a specific conclusion after they initiate to settle their dispute.

## V. Conclusion

The Durand Line came into existence as a result of an agreement known as the Durand Agreement. On November 12 1893, Amir Abdur Rahman Khan and Sir H. M. Durand signed two agreements- One concerning the north-eastern region, and the other relating the south-eastern region of Afghanistan. The latter came to be known as the Durand Agreement. Regarding the validity of the Durand Agreement, specifically after the emergence of Pakistan as an independent State in 1947, certain arguments and contentions arose between Pakistan and Afghanistan. By and large, consecutive governments of Afghanistan have vigorously refused to acknowledge the Durand Line as an official border. Pakistan, on the other side, opposed the contentions raised by Afghanistan and claims that Durand line is the official border with Afghanistan.

Above all, there are arguments that the conditions under which the Agreement was concluded were more fearsome and thus the validity of the Agreement can be questioned on the basis of Article 51 and 52 of the VCLT. However, these assertions have been challenged. As the Amir endorsed the Agreement by holding a *darbar* after signing the Agreement and praised it as an achievement, indicating his consent thereto. Besides, there is no consensus regarding the customary status of Article 52 of the VCLT. The International Law commission has also not confirmed the retroactive effects of Article 52 on the validity of treaties which were concluded before the formation of modern law, the UN Charter law.

Further the legal validity of the Durand Agreement has to be seen with the four other subsequent agreements signed consecutively in 1905, 1919, 1921 and 1930, where Afghanistan accepted the Durand line as its international border. Moreover, the Durand Agreement led to continued annual payments, subsidy, although it is claimed to be an economic coercion and a kind of bribery to the Amir of Afghanistan. For that reason, it may have caused corruption as laid down in Article 50 of the VCLT and the Agreement might be nullified. However, the validity of the Agreement cannot be contested on the ground of corruption as provided in Article 50 of the VCLT, because, during the colonial period, the practice of subsidy was not viewed as bribery and coercion under the VCLT. The VCLT is also restricted merely to the threat or use of force and does not contain economic coercion.

In addition, Afghanistan convened a tribal assembly (Loya Jirga) on July 26 1949 and thereby unilaterally terminated all agreements with the British India, including the Durand Agreement. As withdrawal from a treaty, unlike breach, is an internationally legal act, it should be through mutual agreement until and unless there is a change in the circumstances. Also, the plea of *rebus sic stantibus* or "change in the circumstances" which is one of the grounds to terminate the agreements, cannot be invoked in boundary agreements, particularly, in the context of the Durand Treaty, since Article 62 of the VCLT excludes the boundary treaties from the scope of the Article. Under the principle of *Pacta sunt servanda-* "Every treaty in force is binding upon the parties to it and must be performed by them in good faith."

As far as the question whether Pakistan is the successor of British India is concerned, not only Pakistan claimed being a successor State to British India but also the British Government had accepted at various occasions, including the Indian Independence Act, 1947. Furthermore, the application of the Vienna Convention 1978 depends on expressing the consent to be bound by the present Convention and applies only in respect to the succession of States which has occurred after the entry into force of the Convention and, therefore, does not encompass the validity of agreements. Both Pakistan and Afghanistan are not members to the Convention. Hence, even if the Convention applies, it can only be applicable as rules of customary international law. Although some commentators suggest that the Vienna Convention 1978, codifies customary international law in the field, it is broadly accepted that the Convention does not in fact reflect customary international law.

It is also worth noting that possession of a defined territory is not only significant for being a State under Montevideo Convention, but also is momentous under WTO regime, in particular, the MFN and National Treatment obligations can be fulfilled only when there is a defined territory and these principles will be applicable at the moment goods enter to the territory of a contracting party.

To sum up, all aforementioned arguments are not simply denial of the existence of dispute between Pakistan and Afghanistan. As per the Permanent Court of International Justice (PCIJ) pronouncement; a disagreement on a point of law or fact, a conflict of legal views or interests between two persons can be a dispute. Even the threshold for the existence of a dispute does not require a high degree of intensity between the two countries. Instead, the formulation of opposing positions by both parties can be a sufficient ground. In addition, the mere denial of parties to rebuff a dispute, shall not affect the existence of a dispute. Looking at the divergent views between Afghanistan and Pakistan with regard to the Durand Line, it is safe to call these contentions as dispute. As a result, both States are under two international obligations. First, to resolve and settle their dispute over Durand Border and second, to take into account the pacific settlement of disputes as per the UN Charter instructions. At the end, it is suggested that both parties can agree upon the second Durand Agreement to specify the third party involvement and clearly designate who would have the authority to settle the forthcoming disputes.

## Notes

1. Since there is misunderstanding with regard to the Durand Agreement status, whether it is an agreement or a treaty. On the basis of Vienna Convention on the Law of Treaties 1969 (VCLT), it makes no difference in the legal status of Durand Agreement to be called a treaty or an agreement. A treaty sometimes called a convention, covenant, protocol, charter, pact, agreement etc. *Further* you can read in Villiger (2009, 80).
2. The "clean slate" doctrine is limited by two exceptions. First, those treaties creating rights and obligations relating to the use of a territory are excluded (Art. 12). Second, rules relating to the boundary treaties are also excluded (Art 11). By this, the stability of States would be protected through the principle of *uti possidetis juris*. More on Article 11 can be found in cases like; Temple of Preah Vihear Case (Cambodia v. Thailand), 1962 I.C.J. Rep. 6; Territorial Dispute (Libyan Arab Jamahirya v. Chad), 1994 I.C.J. 6; and Free Zones Case (Upper Savoy and the District of Gex), 1932 P.C.I.J. (ser. A/B) No. 32 (June 7). You can also see O'Connell (1956).
3. The British as a Predecessor State for Pakistan, at least on two occasions confirmed the successor status of Pakistan. Mr. Noel-Baker, the British Secretary for the Commonwealth Relations, speaking in the House of Commons, made a statement on 30 June 1950. Also Mr. Anthony Eden, the British Prime Minister, made a statement in the House of Commons on 1 March 1956. You can see in Sir Olaf Caroe, *The Pathans: 550 B.C.–A.D. 1957* (Union Book Stall, Karachi 1973), p. 465–66

## Acknowledgments

In writing this article, I have incurred a great number of debts to acknowledge them. Above all I wish to thank Dr V G Hegde and Dr Ravidra Pratap for their encouragement and support over years. I am deeply grateful to Dr Srinivas Burra for his invaluable suggestions and comments. He has been for me an inspirational figure, as I am sure for many others. I would also like to take this opportunity to thank Dr Dhananjay Tripathi who reviewed this article and shared his painstaking suggestions with me. I wish to express my heartfelt thanks to Bushra for her constant support I received. Last but not the least I want to thank my family, especially my Dad, for their love and encouragement.

## Disclosure statement

No potential conflict of interest was reported by the author.

## References

Bilder, Richard B. and Others, eds. 1986. *An Overview of International Dispute Settlement. Journal of International Dispute Resolution* 1: 2.

Biswas, Arka. 2013. Durand Line: History, Legality & Future. *Vivekananda International Foundation* 1. www.files.ethz.ch/isn/170887/Durand%20Line_History%20Legality%20%20Future_Final.pdf.

Blarel, Olivier. 2015. Afghanistan-Pakistan: Pashtun. In *Border Disputes: A Global Encyclopedia*, ed. Emmanuel Brunet-Jailly, 1–12. California: ABC-CLIO, LLC.

Brasseur, Brad L. 2011. Recognising the Durand Line: A Way Forward for Afghanistan and Pakistan? *East West Institute*, 5.

Burke, S.M. 1973. *Pakistan's Foreign Policy: An Historical Analysis* (1st ed.). London: Oxford University Press.

Cheng, Tai-Heng. 2006. *State Succession and Commercial Obligations*. New York: Transnational Publishers.

## SOUTH ASIA

Emanuelli, C. 2003. State Succession, Then and Now, with Especial Reference to the Louisiana Purchase 1803. *Louisiana Law Review* 63: 1277.

Ghobar, Mir Ghulam Mohamad. 1967. *Afghanistan Dar Masir-e-Tarikh*. Kabul: Hashmat K Gobar.

Giunchi, Elisa. 2013. The Origins of the Dispute Over the Durand Line. *Internatioanles AsienForum* 44: 25.

Gruber, Christian Hill. 1998. The Admission of New States to the International Community. *European Journal of International Law* 9: 491–509.

Helfer, Laurence R. 2005. Existing Treaties. *Virginia Law Review* 91: 1579.

Helfer, Laurence R. 2012. *The Oxford Guide to Treaties*. Oxford: Oxford University Press.

Hussain, Ijaz. 1985. The Durand Agreementin the Light of Certain Recent International Conventions. *Law and Politics in Africa, Asia and Latin America* 18: 255.

Hutchinson, D.N. 1992. The Material Scope of the Obligation Under the United Nations Charter to Take Action to Settle International Disputes. *Australian Year Book of International Law* 14: 1.

Kakar, M. Hassan. 2006. *A Political and Diplomatic History of Afghanistan 1863–1901*. The Netherlands: Brill's Inner Asian Library179.

Kayathwal, Mukesh Kumar. 1994. Pak-Afghan Relations: Durand Line Issues. *Indian Journal of Asian Affairs* 7: 37.

Khan, Abdur Rahman. 1900*The Life of Abdur Rahman Khan*, ed. Sultan Muhammad Khan. London: John Murray.

Loyn, D. 2008. *Butcher and Bolt*. London: Hutchinson.

Mahmood, Tariq. 2005. The Durand Line: South Asiàs Next Trouble Spot. *NPS California* 1923: 19.

Mavromattis Palestine Concessions (Greece v. U.K.). 1924. PCIJ, ser. A No. 2, at 11 (Judgment of Aug. 13).

Merrills, J.G. 2011. *International Dispute Settlement*,(5th ed). New York: Cambridge University Press.

Murphy, Cornelius. 1974. The Obligation of States to Settle Disputes by Peaceful Means. *Virginia Journal of International Law* 14: 57.

O'Connell, D.P. 1956. *The Law of State Succession*. Cambridge: Cambridge University Press.

Omrani, Bijan. 2009. The Durand Line: History and Problems of the Afghan-Pakistan Border. *Journal of Asian Affairs-Routledge* XL: 177–195.

Qaseem, A.S. 2008. Pak-Afghan Relations: The Durand Line Issue. *Policy Perspectives, Special Issue Afghanistan*. http://www.ips.org.pk/the-muslim-world/986-pak-afghan-relations-thedurand-line-issue.html.

Qassem, Ahmad Shayeq. 2007. Afghanistan-Pakistan Relations: Border Controversies as Counter-Terrorist Impediments. *Australian Journal of International Affairs* 61: 65–80.

Qerimi, Qerim, and Suzana Krasniqi. 2013. Theories and Practice of State Succession to Bilateral Treaties: The Recent Experience of Kosovo. *German Law Journal* 14: 1639–1659.

Qureshi, S.M.M. 1966. Pakhtunistan: The Frontier Dispute between Afghanistan and Pakistan. *Journal of Pacific Affairs* 39: 99.

Rasanayagam, Angelo. 2003. *Afghanistan: A Modern History*. London: I.B. Tauris.

Razvi, Mujtaba. 1971. *The Frontiers of Pakistan*. Karachi/Dacca: National Publishing House Ltd.

Saikal, Amin. 2004. *Modern Afghanistan: A History of Struggle and Survival*. London: I.B.Tauris & Co Ltd.

Salim, Husna. 2007. Durand Line. http://durandline.info/a-study-of-the-durand-line/chapter-2-a-turbulent-relationship-afghanistan-and-pakistan/2-2-strained-relations/.

Schreuer, Christoph. 2008. What is a Legal Dispute? In *International law between Universalism and Fragmentation Festschrift in Honour of Gerhard Hafner*, ed. I. Buffard, et al., 959–980. Netherlands: Brill.

Simma, Bruno. 2012. *The Charter of the United Nations: A Commentary*,(3rd ed). Oxford: Oxford University Press1.

Sumner, Brian T. 2004. Territorial Disputes at the International Court of Justice. *Duke Law Journal* 53: 1779.

Sykes, Percy. 2002. *A History of Afghanistan*, 2nd ed. 2 vols. New Delhi: Munshiram Manoharlal.

Tate, G.P. 1909. *The Frontiers of Baluchistan*. London: Witherby and Co.

The United Nations. 1969. *Vienna Convention on the Law of Treaties. UNTS* 1155: 331.

The United Nations. 1978. *Vienna Convention* on *Succession of States in Respect* of *Treaties. UNTS* 1946: 3.

The United Nations` Charter. 1945. 1 UNTS XVI.

Villiger, Mark E. 2009. *Commentary on the 1969 Vienna Convention on the Law of Treaties.* The Netherlands: Martinus Nijhoff Publishers.

Woolsey, L.H. 1926. Unilateral Termination of Treaties. *The American Journal of International Law* 20: 346.

# No Mountain Too High? Assessing the Trans-territoriality of the Kailash Sacred Landscape Conservation Initiative[*]

Jayashree Vivekanandan

**ABSTRACT**

Regional efforts to preserve mountain landscapes that account for half of the world's biodiversity hotspots raise pertinent questions for existing statist discourses and practices of territoriality. The paper focuses on the Kailash Sacred Landscape Conservation and Development Initiative (KSLCDI), a transboundary Himalayan collaboration involving China, India and Nepal that seeks to conserve an area of shared cultural heritage and rich biodiversity. The UNEP-supported initiative, aimed at integrating regional, national and local actors redefines the role of the state from policy control to policy coordination. This prompts three key questions that the paper seeks to investigate. Firstly, how will states and sub-state actors negotiate divergent interests and approaches to natural resource management? Secondly, to what extent can spatiality be read with citizenship within the framework of transboundary conservation? Thirdly, what are the prospects for cross-border initiatives to reconcile conservation strategies devised at the national and regional levels with indigenous value systems, which have traditionally regulated local resource use? The paper is an enquiry into the Initiative's potential to redefine the spatial and operational remits of state capacity and its implications for mountain governance.

## Introduction

Given its many entanglements with questions of justice, equity and accountability, environmental politics constitutes a deeply contested domain. It has prompted scholars to raise a range of critical questions from interrogating the democratic credentials of the state (Christoff 1996); the credibility of knowledge systems (Jasanoff 2011); the dynamics between science and religion (Kearns 2011) to the fraught debate on resource prioritization. The spatiality and temporality of environmental issues have been emphasized to varying degrees. Not only do they straddle scales, but they also implicate future

---

[*]The paper draws on research undertaken for the project "India's Regional Relations in a Transitioning World: Policies, Priorities and Practices" funded by the Indian Council of Social Science Research (2013–2016). An earlier version of this paper was presented at the annual convention of the International Studies Association on *Spaces and Places: Geopolitics in an Era of Globalization* held in Toronto, Canada from March 26–29 2014; Paper presented at the International Conference on "Borders and Border Studies: The South Asian Perspective", South Asian University, New Delhi, March 6–7 2017.

generations of life systems. These concerns assume added significance in the context of mountain regions where the social and environmental stakes are high. Mountains, which cover nearly a quarter of the world's land area, work as crucial life support systems. They sustain 20% of the world population and are home to half of the biodiversity hotspots globally (*Environmental Science and Policy* 2015, 2). These are landscapes marked by tremendous diversity but limited production scales. For instance, in the Hindu Kush Himalayan region, where an estimated 150 million people inhabit an area of 3.4 million square km, the limited availability of cropland often produces a grave livelihood crisis and food insecurity for the rural poor. Attempts at making decision-making and governance mechanisms ecologically sensitive are particularly shot through with such tensions. Further, efforts to preserve mountain landscapes raise pertinent questions for existing statist discourses and practices of territoriality. Policy attention has been directed towards preserving mountain regions over the last several decades culminating in specific policy documents including chapter 13 on "Sustainable Mountain Development" in *Agenda 21* and a segment on mountains in *The Future We Want*, the report of the Rio + 20 UN Conference on Sustainable Development.

The paper focuses on the Kailash Sacred Landscape Conservation and Development Initiative (KSLCDI), a transboundary Himalayan collaboration established in 2009 involving China, India and Nepal that seeks to conserve an area of shared cultural heritage and rich biodiversity. The UNEP-supported KSLCDI aims at integrating regional, national and local actors to synchronise conservation practices in the Himalayas. Nodal institutions from the three states [Institute of Geographic Sciences and Natural Resources Research, Chinese Academy of Sciences, China; Ministry of Environment, Forest and Climate Change (MoEFCC), India; Ministry of Forests and Environment, Nepal; G B Pant Institute of Himalayan Environment and Development, India; Central Department of Botany, Tribhuvan University, Nepal] were identified to spearhead the research and policy coordination. The coordination of the Initiative is undertaken by the Kathmandu-based International Centre for Integrated Mountain Development (ICIMOD).

The area under focus is a 31,175 square km swathe of the Himalayan range that straddles parts of central India (Pithoragarh and Bageshwar districts), northwestern Nepal (Humla, Bhajang, Darchula and Baitadi districts) and southwestern parts of Tibet Autonomous Region of China (Pulan county). As per ICIMOD's feasibility report in 2011, 15% of the KSL region remains permanently under snow (Zomer and Oli 2011). Much of the million-plus population that inhabits the area is concentrated in Nepal and India while the Tibetan plateau accounts for low population density in comparison. The mountain communities use over a quarter of the total area for grazing purposes, while less than a tenth is agricultural land. The four river systems of the Brahmaputra, Ganges, Indus and Sutlej sustain one of the most ecologically diverse regions of the world that is spread over the ten eco-regions comprising the transboundary landscape (Figure 1).

The paper is an enquiry into the initiative's potential to redefine the spatial and operational remits of state capacity and the key challenges to multilateral cooperation in the region. It sets itself three questions to investigate. Firstly, how will states and sub-state actors negotiate divergent interests and approaches to natural resource management? Secondly, to what extent can spatiality be read with citizenship within the framework of transboundary conservation? Thirdly, what are the prospects for reconciling conservation

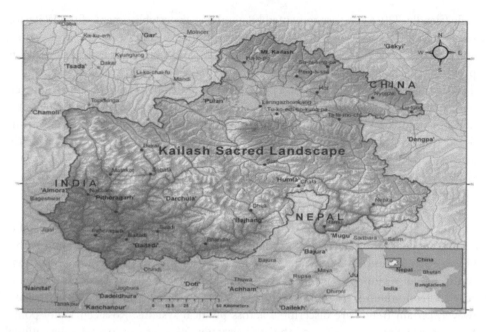

**Figure 1.** The Kailash Sacred Landscape (Pandey et al. 2017, 89).

strategies devised at the national and regional levels with indigenous value systems, which have traditionally regulated local resource use? The paper has three parts to it. The first section offers a contextual overview of transboundary protected areas that foregrounds the discussion on the governance of the Himalayan landscape. The second section enquires into the extent to which conservation practices in the Himalayan region would reinterpret territoriality given that local communities cognize the environment in starkly different terms from the state. The final section examines the key challenges to transboundary cooperation, arguing that the success of the intergovernmental initiative would hinge on its ability to embrace the notion of ecological citizenship.

## Transboundary Conservation and Mountain Governance

States have explored transboundary conservation over the last several decades with varying degrees of success. The notion of transboundary protected areas (TBPAs) received strong ideological validation from the major international agencies including the International Union for Conservation of Nature (IUCN), United Nations Environment Programme (UNEP), World Bank, and Conservation International. The coalescing of expertise, funding and political support proved to be a spur for this model of conservation that was seen to yield other dividends as well. TBPAs were touted as promoting regionalization through cross-border partnerships on a range of issue areas such as water, tourism and trade (Ali 2007; Conca and Dabelko 2002). For instance, the setting up of the Emerald Triangle Peace Park between Cambodia, Laos and Thailand was expected to help in clearing landmines in the area (Barquet, Lujala, and Rød 2014, 2).

The political climate may prove conducive to the creation of TBPAs, as was the case in southern Africa with the end of apartheid in South Africa in 1994. Where relations were already friendly, TBPAs further cemented bilateral ties, the establishment of the Waterton Lakes Glacier by Canada and the United States in 1926 being a case in point. Where relations were fraught, the establishment of peace parks was vigorously promoted to improve prospects for peace among conflicting states.[1] This is especially relevant given that 80% of the world's armed conflicts between 1950 and 2000 occurred within biodiversity hotspots across the world (Cited in Duffy 2014, 820). The mushrooming of transboundary initiatives is on account of this complex blend of strategic state interests and a global conservation agenda. From the mid-1940s, 121 TBPAs were created over the course of two decades. Their number doubled in the 1970s (Barquet, Lujala, and Rød 2014, 2). As of 2007, the UNEP recorded the existence of 227 TBPAs across the world (Brenner and Davis 2012, 500).[2]

The creation of TBPAs has recalibrated spatial practices by easing certain types of mobilities while restricting certain others.[3] However, its implementation across member states has tended to be uneven when different political systems are in operation within a TBPA. Participatory initiatives are more likely to succeed in democratic orders than in authoritarian regimes given that there is greater scope for the protection of rights of borderland communities in the former than in the latter case (van Amerom 2002, 269). However, certain trends are discernible across political systems. Rosaleen Duffy points out to the growing acceptance of the militarization of conservation by international NGOs and states, and its association with effectiveness (Duffy 2014, 822–6).

The agreements establishing TBPAs have, in practice, protected and validated the sovereignty of the participating states (van Amerom 2002, 265). The regulatory state makes its presence felt in a TBPA through several means. Besides the synchronization of national laws necessary to legislate a bioregion into being,[4] TBPAs allow for enhanced state patrolling in the name of keeping poaching and illegal activities in the area under check (van Amerom 2002, 269). Anti-poaching may take on militarized dimensions as conservation agencies resort to coercive measures, veritably signaling a "war for biodiversity" (Duffy 2014, 819). Agreements often state in unequivocal terms that joint conservation efforts do not alter the sovereign rights states have on their respective territories; that the contours of a bioregion do not replace the political boundaries of states. The Great Limpopo Treaty makes clear that "the sovereign rights of each party shall be respected" in an arrangement in which "no party shall impose decisions on an other" (Cited in van Amerom 2002, 269).

While TBPAs are seen as addressing the three criteria of regional cooperation namely, coordinating agency, sectorality and territoriality[5] (*Environmental Science and Policy* 2015, 1), mountain governance brings on board its own complexities to transboundary conservation. Perrier and Levrat examine how the intersection of mountains, borders and governance may prompt "the 'melting' of laws" (Perrier and Levrat 2015, 32). They look at how "hard" national laws soften in the governance of transboundary mountain regions owing to the admixture of regional, subregional and international legal norms on cross-border conservation practices. Besides the legal dimensions, the scholarship has tended to highlight the specific conditions prevalent in mountain regions that set them apart from other bioregions such as wetlands. Yet, the exercise of scale-framing is similar across region types in that bioregions (including mountain regions) are situated within larger global discourses of climate change and the life systems they support (Barquet 2015, 267). The global context becomes a handy frame of reference to underscore the significance of a unique habitat. As an *Environmental Science and Policy* editorial observes,

> What emerges, paradoxically, is that the principal feature that is special about mountain governance is that it is not so special after all, precisely because the process of creating mountains as objects for governance ... is a social process that can be observed in all regional governance. (Environment Science and Policy 2015, 2)

This discursive construction is evident in the case of the Himalayas as well. ICIMOD's policy documents on transboundary cooperation in the Mount Kailash region frame it at the very outset as pertaining to the "Kailash Sacred Landscape" (ICIMOD and UNEP 2009, 2010a). Its identity as a sacred site is articulated thus:

> Famous from ancient times, it represents a sacred landscape significant to hundreds of millions of people in Asia, and around the globe. It is an important cultural and religious landscape with significance for Hindu, Buddhist, Bon Po, Jain, Sikh, and other related religious traditions. (ICIMOD and UNEP 2010c, 1)

The region's cultural geography – its significance to different faiths combined with the remoteness of its location- makes the arduous journey over the mountain passes a popular draw for pilgrims each year. Besides the pilgrimage sites and routes leading up to the sacred mountain Mount Kailash (also known as Kang Rinpoche and Gangrenboqi Feng), there are at least six lakes considered sacred in the area. Lake Mansarovar, a Ramsar site, falls within the Kailash Sacred Landscape. Nepal and China have moved fast to capitalize on its popularity by seeking to integrate it within their respective tourism agendas. While Nepal has focused on improved access through the route that traverses its territory, China is seeking to develop the infrastructure in the Kailash region as part of its larger efforts to integrate Tibet.[6] The once remote area is now accessible by air with the opening of the Ngari Gunsa Airport in 2010.

The growing environmental degradation across the Himalayan region has drawn the attention of environmentalists and policy makers in recent years. The Ganga and Brahmaputra together carry the world's highest suspended sediment load (2180 million metric tons a year) that cause the rivers to drastically alter their course. Engineering interventions have largely failed to take into account these shifts in river courses.[7] A slew of dams planned on rivers such as the Mekong and the Yarlung-Tsangpo/Brahmaputra originating in Tibet are feared to have serious downstream impact on much of Asia. Development interventions such as accelerated national road, rail and hydel projects in the fragile mountain region are taking a huge environmental toll. For instance, the Special Accelerated Road Development Programme (SARDP) to improve road connectivity in India's Northeast as part of the National Highway Development Project (NHDP) aims to litter the length and breadth of the region in a maze of highways. About 44,000 km of roads constructed annually is accelerating the process of deforestation, water and air pollution, displacing an estimated 2650 million cubic meters of debris by landslides across the Himalayas (Khosla 1998). The ecological imbalances have caused the glaciers in the Himalayas and the Hindu Kush to lose mass, a worrying trend the IPCC makes note of in its Fifth Assessment Report (Vaughan et al. 2013, 342). In 2013, a joint team from India and Nepal collected 4.4 tons of garbage left behind by climbers. Besides empty oxygen canisters, food and tents, the team had to dispose of even frozen corpses.

Fledgling institutional measures underway for the conservation of transboundary landscapes in the Himalayan region include the Kangchenjunga Landscape that straddles Bhutan, China, India and Nepal on the eastern flank. As one of the 34 global biodiversity hotspots in the world, the Himalayan landscape of which the Kanchenjunga is a part, has been brought by the states within the ambit of 14 protected areas (henceforth PA). Much of the 6028 square km protected cover lies in India, which accounts for 12 PAs while Nepal and Bhutan manage one each. The initiative aims at establishing connectivity between nine of the 14 PAs that lie scattered across the complex. The proposed conservation corridors, linking the geographically contiguous but splintered "conservation islands", seek to facilitate the movement of wildlife and livestock apart from improving local prospects for timber (Chettri, Thapa, and Shakya 2007). It connects the Mahananda Wildlife Sanctuary and the Neora Valley National Park (NVNP), both in West Bengal, India and a part of the Kangchenjunga Landscape. Given its location, the NVNP provides a link between the Pangolakha Wildlife Sanctuary in Sikkim, India and the Toorsa Strict Reserve, Bhutan. However, the burgeoning tea industry poses a grave challenge by way of increasing encroachments of the forest area within the proposed conservation corridor.

Himalayan communities too have attempted to conserve, and their conservation practices need to be contextualised within local belief systems. For instance, notions of the sacred in the Kumaon region of Uttarakhand, India have been instrumental in ensuring the conservation of the area (Gokhale and Pala 2011). Hill tracts are referred to as the land where gods reside (*dev bhumi*) and certain tree types are revered for their mythical and medicinal significance. Likewise, forest spaces around shrines (*dev van*) in rural Kumaon are believed to belong to the temple deity and as such remain protected spaces (Aggarwal 2010, 134–7).[8] Efforts at community management were constantly frustrated by creeping encroachment and deforestation. It prompted 30 forest councils (*van panchayats)* in Uttarakhand to designate their 2200 hectares forest area in 1998 as under divine protection[9] (Aggarwal 2010, 140). The intention of extending divine protection over these forests was that the fear of divine justice might ensure human compliance that legal measures could not. It should be added that the environmental and social impact of such community interventions is open to debate since the creation of these forests impacted social classes differently.[10] However, new modalities of public action have been critical in governing the Himalayan region. Local initiatives such as the community forestry program in Nepal have worked towards addressing the key challenges to sustainable mountain development, of marginality, poverty and environmental fragility (Tiwari and Joshi 2015, 71).

## Conservation and Territoriality

Statist approaches to conservation need to be understood in light of the civilised-natural binary that continues to find validation in existing policy dicourses. The association of nature with wilderness and untamed elements remains largely unchallenged in policymaking circles in India and China. Its popular and political acceptance ensures that the civilized and the natural remain bifurcated spaces. Sedentarised spaces that indicate toil and control encompass the cultural and the social (*samskrtik*) as against forest spaces associated with the natural (*prakrtik*). Culture as signifying control over nature, brought with the expansion of the *samskrtik* into the *prakrtik*, the symbolism of authority, civilization and order (Fortier 2010, 103).

This sharply contrasts with the manner in which Himalayan communities cognize the environment. Their sense of belonging is defined not by citizenship but by the forests they regard themselves as part of. The social life of indigenous groups like the Raute community in Nepal who forage the forests is defined along multiple nodes. For instance, the community regards the forest as a social and integrated natural domain shared with animals and trees. These are seen as the progeny of the Sun God (*Berh*) that binds them in familial ties with other life systems in the forest. (Fortier 2010, 100) As co-inhabitants of a shared forest space, the self-image of the Rautes is that of the dweller rather than of the hunter. Interestingly, this distinctive ordering of space, wherein they are "the political subjects of the trees" (*Bot Praja*), elevates the forest to the position of a ruler (*raja*). Jana Fortier terms this as "an act of defiance", for, the Rautes "call themselves not simply '*praja*' [subjects] in reference to their relation to the Nepalese state, but '*Bot Praja*' to signal their fealty to the forest rather than the King of Nepal". (Fortier 2010, 105) The cultural scale becomes for them the ordering principle of social life, constructing a complex web of meanings shared by members of the group about resources, life and space that make up the biophysical realm (Guneratne 2010, 6).

It should be added that the multiple ways in which citizenship is interpreted and practised in the Himalayan borderlands do not adhere to a strictly legalistic and territorial understanding. This can be traced to a political understanding arrived at by China and Nepal in 1956 to create a border zone that was not reducible to the exclusive sovereign control of either state. The border zone that extends 20 miles on either side recognized residents living within the zone as "border inhabitants" who were issued "border citizen cards". (Shneiderman 2013) These cards enabled them to "cross" over and travel within the zone without the requirement of legal documentation. The "boundary biography" of the border zone chronicles several such willful transgressions that both states and citizens engage in. Indeed, the border citizen cards formally acknowledged and institutionalized everyday border practices rendering the notion of citizenship fuzzy and messier in the process. State recognition of border-spanning exchanges serves as a useful signpost to rethink sovereignty practices in the region.

It remains to be seen as to what extent the KSL initiative acknowledges the distinctiveness of this border zone. We may ask if the KSL region would be similarly marked off by differentiated citizenship providing a certain right of access and mobility to border residents denied to other citizens residing outside it. For example, customary practices of migratory pastoralism in the Indo-Nepal border could become the basis of such differentiated citizenship rights in the transboundary area. It is customary for the pastoralist community of Byansi Shaukas from Garbyang village in India to migrate to the rangelands near the Tinker and Chhyangru villages in Nepal. In addition to grazing rights, they are permitted to collect the "caterpillar fungus", considered of high value, from this area. The customary rights to graze and collect herbs are robust enough to ensure that no one outside the three villages can do so in the area, a practice that has survived the demarcation of the international border between India and Nepal (Pandey et al. 95). Border citizens have negotiated their identity and multiple senses of belonging with local state agencies in ways that are not be immediately evident in the case of the KSL initiative. Citizenship practices in the Himalayan borderlands point to trans-territoriality as a negotiated state of existence that little approximates the statist interpretation of the border as a firm exclusionary girdle.

## Challenges to Transboundary Cooperation

Successful TBPAs allow for alternative modes of horizontal cooperation that are based on a series of transnational networks. The Alliance in the Alps is one such network established in 1997 that connects over 300 local municipalities across eight Alpine states (Del Biaggio 2015, 46). Networks of this type have been critical in ensuring that a top-down initiative such as the Alpine Convention gains acceptance at the local level. In comparison, the KSLCDI, also an intergovernmental initiative, suffers from a scalar challenge, i.e. of forging effective linkages between local and regional institutions as also from the lack of cross-sectoral policy integration between conservation, livelihood and marginalization. Tiwari and Joshi note that ICIMOD, as the initiative's nodal agency, has failed to create local transnational networks and has largely restricted itself to being a knowledge hub for the member states (Tiwari and Joshi 2015, 71).

A host of sub-national actors have tended to go missing from the ambit of formal institutional frameworks. Studies have pointed towards the entrenched vulnerability of borderland communities engaged in migratory pastoralism in the Himalayas such as the Drokpas, the Humli Bhotiyas and the Shaukas (Namgay et al. 2014; Pandey et al. 2017; Sharma et al. 2014). There are also significant political undercurrents that run beneath the Himalayan conservation initiative that point to fears of institutionalized marginalization. For instance, China's participation in the intergovernmental initiative has stoked Tibetan fears about what the government's proactive role in conserving the Kailash region would entail for the Tibetan population, particularly the nomadic communities. Tibetans point to their institutional underrepresentation in the KSLCDI Regional Workshops as indicative of their marginalized status within the collaborative venture. The mobility of the Tibetan nomads, the sole inhabitants of the core sacred area is seen by the Chinese state as an encroachment into protected areas such as the Changthang National Protected Area that is part of the KSL. Tibetans fear that the conservation rhetoric would serve to delegitimize their nomadic forays and justify the state's strategy to further push for their sedentarisation. The Chinese state has already taken measures to resettle the pastoralists under its *"tuimi huancao"* (Restore Pastures to Grass) policy in 2002. The Grasslands Law, passed the same year, further sought to mainstream pastoralists by inducting them into other professions and employing them as manual labor in areas outside the region (Pandey et al. 2017, 94–5). The sedentarist bias is however not unique to China but is reflective of states at large and the suspicions they harbor about communities that keep borders porous with their mobility, thereby frustrating state attempts to enclose spaces (Kurian 2014; Scott 2009).[11]

Such biases tend to overlook the important ecological role that pastoral communities perform by "curating the land", an organic function that states seek to sunder through their eviction (Lafitte 2011, 3). The success of KSLCDI would hinge on how it addresses these mobilities. Will its professed espousal of a holistic approach extend to recognizing pastoralism both as a form of land use and a vital knowledge source? Clearly, a key challenge facing the KSL initiative then is an epistemological one; of initiating processes that equip both, the science and the development discourses with the capacity to negotiate with traditional knowledge systems[12] (Lafitte 2011, 141). The experiential nature of traditional knowledge makes the social organization of groups inseparable from resource use, a linkage that state interventions in environmental protection can ill-afford to ignore but often do in practice. It also cautions against regarding communities as repositories of knowledge to be selectively engaged with rather than as active agents in how such knowledge is utilized (Figueroa 2011, 239). Participatory modes of engagement that acknowledge the role of indigenous communities have the potential to move beyond set compensation-based mechanisms.

Further, while sacred landscape-based conservation initiatives might seek to incorporate cultural practices such as the above, one needs to be wary of culture becoming "a new policy instrument". It could well become an appendage to preformed conservation plans that are ostensibly geared towards specific development outcomes. At the outset, bringing culture into the conversation runs the risk of assuming, as David Campbell notes, that

> something called 'culture' operates on something else called 'environment'. Holding these abstractions to be separate, objective and symmetrical entities is a strategy for ordering the world that has been extremely powerful in the global history of science, nature and colonialism. (Campbell 2010, 188)

Such an approach tends to streamline cultural identity in ways that privilege frameworks formulated by state and development agencies. In instrumentalising culture along these lines, the local becomes a site of selective engagement and execution. It runs the danger of valuing the local for being just that, overlooking in the process the "progressive contextualisations" that inform its interaction with other scales and, by extension, other actors (Campbell 2010, 190). The often-uncritical assumption of a unitary and coherent indigenous discourse on environment is not borne out in the multiple local realities that villagers routinely negotiate along varying axes of identity and interest.

It is evident that the KSL initiative cannot be seen exclusively through the lens of environmental protection. Indeed, understanding the socio-ethnic composition of local communities in these three multicultural states would be critical to the uptake and success of the initiative. The capacity of communities to participate as effective stakeholders is far from likely to be egalitarian as caste, gender and class identities could add or further entrench complex layers of exclusion. Such identity groups assume particular importance in the environment-development debate given how they differently perceive the imperatives for resource use and conservation in the Himalayas. It is these faultlines that need to be addressed if policies are to be more responsive and effective.

Furthermore, raising awareness and mobilizing support for the KSL initiative could prove to be a double-edged sword. Many sacred groves are facing degradation due to a spike in religious tourism in the region. Changes in everyday religious practices add a new dimension to the degradation of these sacred groves. Local belief systems are fraying at the edges as they are increasingly getting mainstreamed into observing conventional Vedic practices that are abstracted from the environment. Growing ritualism and idol worship has eroded the pagan beliefs that had lent divinity to forests and the link between faith and nature stands weakened. This erosion of environmental identity, amounting to cultural loss, is partly externally initiated through intercultural encounters. But they could also be self-generated given the internal dynamics and adaptive capacities of indigenous groups[13] (Figueroa 2011, 234). It is indicative of how groups interpret the Himalayan habitat loss as one of their ownership, agency and identity.

Lastly, gaps in the knowledge base on the current state of the Himalayas will particularly constitute a grave challenge to the success of any transboundary governance system in the region. Hydrological data and meteorological information about the state of the Himalayan ecosystem remains a severe limitation. Addressing this long-standing lacuna will not prove to be easy since it stems from the abiding reluctance of states to part with information. Even in the event of data becoming available to establish the extent of environmental damage, there is no certainty of any wide-ranging consensus on its policy uptake. The contested climate change debate gives us a glimpse into the limits of scientific concurrence, to the significant extent that it already exists. The limits of scientific consensus and democratic engagement are all too evident in the case of the Himalayan mountain science. The lack of open access information is compounded by scientific controversies surrounding the accuracy of evidence and the use of derivative regional climate models ill-designed in the context of the Himalayas (Bandyopadhyay 2011). The interdisciplinary knowledge base that is vital to understanding the Himalayan ecosystem services under threat remains woefully underdeveloped. The Theory of Himalayan Environmental Degradation (THED) continues to hold currency among the intellectual and political elite in the region (Metz 2010).[14]

While there is no denying that mountain science needs the urgent and sustained attention of states and scientists, social impact assessments remain a neglected area. It partly stems from the popular perception of science as a self-contained field with its own standards of credibility and verifiability. As Alan Irwin notes, "'citizenship' currently only begins when 'expertise' has set the environmental agenda" (Irwin 1995, 79). This raises the more critical question as to whether the call for science to orient itself towards addressing social challenges has indeed allowed for context-specificity. Socially- and policy- relevant science would entail embedding scientific research in webs of institutional accountability with a focus on public engagement.

## A Sum of its Parts?

Will the KSL region be a sum of its parts given that the delineation exercise to demarcate the area was but an aggregate of state inputs? Alternately, can the mandate to collectively conserve escape the dynamics of fragmented polities? Its capacity to do so will turn on both, the resilience and adaptability of its institutions of governance. As Michael Schoon asserts, the institutional beginnings of TBPAs can create path dependencies that result in varying collaborative capacities (Schoon 2013). Bottom-up collaborations that organically lead to the scaling up of conservation, as in the case of the Kgalagadi Transfrontier Park, have proven effective. Top-down initiatives such as the Great Limpopo Transfrontier Park, where conservation is imposed on local communities, have lagged behind in this regard (Schoon 2013).

The KSLCDI is sovereignty conforming [for, the demarcation is undertaken by individual states within their respective territories (ICIMOD and UNEP 2010a, 5–6)] but defines the KSL as an ecoregion [wherein the mutually agreed criteria such as biodiversity corridors, ecosystem contiguity and operational pilgrimage routes determine the area's perimeter (ICIMOD and UNEP 2010a, 5)]. Although the KSL's outer limits do not conform to either international boundaries or domestic administrative divisions, the initiative's emphasis on 'respecting sovereignty' and 'following the laws and regulations of the respective member country' is unmistakable (ICIMOD and UNEP 2010b, 33). The Himalayan region figures in development plans and blueprints of infrastructure projects as a site of statist intent and implementation. As ICIMOD's 2011 feasibility report observes,

> The technical delineation of the KSL ... was completed by each of the partner countries within their own respective borders .... The merged KSL boundary does not include any international or internal administrative boundaries and is only intended to provide the external boundary for the KSL across all three member countries. (Zomer and Oli 2011, 7)

The frame of reference shifts to a space that is mapped but has seldom merited attention outside of states' territorial exclusivities. The transformations are arguably still being directed from a distance but the representation of space has now been regionalized.

But how might we conceive of its many localisations when an all-too-easy fit between universal and local agendas point to the perils of parachuting concepts? For the global governance discourse, navigating the space between localness and universalism will be central. The language of transnational solidarities and the Global South permits interpretations that must necessarily be placed outside the immediacies of particular contexts. It makes possible such interpretations of social exclusion as David Harvey's notion of "accumulation by dispossession" suggests (Routledge 2011, 385). In what ways can we think of ecological sensitization as empowering the local without fetishizing it? As Figueroa notes, "A fine line triangulates the dire need for shared knowledge, collective action, and vulnerability by assimilation" (Figueroa 2011, 239). Self-regulatory practices as living expressions of an engaged citizenship point to possible means by which such tensions could be reconciled.

Calibrating institutions in ways that enhance their democratic content would entail revisiting the formal remits of citizenship especially in sites where citizenship practices of neighboring states encounter one another. It is pertinent in this regard to probe how notions of governance and development that are conventionally tethered to the state could be reworked to now speak to a constituency of the affected who are not always the empowered. The effectiveness of the KSLCDI would depend on its ability to embrace the notion of ecological citizenship that is not confined to legalistic and anthropocentric principles but alters the parameters of rights, responsibility and representation to encompass other species and future generations. (Christoff 1996) It allows us to progress beyond the formal interpretation of citizenship to study its active and living expression by people as they seek to realize their rights and address their needs within its participatory framework. The success of the Himalayan transboundary initiative will largely turn on the extent to which the disenfranchised are made to truly belong to the bioregion.

## Notes

1. The Krakow Protocol signed by Poland and Czechoslovakia in 1924, which eventually led to the three joint parks, was an investment in peace, incidentally the first of its kind.
2. Despite their evident popularity, TBPAs add a degree of complexity that is oftentimes neither foreseen nor desired by states, and might exacerbate existing tensions or induce new ones between them (van Amerom 2002, 265).
3. The shifting fortunes of the Mukuleke community in southern Africa is a case in point. From being evicted in 1969 to allow for the expansion of the Kruger National Park to regaining their lands thirty years later as partners in the management of the transboundary Mukuleke Contractual Park, the clan and its sense of belonging were redefined with the shifting context (Chaderopa 2013, 53).

4. According to the World Resources Institute, a bioregion is "a geographic space that contains one or several nested ecosystems. It is characterized by its land forms, vegetative cover, human culture, and history, as identified by local communities, governments, and scientists" (Cited in Barquet 2015, 266).
5. Each can be plotted along a continuum to yield a variety of permutations. Coordinating agency would range from intergovernmental cooperation to multiple-actor settings; territoriality, from jurisdictional to ecoregional areas; and sectorality, from single-issue to multi-sectoral agreements (Barquet 2015, 2).
6. Scholars have pointed to similarities between the Himalayas and the Alps in terms of both, their rich histories of mountain route networks traversing states and their contemporary experience of infrastructure development. As mountain trails gave way to roads or fell into disuse, the clash between construction and conservation was all too evident, prompting the Swiss state to initiate projects that included collating the "Inventory of Historical Traffic Routes". There are perhaps takeaways from the Swiss experience for the KSL initiative that explore prospects for roads and routes to coexist (Shrestha 2010).
7. The equilibrium regulating the Himalayan ecosystem was assumed as a default state of existence that follows the destabilizing effects of natural and anthropogenic disruptions.
8. The ecological functions such belief systems serve have been well documented. Sacred groves in Kumaon are mostly located in close proximity to farm lands as the deities are believed to cast a benign influence on the agricultural cycle. Topographically, the elevated location of *dev van* assures farmers of a ground water source for their lands.
9. Termed as *dev arpit panchayat* forests, such forests are distinct from *dev van* in that their ownership was not permanently transferred to the residing deity but it continued to be managed by people (see Aggarwal 2010, 142–4).
10. Added restrictions on the collection of fodder compelled poor families to whittle down their cattle size. While they gathered fuel wood from neighbouring forest areas that in turn began to be steadily denuded, richer families could afford to switch to other fuel options such as kerosene (Aggarwal 2010, 144–5).
11. The criminalization of certain hunting and foraging practices of African communities during colonial rule meant that hunting became an illegal activity inviting heavy punishment while, at the same time, protecting the rights of Europeans to hunt game (Duffy 2014, 833).
12. The UN Convention on Biological Diversity defines traditional knowledge as

> the knowledge, innovations and practices of indigenous and local communities, developed and shared through experience gained over time and adapted to the local social structure, culture and environment .... It is usually communicated through indigenous peoples' way of life, stories, songs, folklore, proverbs, cultural and religious values, beliefs, customary laws, practices and traditions, languages and other ways of transmission. This knowledge is normally of a practical nature, and covers areas such as traditional livelihoods, health, medicine, plants, animals, weather conditions, environment and climate conditions, and environmental management. (Cited in Figueroa 2011, 237)

13. Environmental identity as "the amalgamation of cultural identities, ways of life, and self-perceptions that are connected to a given group's physical environment" acknowledges that indigenous community life operates at the intersection of the socio-cultural and environmental realms (Figueroa 2011, 233).
14. THED's claim that a burgeoning population was responsible for the deforestation and flooding in the Himalayas found favor among scholars, policy makers and donors in 1970s. Subsequent work on the area sought to provide more nuanced and empirically rigorous explanations for environmental degradation. The crisis was made amenable to objective analysis by scientists and development agencies and rendered an otherwise complex reality coherent and simple for policy uptake. The discourse collapsed the evolutionary history of the land and its people into the crisis prone present, signaling the redundancy of investigating past patterns of resource use and state policies.

## Disclosure Statement

No potential conflict of interest was reported by the author.

## References

Aggarwal, Safia. 2010. The Role of Religion in Conservation and Degradation of Forests: Examples from the Kumaun Himalaya. In *Culture and the environment in the Himalaya*, ed. Arjun Guneratne, 132–50. London: Routledge.

Ali, S.H. 2007. *Peace Parks: Conservation and Conflict Resolution*. Cambridge, MA: The MIT Press.

Bandyopadhyay, Jayanta. 2011. Knowledge Gaps for an Interdisciplinary Water Science and Policy for Monsoon-fed Himalayan Rivers. Presentation at River Waters: Perspectives and Challenges for Asia, November 18–20, Foundation for Non-Violent Alternatives, New Delhi.

Barquet, Karina. 2015. Building a Bioregion through Transboundary Conservation in Central America. *Norwegian Journal of Geography* 69, no. 5: 265–76.

Barquet, Karina, Päivi Lujala, and Jan Ketil Rød. 2014. Transboundary Conservation and Militarized Interstate Disputes. *Political Geography* 42: 1–11.

Brenner, Jacob, and John Davis. 2012. Transboundary Conservation Across Scales: A World-regional Inventory and a Local Case Study from the United States-Mexico border. *Journal of the Southwest* 54, no. 3: 499–519.

Campbell, Ben. 2010. Beyond Cultural Models of the Environment: Linking Subjectivities of Dwelling and Power. In *Culture and the Environment in the Himalaya*, ed. Arjun Guneratne, 186–203. London: Routledge.

Chaderopa, Chengeto. 2013. Crossborder Cooperation in Transboundary Conservation-development Initiatives in Southern Africa: The Role of Borders of the Mind. *Tourism Management* 39: 50–61.

Chettri, Nakul, Rajesh Thapa, and Bandana Shakya. 2007. Participatory Conservation Planning in Kangchenjunga Transboundary Biodiversity Conservation Landscape. *Tropical Ecology* 48, no. 2: 163–76.

Christoff, Peter. 1996. Ecological Citizens and Ecologically Guided Democracy. In *Democracy and Green Political thought: Sustainability, Rights and Citizenship*, ed. Brian Doherty, and Marius de Geus, 151–69. London: Routledge.

Conca, K., and G. Dabelko. 2002. *Environmental Peacemaking*. Baltimore, MD: Johns Hopkins University Press.

Del Biaggio, Cristina. 2015. Investigating Regional Identities within the Pan-alpine Governance System: The Presence or Absence of Identification with a "Community of Problems" among Local Political Actors. *Environmental Science and Policy* 49: 45–56.

Duffy, Rosaleen. 2014. Waging a War to Save Biodiversity: The Rise of Militarized Conservation. *International Affairs* 90, no. 4: 819–34.

Environmental Science and Policy. 2015. Should Mountains (Really) Matter in Science and Policy? 49: 1–7.

Figueroa, Robert Melchior. 2011. Indigenous Peoples and Cultural Losses. In *Oxford Handbook of Climate Change and Society*, ed. John Dryzek, Richard Norgaard, and David Schlosberg, 232–47. Oxford: Oxford University Press.

Fortier, Jana. 2010. Where God's Children Live: Symbolizing Forests in Nepal. In *Culture and the Environment in the Himalaya*, ed. Arjun Guneratne, 100–13. London: Routledge.

Gokhale, Yogesh, and Nazir Pala. 2011. Ecosystem Services in Sacred Natural Sites (SNSs) of Uttarakhand: A Preliminary Survey. *Journal of Biodiversity* 2, no. 2: 107–15.

Guneratne, Arjun, ed. 2010. *Culture and the Environment in the Himalaya*. London: Routledge.

ICIMOD and UNEP. 2009. *Kailash Sacred Landscape Conservation Initiative: Inception Workshop Report*. Kathmandu, Nepal.

ICIMOD and UNEP. 2010a. *Kailash Sacred Landscape Conservation Initiative: First Regional Workshop Report*. Almora, India.

ICIMOD and UNEP. 2010b. *Kailash Sacred Landscape Conservation Initiative: Second Regional Workshop report*. Sichuan, China.

ICIMOD and UNEP. 2010c. *Kailash Sacred Landscape Conservation Initiative: Developing a Transboundary cooperation framework for conservation and sustainable development in the Mt Kailash Region of China, India, and Nepal*. Kathmandu.

Irwin, Alan. 1995. *Citizen Science: A Study of People, Expertise and Sustainable Development*. London: Routledge.

Jasanoff, Sheila. 2011. Cosmopolitan Knowledge: Climate Science and Global Civic Epistemology. In *Oxford handbook of climate change and society*, ed. John Dryzek, Richard Norgaard, and David Schlosberg, 129–43. Oxford: Oxford University Press.

Kearns, Laurel. 2011. The Role of Religions in Activism. In *Oxford Handbook of Climate Change and Society*, ed. John Dryzek, Richard Norgaard, and David Schlosberg, 414–28. Oxford: Oxford University Press.

Khosla, P. K. 1998. Himalayas Facing Ecological Disaster Depletion of Natural Resources Alarming, *The Tribune*, July 17.

Kurian, Nimmi. 2014. *India China Borderlands: Conversations Beyond the Centre*. Delhi: Sage.

Lafitte, Gabriel. 2011. Mother of all Asian Rivers, Water Tower of Asia. Paper Presentation at River Waters: Perspectives and Challenges for Asia, Conference of the Foundation for Nonviolent Alternatives, India International Centre, Delhi.

Metz, John. 2010. Downward Spiral? Interrogating Narratives of Environmental Change in the Himalaya. In *Culture and the Environment in the Himalaya*, ed. Arjun Guneratne, 17–39. London: Routledge.

Namgay, K., Joanne E. Millar, Rosemary S. Black, and Tashi Samdup. 2014. Changes in Transhumant Agro-Pastoralism in Bhutan: A Disappearing Livelihood? *Human Ecology* 42, no. 5: 779–92.

Pandey, Abhimanyu, Nawraj Pradhan, Swapnil Chaudhari, and Rucha Ghate. 2017. Withering of Traditional Institutions? An Institutional Analysis of the Decline of Migratory Pastoralism in the Rangelands of the Kailash Sacred Landscape, Western Himalayas. *Environmental Sociology* 3, no. 1: 87–100.

Perrier, Benjamin, and Nicolas Levrat. 2015. Melting Law: Learning from Practice in Transboundary Mountain Regions. *Environmental Science and Policy* 49: 32–44.

Routledge, Paul. 2011. Translocal Climate Justice Solidarities. In *Oxford Handbook of Climate Change and Society*, ed. John Dryzek, Richard Norgaard, and David Schlosberg, 384–98. Oxford: Oxford University Press.

Schoon, Michael. 2013. Governance in Transboundary Conservation: How Institutional Structure and Path Dependence Matter. *Conservation and Society* 11, no. 3: 420–28.

Scott, James. 2009. *The Art of Not being Governed: An Anarchist History of Upland Southeast Asia*. New Haven: Yale University Press.

Sharma, L.N., Ole Reidar Vetaas, Ram Prasad Chaudhary, and Inger Elisabeth Måren. 2014. Pastoral Abandonment, Shrub Proliferation and Landscape Changes: A Case Study from Gorkha, Nepal. *Landscape Research* 39, no. 1: 53–69.

Shneiderman, Sara. 2013. Himalayan Border Citizens: Sovereignty and Mobility in the Nepal-Tibetan Autonomous Region (TAR) of China Border Zone. *Political Geography* 35: 25–36.

Shrestha, Chandra. 2010. Why Should we Preserve Trans-Himalaya Heritage Routes? Paper presented at International Workshop on Transport in Mountains, Kathmandu.

Tiwari, Prakash, and Bhagwati Joshi. 2015. Local and Regional Institutions and Environmental Governance in Hindu Kush Himalaya. *Environmental Science and Policy* 49: 66–74.

van Amerom, Marloes. 2002. National Sovereignty and Transboundary Protected Areas in Southern Africa. *GeoJournal* 58, no. 4: 265–73.

Vaughan, D.G., et al. 2013. Observations: Cryosphere. In *Climate Change 2013: The Physical Science Basis. Contribution of Working Group I to the Fifth Assessment Report of the Intergovernmental Panel on Climate Change*, ed. T.F. Stockeret al., 317–82. Cambridge: Cambridge University Press.

Zomer, R., and K.P. Oli, eds. 2011. *Kailash Sacred Landscape Conservation Initiative: Feasibility Assessment Report*. Kathmandu: ICIMOD.

# Analysis of a Parallel Informal Exchange Rate System in Indo-Bhutanese Border Towns

Ankur Sharma

**ABSTRACT**

The Bhutanese Ngultrum and the Indian Rupee follow a fixed exchange rate system but within the border towns between India and Bhutan, an informal exchange rate system exists, which in contrast, is primarily based on market value system. The researcher aimed to study the underlying dynamics associated with an informal exchange rate system co-existing with the official market rate within the borderland regions of India and Bhutan. This research was focussed primarily upon intensive research methodology through interactive interviews, qualitative analysis and, primarily, in-site participant observation research techniques.

## Introduction

The classification system of the International Monetary Fund for exchange rate arrangements distinguishes among four major categories: hard pegs, soft pegs, floating regimes, and a residual category known as other managed (International Monetary Fund 2017, 5). There are five countries that are currently classified under soft pegs which maintain a conventional pegged arrangement based on an exchange rate anchor to a single currency which is not the US Dollar or Euro (International Monetary Fund 2017, 6). Among the five countries, the exchange rate anchor for three countries: Lesotho, Namibia, Swaziland is the South African Rand and the exchange rate anchor for two countries: Bhutan and Nepal is the Indian Rupee, and a common reason for such according to the International Monetary Fund is that the pegged countries either partially or exclusively border the country whose currency they use as their exchange rate anchor (International Monetary Fund 2017, 11). There are however two main differences between the South African Rand and the Indian Rupee—firstly in the manner in which their conduct as an exchange rate anchor is administered and secondly in their normative behavior in borderland regions. The administration of South African Rand as an exchange rate anchor is based on a multilateral format whereby South Africa, Namibia, Lesotho, and Swaziland have formed a monetary union known as the Common Monetary Area wherein the South African Rand is a legal tender in all member countries and the respective currencies of Namibia, Lesotho and Swaziland are pegged at 1:1 with South African Rand (Wang et al. 2007). The administration of the Indian Rupee as an exchange rate anchor is based on a bilateral format whereby Nepal and Bhutan have maintained a separate bilateral arrangement with

India wherein the Nepalese Rupee and Bhutanese Ngultrum are pegged at different rates to the Indian Rupee and only selective currency notes of Indian Rupee can be utilized for legal financial transactions in Nepal and Bhutan respectively. The second difference is that of normative behavior in particular the volatility of the exchange rate from its fixed attribute in border regions. A report of the Bank of International Settlements describes the normative behavior of the South African Rand and Lesotho's Maloti as:

> The Lesotho–South Africa currency arrangement has shown no evidence of parallel markets for rand in Lesotho, and maloti continue to be converted into rand at the official exchange rate of one-to-one in shops, department stores, petrol stations and other public trading places. There is no evidence that individuals are hoarding rand. More interestingly, even though maloti are not formally legal tender in the RSA, traders in RSA border towns are increasingly accepting them. (Foulo 2003)

This is similar across South Africa's border regions with Swaziland and Namibia and is significantly driven by the formation of a Common Monetary Area that seeks stability of exchange rates (Zyl 2003). While in India–Nepal and India–Bhutan border regions, the exchange rate of the Indian Rupee with the respective currencies would fluctuate irrespective of being pegged at a fixed rate. An informal currency exchange rate system therefore co-exists with the official exchange rate within the border regions of India with Bhutan and Nepal.

This presence of a volatile parallel informal exchange rate system in the border regions of India with Nepal and Bhutan therefore differentiates it from the stability of the official exchange rate within the border regions of South Africa with Namibia, Lesotho and Swaziland. The researcher therefore intends to showcase the underlying dynamics that are causal to the parallel informal exchange rate system within the Indo-Bhutan borderlands. The research was confined to the border towns, Jaigaon, India and Phuentsholing, Bhutan and was based primarily upon intensive research methodology. Intensive method's research questions rest on how a process works in a particular case and what produces a certain change (Pongsawat 2007). The relations that intensive research looks at are substantial relations of connection especially in terms of causal relations. It aims at producing causal explanations of the production of certain objects or events, though not necessarily a representative one. The methods used in this research were studying of individual agents in their causal contexts through interactive interviews, qualitative analysis, and, primarily, in-site participant observation research techniques.

## Background to India–Bhutan Currency Arrangement and Border

The Ngultrum (BTN) is the official currency of Bhutan and the Rupee (INR) is the official currency of India. Bhutan follows a dual currency system whereby the Indian Rupee is a legal tender currency in Bhutan and is allowed free circulation limited to the denomination of INR 100. This system is described as an informal currency union with India (Royal Monetary Authority, 1982). Since the introduction of the Ngultrum, the Bhutanese government has pegged it at par with the Indian Rupee and both currencies follow a fixed exchange rate system at 1:1. In India, the use of BTN for transactions is illegal. Prior to March, 2012, Indians were permitted to open a bank account in Bhutan where both BTN and INR can be used for transactions, subject to certain guidelines. Most individuals residing in border regions between India and Bhutan opened their bank accounts in

Bhutan as it provided them a means to deposit Ngultrum they have received from daily trade with Bhutanese citizens from across the border and subsequently withdraw INR (Dorji 2012) (Wangmo 2012).

In March, 2012, the Royal Monetary Authority of Bhutan (RMA) closed all existing depositing accounts of non-resident foreigners among whom primarily were Indians, a reactionary measure provoked by the "Rupee Crunch" in Bhutan (Bisht 2012). As of now, an Indian is allowed to open a bank account in Bhutan provided the individual either holds a valid work permit/Bhutanese Business License and/or is married to a Bhutanese and holding a valid marriage certificate. In India, a citizen of Bhutan is allowed to open a bank account where only INR can be used for transactions, provided the "Know Your Customer" norms of the bank are fulfilled (Reserve Bank of India 2015). A Bhutanese citizen when traveling to India is entitled to purchase a specific amount of INR subject to a monthly limit, which is increased for those traveling for medical treatment. There is no limit on INR that a person may send or take from Bhutan to India but the amount is subject to a limit of denomination of INR 100. Persons going to a third country from Bhutan should not carry more than INR 5000. An individual traveling from India to Bhutan may carry any denomination of INR subject to a limit, while no limit exists on denominations of INR 100. Exchange counters were formed by the RMA of Bhutan that allowed conversion of INR and BTN (Lamsang 2016) and this facility was also extended by banks in Bhutan but post-demonetization in India in 2016, strict conditions were imposed by the RMA on exchange of BTN and INR.

The border between India and Bhutan is 699 km long and the border with India is the only land access to enter Bhutan since the border with China is closed. Phuentsholing is called the gateway of Bhutan since a large portion of Bhutan's trade with India and with third countries is done through Phuentsholing's border and it also handles a large volume of tourist traffic to/from Bhutan (Consulate General of India, Phuntsholing, Bhutan 2018). Phuentsholing is the Bhutan financial, industrial and trading capital and the cross-border trade with Jaigaon has resulted in a thriving local economy. Jaigaon is similar to many other West Bengal centers of commerce, albeit with many Bhutanese shoppers (Chhukha Dzonghag Administration 2019). Phuentsholing Gate upon the border of India and Bhutan is formed on the sole road that connects India with Western Bhutan and is located between the opposite towns of Jaigaon and Phuentsholing. This corridor currently handles 68.52% of Bhutan's export and 80.93% of its imports from India, and 72.77% of Bhutan's exports and 82.53% of its imports from countries other than India (Ministry of Finance, Royal Government of Bhutan 2019, 3). The thriving local economy and the commercial significance of the border region therefore also attract ample formal and informal labor from both countries to the region. The presence of a parallel informal exchange rate system is observed across border towns located on the India–Bhutan border (Rai 2015) (Telegraph India 2016), however the importance of the Phuentsholing –Jaigaon border corridor for trade and commerce between India and Bhutan makes it an appropriate site of study above other locations.

## Parallel Currency Markets: Theoretical Perspective

An informal exchange rate is the existence of a parallel or dual exchange rate, separate from the exchange rate fixed by the government. A parallel market is a structure generated in response to government intervention through legal restrictions on sale, official price ceilings or both which creates a situation of excess supply or demand in a particular product (Agenor 1992, 6). Parallel markets for foreign exchange can emerge only when the government imposes exchange controls, that is, restrictions on the volume of certain foreign exchange transactions or on the price at which such transactions are made (Ghei and Kamin 1996, 500). Therefore an illegal parallel market system emerges when private agents attempt to evade restrictions on the price or quantity of foreign exchange transactions (Ghei and Kamin 1996, 500). The demand for foreign currency in the parallel market reflects generally three activities: legal and illegal imports, portfolio diversification and capital flight and residents traveling abroad (Agenor 1992, 10). The impositions of tariffs and quotas create incentives to fake invoices and smuggle, thereby illegal trade creates demand for illegal currency, which in turn, leads to the creation and establishment of a parallel currency market, while the demand for foreign currency for legal imports stems from the existence of rationing of foreign exchange by the central bank (Agenor 1992). Portfolio diversification in foreign exchange may also take place through the parallel market when countries impose restrictions on private-capital outflows (Agenor 1992, 12). The supply of illegal foreign currency comes in general from five possible sources: smuggling of exports, under-voicing of exports, over invoicing of imports, foreign tourists and diversion of remittances through nonofficial channels and through government officials who allow diversion of foreign exchange from the official to the parallel market in return for bribes and favors (Agenor 1992, 8).

Pierre-Richard Agenor (Agenor 1992, 12) considers four adverse effects of parallel markets: First, there is a cost of enforcement to counteract illegal activities and punish offenders. Second, there is a loss of tariff revenue as a result of smuggling and under-invoicing, a loss of income taxes and domestic indirect taxes and a reduced flow of foreign exchange to the central bank, which lowers the government's capacity to import. Third, parallel markets encourage rent-seeking activities (corruption of government officials, for instance), which lead to suboptimal allocation of scarce resources. Fourth, the existence of a parallel market facilitates the switch from domestic-currency assets to foreign currency assets and may reduce the seigniorage revenue accruing to the government. Despite the adverse effects, parallel markets are tolerated in developing countries. The typical argument used to justify them is that governments realize that as long as there is demand rationing in the official market for foreign exchange, there is bound to be a secondary market, which can be eliminated at a prohibitive cost. Viewed this way, a parallel market is taken to be socially desirable because the parallel market meets the demands of operators rationed in the official market (Agenor 1992, 12).

## Narrative Analysis Method

The researcher employed narrative methodology to analyze the informal exchange rate system as it provides an ability to produce causal explanation of a system which yearns to hide its causal production. Quantitative analysis, a preferred research method in economics, is restricted by the confidentiality of transactions in the parallel market and the absence of reliable data available. This is a common problem which is highlighted when researching upon parallel exchange markets whereby Pierre-Richard Agenor states that the nature of parallel markets precludes collection of detailed and reliable data (Agenor

1992, 1), similarly a case study on parallel currency market in Nigeria has also highlighted that the central methodological problem of any research on the informal economy, in particular the informal exchange rate, is quantification and availability of data (Hashim and Meagher 1999). Parallel currency markets are in general dominated by a small number of large players who fix the exchange rate, are followed by a large number of intermediaries who are physically present in the market on a daily basis and, because of this intermediation, the actual size of the market is difficult to evaluate and estimates are subject to wide margins of error (Agenor 1992, 7). Therefore, any qualitative assessment that may be concluded in this paper will have to be corroborated through a theoretical model in economics rather than through quantitative data.

There exists a gap in the academic literature on the Indo–Bhutan borderland and particularly so on the system of informal exchange rate system that is followed between India and Bhutan. Interviewing might often be the only means for establishing causation in cases, particularly when the phenomenon of study is relatively recent and there are no reliable alternative sources for judging motivation (Rathbun 2008, 692). Due to the often illegal nature of transactions in parallel markets, information of their functioning is neither readily available nor very reliable. Interviewing is often regarded as the method used when social scientists do not have fully formed ideas or theories thereby interviewing allows them to go in-depth in a way that second-hand sources, archives or surveys do not allow (Rathbun 2008, 685). The interactive interviews will help to produce intersecting and divergent voices and help in locating the agreed upon and contested arguments. Lived experiences of individuals at the border provide conscious narratives of unconscious performances and practices (Prokkola 2009). The experience of the borderland citizens, both as participant and/or as observer, provides an articulation of the intersecting and agreed upon arguments to form intersectionality that makes the informal tangible in analysis because the reality is that the informal economy exists. The used interview method is a narrative interview in which the interviewee is encouraged to and gives his own opinion of the subject. Although the status of data derived from interviewing is objected to as it is by nature subjective and imprecise and therefore subject to multiple interpretations (Rathbun 2008, 685). Yet interviews, despite the flaw, provide an opportunity to agency to describe the structure and the drawback of subjective reality was attempted to be circumvented by conducting multiple interviews from both sides of the border and of individuals with varying profession and experiences to obtain an overall perspective. Interviews also carry a problem of selective memories leading to perils of strategic reconstruction by respondents but that can be minimized by finding multiple sources for the same data either written or interview based and will reinforce one's belief that what one is hearing is more than just opinion or that it is just a particular interpretation of ambiguous information (Rathbun 2008, 694). By asking the same question across a section of respondents and deciphering the common pattern in differing accounts will help in separating opinion from facts. The information provided by the RMA of Bhutan and Reserve Bank of India (RBI) will further augment opinion as an official fact.

The interview transcripts may also serve as primary data for further study on the informal exchange rate system in Indo-Bhutanese borderlands. The interviewees were informed prior to the interview that it would be recorded and due to the nature of the topic, any implication of incrimination of self or others should be avoided. Prior to their interview, the interviewees were also given the opportunity to view the questions to be asked, to view the transcript after the interview, to record the interview and, if required, a copy of the interviewer's recording. Some interviews were conducted in Hindi and have been translated by the author into English while being careful to maintain the essence of the interviewee. Parentheses have been used to expand abbreviations used or where the object implied by the interviewee is unclear. Vocalized pauses which may have arisen in the conversation have been removed from the transcript. The name of the interviewee has not been provided to ensure privacy however the occupation has been provided to provide context towards their opinion.

## Narratives

An interview was conducted with a resident of Jaigaon who is a merchant in an electronic store in Jaigaon, in which the medium of language was Hindi. The transcript of the interview is as followed:

*Ankur Sharma:* "The traders in Jaigaon and Phuentsholing who receive Bhutanese currency, how do they convert it into INR?

*Interviewee 1:* "If you have more than (Nu) 50000, then a soft copy bill of tax invoice plus pan card and if possible voter I.D. card needs to be submitted (in a Bhutanese Bank), for which you will receive a demand draft (in INR), which you take to a bank (in India). If it is below (Nu) 50000, you take the copy of voter card and deposit the money and take D.D. (Demand Draft)."

An interview was conducted with a resident of Phuentsholing who is a bureau correspondent with a Bhutanese newspaper "Kunsel." The medium of language was English and the transcript of the interview is as followed:

*Ankur Sharma:* "What is the cause of informal exchange rate in Jaigaon and Phuentsholing?"

*Interviewee 2:* "You know, it was not like this before. In 2011, you know, when government, ruling government, brought measures, they banned bank accounts and all that, you know. That caused a lot of Rupee crisis in the country, ok. There was an overflow of Bhutanese currency in market and the demand for rupee started up and that is how it started in a nutshell. And then, I think, you know, in the border's, since this is the biggest border, right, and now Indians wanted INR so they started to, you know, in Jaigaon, started to hide (INR) and because of that IC (Indian currency) was less in their hand, circulation was little less and top of that, beyond Hasimara, any place in India, you need INR. While IC (Indian currency) was already in short in market and border areas erupted as illegal destination. Many people, I am not blaming the people but scenario of market, Indian people, Bhutanese people needed INR, desperate for INR, they have to buy and in that desperation, they paid certain charges, right, and initial stages, illegal sellers charged up to 20–25%. This is how it started but over the years it was controlled but again after demonetization, again it started.

*Ankur Sharma:* "What do Indians unofficially do with Bhutanese currency?"

*Interviewee 2:* "Many ways actually, ok. Reflective of region, the relations are, people know very much each other, if one Indian comes, you know there is fronting?"

*Ankur Sharma:* "Yes"

| | |
|---|---|
| *Interviewee 2:* | "So, if one Indian comes and he knows someone very well, he can give them and can officially convert that to INR. That kind of things happens. But a racket is there, still there." |
| *Ankur Sharma:* | "So for that conversion, a commission would be taken?" |
| *Interviewee 2:* | "Yes, yes." |
| *Ankur Sharma:* | "How does fronting lead to informal exchange rate in Jaigaon and Phuentsholing? Can you also explain fronting?" |
| *Interviewee 2:* | "Fronting, by the way, whole country is not in sync to define fronting. Because there are certain acts that are not clear and a discussion has been taken in parliament and we are really in process of defining fronting. So that is my definition of fronting (laughs). So the general understanding is that, like, I being a Bhutanese might not have capital to invest and might not even have the idea but I would go across the border and if I know you from say Jaigaon, you can't operate in Bhutan with Indian licence, right. And of course there are many people from say Phuentsholing border who have authentic Bhutanese licence or those across the border who were given way back in, 4–5 decades ago and they are still operating. But new ones who have money there and want to operate in Bhutan, they identify certain people and I, Bhutanese will take licence and investment, will come across that border. The licence holder will get some commission. The second part of question was?" |
| *Ankur Sharma:* | "How does fronting lead to informal exchange rate at border towns?" |
| *Interviewee 2:* | "Because somebody gets commission and that is black money and for that they would need to borrow money from border markets that is not official, that would cause the system, exchange rate system to become informal. The whole thing about the exchange rate is, up and down is all due to black market." |
| *Ankur Sharma:* | "Do Indian traders charge higher for accepting Bhutanese currency like Nu. 115–120 for a Rs. 100 product?" |
| *Interviewee 2:* | "Not always. Whenever there has been a whole drama of INR crisis or time of demonetization." |

An interview was conducted with a resident of Jaigaon who is the former president of the Jaigaon Merchant Association. The medium of language was Hindi and the transcript of the interview is as follows:

| | |
|---|---|
| *Ankur Sharma:* | "Uncle, can you tell, as Indian currency and Bhutanese currency are fixed but at the border areas, in Jaigaon and Phuentsholing, as to why it fluctuates?" |
| *Interviewee 3:* | "The reason for fluctuation is that in Bhutan, from Bhutan side, the buyers bring Bhutanese currency, they carry Bhutanese currency as even in Bhutan, Indian currency is not available. Anyways Rs. 500 and Rs. 2000 note is not accepted, due to which the only currency available is in Rs. 50 and Rs. 100 notes. Anyways they are Bhutanese citizens, they don't receive as needed and that is why they bring it (Bhutanese currency) here. There is facility at their side, those Indians at the border side, if we accept Bhutanese currency, if we don't have any other source of payment then what would we do by taking Bhutanese currency. The Royal Monetary Authority (RMA) of Bhutan invited us, asked for suggestions, so we said that with the same honour we take Bhutanese currency, in the same way. Before 9th March, 2012, we had accounts in Bhutan, we could deposit Bhutanese currency there, and then it got completely closed. Then people couldn't doRTGS (Real Time Gross Settlement System) nor |

| | |
|---|---|
| | draft. About two and half years back, RMA. started a new facility that those who have Bhutanese currency, they can go to a bank in Bhutan, have an RTGS or draft (Demand Draft), whatever it is, plus what we have voter ID, they convert Nu 50000 in a month, BC (Bhutanese currency) into IC (Indian currency). This became easily available and then on 8th November the devolution happened. It didn't happen?" |
| *Ankur Sharma:* | "Demonetization." |
| *Interviewee 3:* | "Demonetization! What happened was that the system of cash exchange got closed. Though the system of RTGS and draft (Demand Draft) continued. Due to this, those who had small amounts, those who are hand to mouth, those who did not have an official account, there is a source here, which is also called an unofficial source in our lingo. They kept currency available and continued exchanging. Because they exchange, that is why fluctuation happens. Due to availability, demand and supply." |
| *Ankur Sharma:* | "In India, Bhutan's currency is not allowed to be used ... " |
| *Interviewee 3:* | "It is not allowed but consider, border is very close and when we know, they take Bhutanese currency, from ages this is happening. This is not a system of India and Bhutan, its local. Maybe in Hasimara or Alipur, our officials from Indian side used to control, they had it closed down also. But see, in border area, we are close, you can't tell the difference from 3 km above as to where is Jaigaon and Phuentsholing. It's extremely close, total business of Bhutan is dependent. Bhutan is also giving this facility because they know, if they stop, we will stop accepting BC (Bhutanese currency)." |
| *Ankur Sharma:* | "Those who are unofficially converting BC (Bhutanese currency) into INR, they also take commission for this?" |
| *Interviewee 3:* | "Yes. Rate is also monopolized, there is no determined rate. It also happens that Bhutanese come and ask for BC (Bhutanese currency). This is acknowledged by few people but this is also true. After demonetization, Rs. 1000 and Rs. 500 notes were banned and those who had official banking channels, they kept the Bhutanese currency and got it converted through their bank and it went where it needed to go. Before demonetization, the rate was normal, handling charges, something has to be taken." |
| *Ankur Sharma:* | "Why would Bhutanese citizens purchase their own currency?" |
| *Interviewee 3:* | "Bhutanese citizens as they are not able to withdraw money from their own country (source Ngultrum for illegal usage), find it safer to take money through informal means." |

A request for information was sent to the RMA of Bhutan. The transcript of the questions asked and the respective replies received from is as follows:

Q: What is the procedure for Indians to convert Ngultrum into Indian Rupee through banks in Bhutan?

R: The following documentations are required for Indian Nationals to access INR in Bhutan. (i) A valid work permit or the Bhutanese business license. (ii) Indians married to Bhutanese and holding valid Marriage Certificates.

During travel to India, they shall be permitted to purchase INR 10,000 per day subjected to a limit of INR 50,000 per month. Those travelling for medical treatment shall be permitted to purchase cash up to Indian Rupee 100,000.

Q: What verification papers are taken from Indians to proceed with the conversion?

R: (i) A letter from the employer. (ii) A copy of valid work permit. (iii) A copy of confirmed air-ticket or in case of travel via road, the applicant must submit copies of relevant travel document.

*Q:* When the demand draft is formed in the bank in Bhutan for Indians, is it compulsory for the account holder to be the depositor?

*R:* It depends upon the KYC (Know Your Customer) norms of the individual banks.

*Q:* Is an Indian required to have an account with a bank in Bhutan to make a demand draft?

*R:* Yes, it's a mandatory requirement.

*Q:* Can the demand draft be formed in the name that is different from the depositor and the name on the verification I.D provided?

*R:* Again, it depends upon the KYC norms of the individual banks.

An interview was conducted with a video journalist operating in Jaigaon. The interview was initially conducted in person and the interview transcript was shared with the individual upon his request. Subsequently, the interviewee emailed his answers to the same questions asked, with minor changes. The subsequent transcript with the questions and replies is as followed:

*Q:* What are the unofficial procedures for Indians to convert BTN into INR?

*R:* Circulation of Indian and Bhutanese currency is a day-to-day matter for the one residing here who would like to bring the other part of a coin in a simple and precise manner. Indians residing at Jaigaon usually follow the standard procedures to convert BC (Bhutanese currency) into IC (Indian currency) i.e., to convert a specific sum (up to Nu 50000), residents and business communities prefer demand drafts issued from any Bhutanese banks but once the given limit exceeds, they are left with no other options rather than to get IC (Indian currency) from some other/unofficial means. Usually one can easily exchange BC into IC at most of the *Paan* (Betel) shops who function as unauthorized commission-based exchange counters, readily available in Jaigaon. The rate of exchange varies from 1% to 7% depending upon availability of IC in the market. Such counters are also a lifeline of residents from either nation, who are in need of IC within a very short span of time for any given reasons. During the demonetization issue, the rate of exchange was between 10–15% at some counters

*Q:* Why is there an informal exchange rate system in Indo-Bhutan border regions?

*R:* Some of the business people at Jaigaon avoid so called *Pakka* (Official) bill, if not asked for one and in return, they never hesitate to accept Bhutanese currencies. As the transaction becomes void without the notice of taxation authorities. They don't mind to pay the unofficial exchange rates for the conversion from BC to IC. This system has been going on since 2012.

*Q:* Can you throw some light on black money circulation and role of smuggling in the informal exchange rate system in Indo-Bhutan border regions?

*R:* Such unauthorized and so-called illegal transactions further lead to circulation of black money, ruining the economy of India and Bhutan. A few Bhutanese also come down to border areas and they literally sell the IC and take BC. They are also not always aware of the unofficial exchange rates, for them any percentage besides their principal amount is profit.

Two separate requests for information under the Right to Information Act were sent to the Reserve Bank of India (RBI). The transcript of the questions asked and the respective replies received from RBI is as followed:

*Q:* Please explain the procedure for an Indian to convert Bhutanese Ngultrum to Indian Rupee within India.

*R:* The person may approach any Authorized Person dealing in Bhutanese Ngultrum.

*Q:* Are Indian banks authorized to convert Bhutanese Ngultrum to Indian Rupee?

R: There is no restriction on any Authorized Person regarding conversion of Bhutanese Ngultrum into Indian Rupee.

Q: Is Bhutanese Ngultrum a convertible currency into Indian Rupee in India?

R: There is no restriction in India, on any Authorized Person regarding conversion of Bhutanese Ngultrum into Indian Rupee.

## Analysis of Narratives for Underlying Dynamics

The narratives provide multiple aspects of causation of the presence and requirement of an informal currency exchange system and an informal currency exchange rate in the Jaigaon-Phuentsholing borderland.

*It facilitates local trade:* There is a mutual dependency between the residents of Jaigaon and Phuentsholing. The residents of Phuentsholing are dependent on Jaigaon for goods and services, even basics such as fruits, plumbers, among others. Bhutanese citizens form the largest customers for the residents of Jaigaon and Bhutanese citizens when purchasing goods or services from Jaigaon prefer to primarily use BTN as it forms the dominant currency they hold and is acceptable by Jaigaon merchants. Jaigaon merchants and traders accept BTN even though it is illegal in India as Bhutanese citizens form their largest customers and because of the indifference of the authorities.

*INR Rationing:* INR is rationed by both the government and the citizens of Bhutan because Bhutan imports the majority of its required products from India and therefore there is a large outflow of INR from Bhutan to India for the purchase of these products. It has therefore become a major reason for Bhutanese citizens on insisting in paying in BTN in Indian border towns for purchase of products, but it causes a system of informal exchange rates to be formed for Indian merchants to have the BTN converted to INR.

*Tax avoidance:* In Jaigaon, if being paid in BTN, a form of Kuchha (Temporary) bill is given which allows the merchant to evade taxation and which in turn forms a source of black money. In rare instances, an individual in border areas will have to pay an amount higher than the Maximum Retail Price on a product if paying in BTN such as Nu. 115–120 for a Rs. 100 product or service, which entails both an evasion of taxation through a Kuchha bill and an illicit surcharge amounting to a source of black money. This black money that is being held in BTN is converted into INR through the parallel exchange market by paying a commission. The commission is in general lower than the percentage of tax evaded and the illicit surcharge imposed.

*Fronting:* When a Bhutanese license holder and a capital investor collude in a mutually beneficial arrangement, whereby the license holder acts as a "front" by illegally leasing the license to the investor, it is, in simple terms, known as fronting. For this the license holder receives a commission and the investor gets an opportunity to enter Bhutan's market. In border towns, the profit earned in hard cash from this endeavor if BTN is then smuggled out of Bhutan to the investor through the parallel currency market. The commission which forms a source of black money is also traded through the parallel currency market as it ensures secrecy.

*Economic shocks:* The government of Bhutan because of unanticipated events such as the "Rupee Crunch" in Bhutan or demonetization in India has imposed certain restriction on transactions and outflows of INR. To circumvent the private-capital outflow restrictions on INR, a Bhutanese citizen can exchange BTN for INR by paying a commission in the parallel currency market, a system only openly available at the borderlands.

*Ease of local banking:* An Indian may approach a bank in Bhutan either in-person or through a representative, furnish a copy of an Indian voter I.D. card and deposit an amount less than Nu 50000 and receive a demand draft which is payable at a bank in India in INR or have the amount RTGS to an account in India and then withdraw INR of the same amount. For this transaction, it is not compulsory for the Indian to have an account with the bank in Bhutan and also no transaction cost is imposed. It is also not mandatory for the depositor to be the beneficiary in the demand draft or RTGS and it also not mandatory for the depositor or beneficiary to submit their own voter I.D. card. This relaxation in Know Your Customer norms have been unofficially given to the citizens of Indo-Bhutan borderland. This system allows Indians that have received BTN as a means of transactions in the borderland to convert BTN into INR and it allows the citizens and banks in Bhutan to maintain its INR reserves as the payment and transactional cost of conversion are borne by Indian banks which receive the demand draft and RTGS. This system, inevitably allows individuals involved in the informal currency exchange system to convert BTN they receive into INR, a consequence of which is the circulation of black money into the official banking system.

*Illegal trade:* Another aspect is the alleged smuggling that occurs between India and Bhutan, invariably linked to China and South East Asia. Individuals in general require INR and BTN to conduct smuggling between India and Bhutan and generally receive INR and BTN as profit from such. Illegal trade generates illegal currency which can be converted through illegal means. Therefore, the parallel currency exchange market located at borderlands provides an option for this conversion and to change the nature of illegal currency into a legitimate form.

*Daily wage conversions:* Indian day laborers who work in border areas of Bhutan receive a small wage in BTN, mostly on a daily basis. If they require, they prefer to convert BTN into INR through the available "Paan" (Betel) shops as compared to banking channels which consumes valuable time through deposit and withdrawal.

*Lack of official currency converting facility:* The RBI has asserted, in vague terms, that an Authorized Person or an Indian Bank may convert BTN to INR but the borderland citizens have given official and unofficial talks asserting the contrary. There lacks an authorized facility in Jaigaon or nearby Indian cities to where an Indian may take BTN and convert it into INR and the reason for this absence has yet to be given by the Indian Government and will be a matter of speculation for others such as the borderland citizens and the author to make.

## Conclusion

The nine listed reasons as causal to the parallel informal exchange rate system within the Indo-Bhutan borderlands correspond with the reasons stated for the existence of parallel currency markets in the theoretical perspectives on parallel currency markets—exchange controls (Ghei and Kamin 1996), and private agents attempt to evade restrictions, illegal imports, economic shocks, capital flight, fake invoices and smuggling, rationing of foreign exchange and diversion of remittances through nonofficial channels (Agenor 1992). This paper therefore showcases the specific local dynamics of the Indo-Bhutan borderland that lead to causative factors for the rise of a parallel informal exchange rate system.

The parallel currency exchange system adopts a parallel exchange rate whenever a commission is taken for converting BTN and INR. Within the borderland, based on mutual trust, an Indian who has BTN may ask a Bhutanese to convert BTN into INR by depositing BTN within their account and withdrawing INR, for which they may take a commission. An act done without commission inconsequentially forms a parallel currency exchange system but follows the 1:1 exchange rate, it is when a commission is taken that a parallel exchange rate is formed.

The authorities in India and Bhutan understand the actual need for a parallel market and that the cost in terms of social capital and monetary capital required for legal enforcement to confront the parallel system would be excessive. The laxity in perceived security threat to territorial integrity by the proliferation of foreign currency in borderlands invariably depends upon the national identity of the currency. This can be considered with the assumption that the reaction of the Indian authorities would have been quite different if it had been the Chinese Renminbi or Pakistani Rupee rather than Bhutanese Ngultrum that had crept into the Indian borderlands.

The borders in South Asia have their own specific character, firmness and unaltered definition (Tripathi 2015, 197). The India-Bhutan borderland region provides a unique contextual understanding of functioning of an informal exchange rate system that occurs in parallel to an official fixed currency exchange system. This research can further be utilized for comparative understanding of the presence of a similar informal exchange rate system that exists between India and Nepal border region in parallel to an official fixed currency exchange system. Another future utilization would be to understand the factors that differentiate India and South Africa in maintaining stability of exchange rate in border regions with those countries with which they follow a conventional pegged arrangement of exchange rate system respectively.

In International Studies literature, border is taken as a line that separates nations and its sovereign institutions. But in Indo-Bhutan borderlands, the identity of the currencies is not territorially confined and borderland citizens can identify with coinciding currencies. The institutional identity of the currencies produces a dichotomy which is often being renegotiated at the border in parallel to the fixed institutional discourse. The parallel currency market that might be an anathema to the state, ensures regularity in the borderland economic structure. The informal structure is in itself a causation of the institutional identity of currency, with the latter being dictated by State to adhere to the borders established yet it challenges by forming the means to transcend the confronting border.

## Disclosure Statement

No potential conflict of interest was reported by the author.

## References

Agenor, Pierre-Richard. 1992. *Parallel Currency Markets in Developing Countries: Theory, Evidence and Policy Implications*. International finance section, Princeton University. Princeton: Princeton University Press.

Bhutan Benefits in Border Markets. 2016. *The Telegraph*, November 16. https://www. telegraphindia.com/1161116/jsp/siliguri/story_119418.jsp#.WK1j3m-GPIW (accessed January 9, 2017).

Bisht, Medha. 2012. The rupee crunch and India-Bhutan economic engagement. Issue Brief, Institute for Defence Studies & Analyses, New Delhi.

Chhukha Dzonghag Administration. 2019. *Phuentsholing, Dungkhag*, May 20. http://www. chhukha.gov.bt/dungkhags/phuentsholing (accessed May 20, 2019).

Consulate General of India, Phuntsholing, Bhutan. 2018. *Consulate general of India, Phuntsholing, Bhutan*, January 9. https://consulatephuentsholing.nic.in/?0626?000 (accessed May 10, 2019).

Dorji, Minjur. 2012. The Bhutanese. *Non-resident foreigners' bank accounts in country is money laundering: RMA Governor*, April 21. http://thebhutanese.bt/non-resident-foreigners-bank-accounts-in-country-is-money-laundering-rma-governor/ (accessed January 10, 2017).

Foulo, Tabo. 2003. *Regional currency area and the use of foreign currencies: Lestho's experience*. BIS Papers 17, Basel: Bank for International Settlements.

Ghei, Nita, and Steven B. Kamin. 1996. *The use of the parallel market rate as a guide to setting the official exchange rate*. International Finance Discussion Papers 564, Board of Governors of the Federal Reserve System (U.S.).

Hashim, Yahaya, and Kate Meagher. 1999. *Cross-border Trade and Parallel Currency Market*. Uppsala: Nordiska Afrikainstitutet.

International Monetary Fund. 2017. *Annual report on exchange arrangements and exchange restrictions 2017*. Washington: International Monetary Fund.

Lamsang, Tenzing. 2016. RMA & Jaigaon merchants association declare Nu-INR parity fully restored. *The Bhutanese*, May 3. (accessed January 10, 2017 http://thebhutanese.bt/rma-jaigaon-merchants-association-declare-nu-inr-parity-fully-restored/.

Ministry of Finance, Royal Government of Bhutan. 2019. *Bhutan trade Statistics, 2018*. Trade Statistics, Thimpu: Department of Revenue & Customs, Ministry of Finance.

Pongsawat, Pitch. 2007. Border partial citizenship, border towns, and Thai-Myanmar cross-border development: Case studies at the Thai border towns. PhD Thesis, University of California, Berkley.

Prokkola, Eeva-Kaisa. 2009. Unfixing Borderland Identity: Border Performances and Narratives in the Construction of Self. *Journal of Borderlands Studies* 24, no. 3: 21–38.

Rai, Rajesh. 2015. Illegal BTN-INR exchange rate jacked up in Jaigaon. *KuenselOnline*, February 9. http://www.kuenselonline.com/illegal-btn-inr-exchange-rate-jacked-up-in-jaigaon/ (accessed January 10, 2017).

Rathbun, Brian C. 2008. Interviewing and Qualitative Field Methods: Pragmatism and Practicalities. In *The Oxford Handbook of Political Methodology*, ed. Robert E. Goodin, 685–701. Oxford: Oxford University Press.

Reserve Bank of India. 2015. Supplement on 'exchange control regulations applicable to Nepal and Bhutan'. *Reserve Bank of India*, May 31. https://www.rbi.org.in/Scripts/ECMUserView.aspx?Id=56 (accessed January 10, 2017).

Royal Monetary Authority of Bhutan. 1982. *Monetary policy framework*. (accessed January 10, 2017 https://www.rma.org.bt/EXTERNALWEB/duties_fun.htm.

Tripathi, Dhananjay. 2015. Interrogating Linkages between Borders, Regions, and Border Studies. *Journal of Borderlands Studies* 30, no. 2: 189–201.

Wang, Jian-Ye, Iyabo Masha, Kazuko Shirono, and Leighton Harris. 2007. *The common monetary area in Southern Africa: Shocks, adjustment, and policy*. IMF Working Paper, Washington: International Monetary Fund.

Wangmo, Tashi. 2012. Rupee crunch leads to soaring informal exchange rates in border towns. *The Bhutanese*, March 21. http://thebhutanese.bt/rupee-crunch-leads-to-soaring-informal-exchange-rates-in-border-towns/ (accessed January 10, 2017).

Zyl, Lambertus van. 2003. *South Africa's experience of regional currency areas and the use of foreign currencies*. BIS Paper 17, Basel: Bank for International Settlements.

# Gaining a Ghetto: The Resettlement of Partition-affected Bengalis in New Delhi's Chittaranjan Park

Anubhav Roy

**ABSTRACT**

The Bengali sufferers of the tragic partition of India in 1947 have arguably failed to garner the political, policy, and discursive attention received by their West Pakistani or Punjabi counterparts. A case in point, Chittaranjan Park – a sub-urban neighborhood or colony of New Delhi granted as a ghetto to the Bengalis rendered rootless by the formation of East Pakistan – is rarely a muse for forays in partition studies or borderscaping. This paper, as an attempt to fill this void, traces the civil society-led lobbying movement for the carving out of Chittaranjan Park at the heart of India's national capital, by largely relying on archived editions of the colony's first newsletter. The narrative is linked to its contextual undercurrents of identity consciousness, state rehabilitation policy, civil-state relations, and local politics and economics by historical-evaluation. First, after highlighting how the Bengal chapter of the partition is often overlooked, this paper highlights the benefits that the then expanding city of Delhi offered its refugees in India. Second, it contrasts the Indian state's policy response to the partition's refugees from West Pakistan to those from the east. Third, it unpacks the idea of, and lobbying bid for, Chittaranjan Park, and examines if the colony qualifies as an ethnically-exclusive bordered space within a city.

Tucked in the southeast corner of India's capital city, New Delhi, the neighborhood or colony of Chittaranjan Park has etched itself as a home-away-from-home for Bengali-speaking Hindus (hereafter, Bengalis) within India's Hindi-speaking heartland. It is romanced as a demographic and cultural microcosm of Calcutta (now Kolkata), the colonial-era Bengali megalopolis. This portrayal of the colony, however, eclipses the complicated backdrop of its creation and sustained communitarian composition. Given that its present landscape upholds metropolitan modernity, and it is largely inhabited by *bhadraloks* (the elite Bengali gentry), Chittaranjan Park can hardly be imagined as a once sub-urban ghetto secured, after much effort, for the Bengali *baastuhaaraas* (an umbrella term to describe a person rendered rootless or homeless by the partition of British India's Bengal region in 1947). The acknowledgement of the colony's past is arguably limited by the fact that it was granted to those affected by the eastern theater of the partition, an appendage in the popular memory of the tragedy. A price for its decolonization, the partition of India triggered the largest concerted mass migration in history, costing as many as 2 million lives and the painstaking two-way exodus of about 20 million refugees compelled to choose between India and Pakistan. The worst brunt was borne by its western theater in bifurcated Punjab, where communal heat between Hindus, Muslims, and Sikhs spiraled into bloodbath and displacement en masse. In the east, the violence resulting from the similar bifurcation of Bengal was largely restricted to certain pockets such as Calcutta and Noakhali, and the consequent exoduses occurred in waves spread over several years (Chatterji 2007, 110–111). The crisis in Punjab, thus, deserved and received larger and swifter policy responses. The middle-class and rural victims of Bengal's partition, however, did face grave and prolonged challenges upon migrating with little but hope into India. Yet, Punjab remains the primary *lieux de memoire*[1] of India's partition in popular and academic discourses. India's lone Partition Museum, as a sample, is based at Amritsar in Punjab.

That Bengal's story often takes a backseat in India's memory of the partition is demonstrated by Indian cinema, a beloved platform for the popular. The Hindi film *Begum Jaan* (Madam Dearest, 2017) – an evocative tale of a brothel whose occupants refuse to relocate to facilitate the partition – is an adaptation of *Rajkahini* (A Tale of Kings, 2015), the Bengali original. Interestingly, Srijit Mukherji, the director of the 2015 original set in partitioned Bengal, had to direct this Hindi remake set in partitioned Punjab in order to "bring in a renewed focus" on the turbulence of those times (IANS 2017). While it must be argued that mainstream Hindi Bollywood films have wider outreach than regionally restricted Bengali cinema, the argument may appear simpleminded. Since 1965, three films – *Garam Hava* (Hot Winds, 1973), *Tamas* (Darkness, 1987), and *Pinjar* (The Cage, 2004) – based on the western half of the partition's aftermath have won India's pan-linguistic National Film Award for National Integration. None of their Bengali counterparts have managed to make the cut. In fact, while all three acclaimed films enjoy cult status among Indian audiences, Ritwik Ghatak's laudable Bengal partition trilogy – *Meghe Dhaka Tara* (The Cloud-Capped Star, 1960), *Komal Gandhar* (A Soft Note on a Sharp Scale, 1961) and *Subarnarekha* (A Streak of Gold, 1965) – eludes even tasteful recommendations on the cinematic depictions of the partition's impact.[2]

Mainstream Indian literature in English, too, has not been quite keen on Bengal's partition plight, with memorable novels like Amitav Ghosh's *The Shadow Lines* (1988) being a rarity. Most recently, it took a semi-fictional comic strip by Ghosh and Sen (2015), in a volume edited by Urvashi Butalia on life after partition, to reflect, even if briefly, the travails and aspirations of Bengali partition victims within transitioning urban refugee-havens like Raipur. As for India's capital city, it might be argued that the popular imagination of New Delhi, quite acceptably, does not identify with its tiny Bengali community (Dasgupta and TNN 2018). In a novel set in New Delhi, for instance, Singh (2011, 5–10) embodies the traditional ethnic composition of the city with his story's primary protagonists: a Hindi-speaking Hindu Brahmin, a Sunni Muslim, and a Sikh. This normalized identification is also reflected in writings on post-partition Delhi (which, at the time, included the British-built New Delhi or Lutyens' Delhi area and the adjoining Mughal-era Old Delhi). Kaur's (2017) richly nuanced inspection of the city's post-partition endurance focuses solely on the Hindu and Sikh migrants from West Pakistan. Contrastingly, Jaffrey's (2016) more casual exercise in food anthropology, centerd on post-partition

Delhi, concentrates on the "*koftas* and *karhi,* the *paneer* and *pooris,*" which are hardly staple Bengali delicacies.

As Kaul's (2001) edited volume exhibits through its essays, the partition of India – and the consequent question of choosing a homeland amidst upheaval and uncertainty – impinged upon the lives of most prominent communities in the northern half of the Indian subcontinent, cutting across religious and caste affiliations. Yet, as Yong and Kudaisya observe (2004, 24), the "existing literature [on the partition] has been Punjab-centred." Compared to the rich and multi-faceted academic assessments commanded by the Punjab partition, few scholars have shone exclusive light on the tragedy's impact on other groups such as the Bengalis. Among those who have, Joya Chatterji (1994); Chakrabarty (2004); Frasier (2008); Ghosh (2010); Dasgupta, Togawa, and Barkat (2011); Basu and Roland (2013); Debjani Sengupta (2015); and Paulomi Chakraborty (2018) explore the communal, political, economic, gender, literary, and psychological dimensions of Bengal's bifurcation with exhaustive detail. Yet, even these works spare partial attention to the complicated rehabilitation of Bengali *baastuhaaraas,* often reserving a chapter or two for that aspect, once the partition's causes, commotion, and immediate aftermath have been assessed. Noticeably, several authors on the Punjab partition, such as the likes of Rai (1986); Menon and Bhasin (1998); Nair (2011); and Butalia (2017), also use this template in narrating the rehabilitation experiences of refugees from West Pakistan. In this respect, Joya Chatterji has emerged as a champion of mapping the impact of the partition on the *baastuhaaraas* and their impact, in turn, on their host nation-states. Her exhaustive writings on the subject extend from investigating the policy and socio-economic challenges of rehabilitating the refugees (Chatterji 2001) to their relevance for the rearranging politics in the Indian portion of Bengal after 1947 (Chatterji 2007). Chatterji is particular about not marginalizing the Muslim voices of Bengal's partition (Chatterji 2016), and has also delved into aspects of the Bengal partition as microscopic as the class-centric concerns of Calcutta's *bhardralok* diplomats (Chatterji 2018). Her works do not, however, draw the reader's gaze towards the partition-affected Bengalis in Delhi. Likewise, Yong and Kudaisya (2004, 159), who evaluate the partition's impingement on "South Asia's capital cities," fail to note the tall shadow of the tragedy behind New Delhi's Chittaranjan Park.

This absence of acknowledgement may be traced to a few peculiarities that may devalue the colony's worth as a specimen for partition studies. First, Chittaranjan Park began shaping up in the 1960s, over a decade after the partition and the violence linked to it displaced the first and largest wave of migrants into India. Second, the lobbying movement for the colony's creation did not involve or bail out the lowest stratum of Bengali refugees from the pitiable post-partition transit camps along the then newly redrawn border of east India. Third, the colony is nowhere near the border that split Bengal. The booming discourse on borderscaping may prove a welcome intervention in this regard. Although border studies has conventionally prioritized cases of zones spatially congruous to formal or informal borders separating states or peoples, the ambit of the borderscape has, more recently, grown to include imagined and microcosmic borders within, and not only peripheral to, states. As Strüver (2005, 170) observes, borderscaping no longer implies "the shaping [of] border[s] on the ground, but [also] in people's minds." In fact, any area bound by a border is likely to have been "shaped [as] a constructed reality," from above by those administering it or from below by those inhabiting it

SOUTH ASIA                                                                                    111

(Houtum, van der Velde and Jacobs n.d., 5). Such arguments are only aided by the classical conception of nations as "imagined communities" by Anderson (1983), who tests his idea of the imagination of a nation preceding its physical existence on the tiniest countries in the world. Thus, it is unsurprising that Lazzirini (2015, 179) interprets even cities as spaces with borders, since "founding a city means, first of all, marking boundaries separating it from what is not a city." In accordance, could a part of city, such as a colony – especially one initially carved out as a mono-ethnic ghetto, such as Chittaranjan Park – also be imagined as a bordered landscape? Before addressing this question, the contextual backdrop and rationale behind the insistence for, and the birth of, a colony in Delhi for the *baastuhaaraas* directly or indirectly affected by the partition of Bengal deserves to be explored in detail.

Between 1947 and 1967, six million Bengali-speaking Hindus migrated in waves into West Bengal (the Indian portion of Bengal) from "*Opaar Bangla*" (the other side of Bengal or East Bengal), which remained East Pakistan until seceding as Bangladesh in 1971 (Chatterji 2007, 2). West Bengal, the Indian half of Bengal, became the instinctive bet for survival for most migrants from the Pakistani half due to the cultural continuity of both halves. Thus, those that the Indian state tried to scoop away from the region for resettlement elsewhere were quick to return, wary of "congenial and strange surroundings," admitting an inability in "acclimatising themselves to the new environment," and flagging the inadequacy of skills to adapt to untried occupations, especially the tilling of unkind terrains such as the dry-lands of Dandakaranya (EW 1954, 1173–1175). Yet, India's Ministry for Rehabilitation pressed ahead with its attempts to scatter the Bengali refugees, shipping a chunk of them away from the Indian mainland to the Andaman and Nicobar Islands in the Bay of Bengal.[3] Why, in that scenario, did a handful Bengalis who identified as *baastuhaaraas* spark a campaign for an exclusive ghetto in Delhi, then a nascent city spatially and culturally distant from Bengal's borderlands? For aspiring Bengalis in decolonizing India, Delhi's prospects had begun rivaling Calcutta's.

## I. Delhi: the Coveted Refuge

Postcolonial Calcutta stood saturated and strained. Although West Bengal did not require a major linguistic redrawing unlike India's other colonial-era provinces and presidencies, only half the workforce in and around its largest city, Calcutta, ethnically identified as Bengali. That the populace of skilled labor was over double the size of unskilled labor in the city's industries and merely 38% of its employees were "gainfully employed in white-collar jobs," affirmed the metropolis' cut-throat climate. Lubell (1974, 40–54) observes that "the situation of the educated unemployed in Calcutta was already one of crisis in the 1950s." This made the ageing metropolis a tough arena for hopefuls from East Bengal, amongst whom, "there was a heavy concentration of educated persons who sought jobs." Worse, while Calcutta's then prevalent "unemployment rates were low for ordinary migrants, [they stood] extremely high (over 35%) for displaced migrants from East Pakistan," often due to the prevalent distrust for the outsiders.[4] Joya Chatterji (2007) and Paulomi Chakraborty (2014) have accounted the tremendous hindrances in Calcutta's bid to absorb Bengali refugees.

Amongst the world's largest and busiest cities, Calcutta housed roughly 4.5 million people by 1950 (Mantri 2011). Meanwhile, a then largely limited Delhi had a population of only 1.4 million despite being India's political capital (Rajadhyakshal 2013). Unlike its elder, colonially-crammed metropolises, Delhi was not bursting at its seams and promised an accommodative boom capable of absorbing mass migration. A crucial factor that made it a coveted space was its cost of living, which, for the era's working class, was around 46% of Bombay's, 42% of Madras', and noticeably, 39% of Calcutta's.[5] Distant Delhi, as an elementary dividend, assured survival at half the cost offered by other Indian metropolitan cores. More lucratively, the city promised opportunity with urbanization. First, as a young metropolis demanding skilled labor, Delhi allowed anybody with even basic typing skills a shot at employment. Second, as the seat of national governance, it was the *mecca* to those aspiring for public sector jobs.[6] Third, as India's political core, Delhi availed valuable proximity to the corridors of power and bureaucracy that pervaded past red tapes. These corridors included ample Bengali officers who had been transferred from Calcutta to Delhi, the last capital of British India, since 1911 (Nakatani 2015).

As was familiar in most transitional postcolonial societies, the colonial ills of nepotism and cronyism were conveniently inherited in India. For those displaced from Pakistan thronging the transit camps of Delhi, however, altruistic favors often proved to be miracles. In 1953, for instance, Balraj Bahri Malhotra, a financially-fraught Punjabi refugee, mustered the allotment of a space for a shop at the city's heart in Khan Market only with an acquainted politician's aid. The shop evolved into *Bahrisons* – the favorite bookstore of Delhi's elite – as "Khan Market went from being a refugee market to a posh market" over the years (Sahni and Mehta 2011). Even migrants who were better off profited similarly. Kundan Lal Gujral, the gourmet owner of Daryaganj's new Moti Mahal diner, managed to clinch banquet contracts from the Prime Minister's office with the endorsement of a client from his pre-partition business in Peshawar: Mehr Chand Khanna, who cemented his political clout in Delhi as the Jawaharlal Nehru cabinet's Minister for Rehabilitation by 1954 (Gujral 2004, ch. 1). Delhi's nursing of partition victims could hardly avoid politicization. The influx of Hindu refugees stimulated the activism of the majoritarian Hindu Right-wing, which had suffered a loss of legitimacy since *Mahatma* Gandhi's controversial assassination by a militant majoritarian. The rivalry between the ruling Centre-Left Congress Party and the Hindu majoritarians began to heat as the former camp "co-opted" Khanna, a "key figure of Hindu politics in the Northwest Frontier Province before 1947," under the Hindu Mahasabha's nose (Jaffrelot 2010, 292). The Hindu Right, nevertheless, was mindful of "the potential of the refugee support vote base" and strove to secure substantial presence within the constituency. Thus, from a seasoned Balraj Madhok to a young Madan Lal Khurana (R. Sengupta 2008, ch. 4), some of the most approachable advocates of migrants' interests emerged from the camp leaning Rightwards.[7]

## II. Disproportionate Dividends

Preceding Khanna's ascent to the forefront of refugee affairs, the discord along the political spectrum had spiked with the atrocious Barisal riots of 1950, which compelled the largest exodus wave of two million refugees from East Pakistan to India. The tragedy coincided with and soured the spirit of the Liaquat-Nehru Pact, a bilateral understanding between the heads of governments of India and Pakistan seeking to amicably settle "the security of […] religious minorities [in either state] and put a permanent end to migrations."

Days after the agreement got signed despite the bloodbath at Barisal, the Bengali hardliner, Shyama Prasad Mookerjee, resigned from the Nehru cabinet in protest, and led an All India Refugee Conference to found the Bharatiya Jana Sangh (the predecessor of today's Bharatiya Janata Party). While catalyzing the Hindu Right's revival in Delhi, the agitation provided little benefit to the freshly displaced Bengalis in West Bengal (Jaffrelot 1996, 96–98).

*Dil-waalon ki Delhi* (the Delhi of the large-hearted), meanwhile, was becoming a resort for migrants. Those packed at the crude camps between the Kingsway Camp and Kalkaji areas saw devoted residential ghettos emerge, prompting the city's urbanization beyond its colonial core. 2000 acres of land were allotted by the state for settlements in north Delhi alone, which led to the founding of the Vijay Nagar and Model Town colonies. The neatly built refugee hubs of Patel Nagar and Moti Nagar "became the template for subsequent neighbourhoods." Meanwhile, "the deserted south side of Lodhi Road" became the rather habitable Jangpura and Nizamuddin. To the south, agrarian patches were converted to Lajpat Nagar and Defence Colony. More than the *bazaars* of Khan Market and Lodhi Colony, the new industrial belts of Malviya Nagar and Okhla were the instruments of the resurgence of migrant-turned residents. In its benevolent evolution, however, India's capital "had, by the 1950s, emphatically become a Punjabi city," as historian VN Dutta (Alluri and Bhatia 2016) testifies. Its "boisterous, hearty, and enterprising" complexion was driven by aspiring migrants from West Pakistan. Ranjana Sengupta (2008, ch. 4) recalls that "the Kapoors, Khannas, Chopras, Malhotras, Seths, Puris, and Tandons, […] as their fortunes improved, moved into the new [and uptown] south Delhi colonies that were coming up – Golf Links, Vasant Vihar, Greater Kailash, and Maharani Bagh." A large share of the credit for their prospering was owed to Mehr Chand Khanna, the champion of Delhi's refugees. His personal push for the development and regularization of the refugee-owned houses and shops in Lodhi Colony and BK Dutt Colony inspired the area's Khanna Market and Mehr Chand Market. Khanna's plans for Bengal's *baastu-haaras*, however, proved contrastingly short-sighted initially.

Unlike the messier Punjab theater of the partition, in the east, a wave of *bhadralok* Bengalis had migrated to the inner sanctuaries of India before the violence peaked, leaving the *dalits* (lower castes) and the impoverished to bear the heavier brunt of the communal bloodletting that followed.[8] Moreover, the most worrying influx of Bengali migrants to India emerged only in 1950, by when the Indian state had attained ample experience in refugee management. Yet, the situation of the displaced Bengali was undeniably grave and the defects in its redressal were quite stark. Contrasting the optimism of developing Delhi was the disastrous instance of the Dandakaranya project. As West Bengal, Assam, and Tripura brimmed with Bengali migrants, the Indian state sought an additional 100,000 acres of land for them, embarking on "arguably the largest colonization operation undertaken in independent India" for their resettlement in the afforested belt contiguous to what was then Madhya Pradesh, Andhra Pradesh, and Orissa (Tiwari 2010, 115–117). Tiwari's (2010) study of the proposed project unveils its lacunae. First, the Ministries of Rehabilitation, Finance, and Home Affairs – the responsible state arms – could not chalk a proposal and conclude their logistics before 1958. Second, the tracts chosen for such a large settlement were Scheduled Areas that constitutionally assured special rights to the development-averse indigenous forest tribes that dominated the region. The possibility of the project being an assimilationist threat loomed large, as Khanna's Ministry for

Rehabilitation envisioned Dandakaranya to evolve into an industrialized belt for entrepreneurial Bengali migrants, just as Delhi had for their Punjabi counterparts. Third, the state decided to hastily shut the fiscally burdening refugee transit camps in West Bengal by July 1959. Despite the infeasible project failing to become a reality on ground, "25,000 families," mostly poor, were "cajoled, browbeaten, or forced" to relocate to Dandakaranya's unkind terrains by 1973. When their reverse exodus started, the red-faced state and the populist press blamed the "laziness and [...] stubborn resistance" that had come to be stereotypically ascribed to the Bengali refugee, who was painted pale in comparison to "the 'sturdy' and 'enterprising' peasant refugees from Punjab" (Chatterji 2007, 135–137).

Adding the worst blow, in 1979, West Bengal's Left government deployed police firing to drive out a cluster of embittered settlers at the Marichjhapi island in the Sunderbans, killing "several hundred men, women, and children" (Mallick 1999, 111). They had returned from Dandakaranya, lured by "poll promises" of improved living conditions (Bhattacharya 2011). Bengali refugees stranded elsewhere, too, faced existential threats. The "*Bongal Kheda* (drive away the Bengalis) agitations" in Assam in the 1960s led "half a million Bengalis" to flee from its Brahmaputra valley to the state's "Bengali dominant Barak Valley" (Bhaumik 2008, 252). In 1980, Tripura's native rebels drummed up a sons-of-the-soil campaign against its Bengali refugees. Their movement for the "expulsion of the foreigners" erupted into "700 people, mostly Bengali, being killed in over two dozen places." Among the anti-Bengali pogroms in Tripura, the most harrowing was the massacre of June at Mandai, where around 350 people were slaughtered in the village near Agartala, with the barbarism stretching to the extent of the "bodies of children [being] spiked through" (NYT 1980). As an emblem of poor policy, Bastar, the pilot district for the Dandakaranya project, is a den of Left-wing guerrillas.

## III. Finding a Footing

The educated, middle-class Bengali migrants who managed to relocate to Delhi had their own hurdles. Paritosh Bandopadhyay, who went on to become an activist, captures the struggle of his kind. An average *baastuhaaraa*, he moved to Delhi from West Bengal with meagre means in December 1956, after securing a public job from the Indian state's Union Public Service Commission (UPSC).[9] Lodging with an acquaintance in Delhi's Vinay Nagar locality, he was astounded to hear his Bengali benefactors fluently carry their conversations in Hindi, a language unfamiliar to him. In two years, however, Bandopadhyay proceeded to ace his Hindi clerical test. The monetary reward for his efforts was adequate to help him upgrade his modest wardrobe for Delhi's bitter winters, a weather pattern unfamiliar to him. Shortly after, when he moved to a privately-run hostel in central Delhi's Gole Market, he cherished his freedom, but regretted the lack of quiet needed for studying. Repulsed by a spent *beedi* (a crude cigarette) in his lunch, he soon shifted to a cabin in south Delhi's Laxmi Bai Nagar, only to find its owner in a haste to sell it off and leave Delhi. Before that winter could end, Bandopadhyay went back to square one: a rented quarter at Vinay Nagar (P. Bandopadhyay 2016).

The term *vinay* (submissive humility) reminded the public officials residing in Vinay Nagar of their subservience within the colonial bureaucratic hierarchy, which triggered the eventual renaming of the colony to Sarojini Nagar. Yet, the acceptance of *vinay* defined the course of Bengali migrants in Delhi, whose ambitions of upward mobility kept being circumstantially and structurally challenged. Their counterparts from West Pakistan, who had their own bitter pills to swallow, found answers to their doubts of housing and employment in the receptive response of the Indian state. Vinay Nagar, for instance, was not a refugee-only locality, but most shops in its community market were allotted to those from West Pakistan (Trikha and Wadhwa 2016). In contrast, skilled middle-class Bengali migrants landing in Delhi to occupy white collar vacancies remained tenants on others' properties for years. Having abandoned ancestral assets in their *janmabhoomi* (place of birth), which had become East Pakistan, and failing to gain fixed assets in their *karmabhoomi* (place of work) of Delhi, most of the city's Bengali migrants remained rootless despite having revived their careers after the partition. The likes of Bandopadhyay could afford to own a house only in Chittaranjan Park.

The initial aversion of the Indian state towards the Bengali refugee question was reflected by the glaring lack of its mention in the Displaced Persons (Compensation and Rehabilitation) Act passed by the parliament in October 1954 (Kanoon n.d.) and the First Five-Year Plan (1951–1956) that preceded the law (PCI 1951, ch. 38). As if in anticipation, handful Bengali migrants employed at the Indian Meteorological Department began meeting, by February 1954, on their Lodhi Road office's terrace to discuss the future of their community. Led by Jahnabi Charan Chakraborty, the bunch – routinely found basking in the sun during their lunch recess – labeled itself the "Sunshine Club" (Majumdar 1977) and expressed a mutual urge to seek solutions for the woes of Delhi's Bengali migrants. In one such deliberation, Chakraborty observed:

> With the Nehru-Liaquat Pact, [our] dreams of returning to East Bengal came to an end. Has anyone thought where we shall settle now after retirement?

To his serious inquiry, a pessimist quipped, "in hell," while an optimist teased, "on the moon" (Majumdar 1977).

The club went on to vote for Chakrabarty to file an official plea with the Indian state in that regard. Along with his colleague, Manindra Lal Dutta, he pitched a three-page file to the Ministry of Rehabilitation, requesting it to arrange for the compensatory permanent resettlement in Delhi of those Bengali government officials who had no hometowns left in post-partition India to go back to. With that, the path for the "Sunshine Club" to become the "Association of Central Government Servants Dislodged from East Pakistan" (hereafter, the association) was paved, with its mission being a citizen-led grassroot lobbying movement (hereafter, the movement) for a slice of East Bengal – as they continued to call East Pakistan, propelled by nativism – on Delhi's soil. The aspiring seven-member pressure group convened its inaugural formal meeting on 16 March 1954 (Majumdar 1977). Their priority was to expend the association's size by enrolling similarly motivated *baastuhaaraas* in Delhi, who were scattered across "Lodhi Road, Vinay Nagar, Gole Market, Paharganj, Minto Road, and Karol Bagh." The fee for enrollment was a nominal Re. 1 per head and the mode of survey was door-to-door. Commuting miles on bicycles or on foot, the expectant surveyors met apathy, scepticism, and even bitter repulsion at many a doorstep. Yet, by their second meeting in April, the persistent volunteers gathered 460 supporters and the attention of several other Bengali *babus* (public officials) at a parsimonious promotional expenditure of Rs. 40.75. Inspired, the association chose to send its leading representatives directly to Mehr Chand Khanna soon after he became India's Minister for Rehabilitation. The meeting, however, flopped, as Khanna subtly asserted his displeasure by reprimanding Chakraborty and Dutta, both state employees, for their alleged disregard of communication lines and bureaucratic protocol (Majumdar 1977), while playing the card of "administrative difficulties" to discourage their demand upfront (Acharya 1972).

Khanna raised a stronger objection eventually. Most *baastuhaaraas* seeking permanent resettlement in Delhi were employees of the state entitled to pensions and other benefits after retirement, and thus, were relatively privileged compared to the refugees who had fled to the city from West Pakistan and deserved greater state support (Acharya 1972). The argument, however, was unsatisfying. First Bengali *babus* were stationed in the national capital before, during, and after the partition, and the official quarters allotted to them were a temporary perquisite, to be vacated upon discharge. Consequently, those who could not amass enough wealth to purchase lands by their retirement risked becoming landless, with that risk looming largest over migrant Bengali *babus* who lost their ancestral lands to the partition. Second, most Bengali migrants who had freshly been employed by the Indian state in Delhi after partition – like Bandopadhyay's case cited earlier – had to seek temporary shelter as tenants till they could become eligible for official quarters or save enough to purchase private plots. Third, pensions and retirement benefits could hardly compensate for the loss of ancestral lands, especially as colonies for landless refugees from West Pakistan propelled Delhi's urbanization. The state's initial disdain, nevertheless, temporarily punctured the prowess of the association.

The local authorities of West Bengal were not helpful too. By 1955, two appeals to Bidhan Chandra Roy, the then Chief Minister of West Bengal, fell on deaf ears. During a meeting of the association with Air Marshal Subroto Mukherjee – a Bengali veteran and the outgoing chief of the Indian Air Force – a pitch to Renuka Roy, West Bengal's regional Rehabilitation Minister, yielded no favors too. The movement's dipping morale was reflected by the lack of a willing volunteer for the association's secretarial post by July 1956. Whispers of Mahindra Lal Dutta's transfer contributed further to the disheartenment. With desperation rising, Devi Prasanna Acharya – a senior member of the association – persuaded social activist, Jyotirmay Sinha, to volunteer as its secretary. Sinha, a textbook *Ghoti* (West Bengali) *bhadralok* from Calcutta, reserved deep sympathies for the *Baangaal* (East Bengali) migrants and had the influence to turn the movement's tide (Majumdar 1977). Sinha fetched additional funds for the association, and convinced Ila Pal Choudhury, the Congress MP from West Bengal's Nabadwip, and SP Sen Verma, the serving Chief Election Commissioner of India, to become members of the association (Acharya 1972). The grassroot lobbying movement, thus, gained its most prominent advocates and a boost to its legitimacy.

Pal Choudhury began routinely raising the agenda of the association directly with Prime Minister Nehru. She also facilitated appointments for the movement's frontmen with MPs like Sucheta Kriplani and Satish Chandra Samanta. Soon, the association managed to grab the attention of Arun Chandra Guha, the chairman of the Ministry for Rehabilitation's review committee for refugee rehabilitation (Acharya 1972). The MP from West Bengal's Barasat and a veteran of the Indian independence movement, Guha was reportedly dismayed at the contrast between the budding *pucca* (concrete) colonies for West Pakistani refugees in Delhi and the stagnant "slums" dotting West Bengal for their East Pakistani counterparts. He was, most encouragingly, among the few political leaders who saw urbanization as the only route for the upward mobility of the *baastuhaaraas*. In July 1957, at an assembly of the Congress Party summoned in Calcutta by its president UN Dhebar, Guha tabled the matter and catapulted the association's agenda into the mainstream policy discourse for the first time (Guha 1973). A year since its lowest point, the movement had, indeed, turned its tide.

Citing the land and resource saturation in Calcutta, Guha advised that a colony be established in Delhi to at least allow 3,000 *baastuhaaraa* families a shot at rebuilding their lives. The motion was interrupted by Atulya Ghosh – a member of the dubious inner "syndicate" of the Congress Party that caused its split by 1969 – on technical grounds, perhaps to pre-emptively curb press suspicions of the West Bengal government's refugee crisis management shortcomings. Guha insisted that the matter was vital to proceedings since Mehr Chand Khanna was in attendance. When Dhebar sought Khanna's view, the latter politely refused to comment and asked Guha to see him at his Delhi office. In Delhi, Khanna passed the buck by urging Guha to seek a nod from the Congress Party's working committee. The committee included several prominent migrant leaders from West Pakistan who doubted Guha's proposition. Yet, Lala Achint Ram, the Gandhian Punjabi MP, differed. Having witnessed the pitiable conditions at Bengal's transit camps, Ram vetoed all scepticism against Guha's proposal and ensured its ratification by the inner core of India's ruling party (Guha 1973).

## IV. Towards the Promised Land

Upon receiving the approval from the top echelons of his party, Khanna and his ministry sprang into action. His secretariat brainstormed with Guha a vision for an exclusive colony in Delhi for the *baastuhaaras*. As a token of the Indian state's fairness, it was to be set up adjacent to Kalkaji, an upcoming settlement for West Pakistani refugees in southeast Delhi. As an expression of its generosity, the colony not just aimed to settle partition-affected state employees, but assured to accommodate all migrants irrespective of their occupational credentials, true to the egalitarian ideals of Nehruvian socialism. Sceptics, however, continued to press Prime Minister Nehru against the so-called fiscal laxity by playing up the possibility of Delhi's labor market being saturated by aspirant Bengali migrants attracted to the city by the promise of urban plots. Khanna, however, was directed not to lose the progress made on the decision. To bridge demand and dissent, he prescribed the compromise of allotting plots in the proposed colony to only those *baastuhaaraas* who could prove being "gainfully employed" in Delhi, in order to avoid stoking unemployment in the national capital (Guha 1973). This, problematically, restricted the colony's ability of bailing out Bengali migrants to the educated or skilled. By then, despite the state's efforts to scatter Bengal's refugees, "one in four residents" of Calcutta and its suburbs was a migrant, as its periphery got dotted with nearly 150 squatter colonies built overnight through self-help, without permit, and on encroached lands. In West Bengal, unlike in Delhi, even migrants with some education and political connections lived in bamboo-made shanties. Most were able to secure gainful employment only in Calcutta, and thus, failed to qualify for the proposed migrants' colony in Delhi. They went on to embrace the Communist Party of India's Jyoti Basu as their leading advocate and helped propel him as West Bengal's Chief Minister by 1977 (Choudhury 2017).

For settlement in the proposed colony, nevertheless, those working in Delhi's private sector had eligibility at par with their counterparts on the state's payroll (Guha 1973). In order to embark on the larger task of scouting and attracting a batch of allottees from diverse sectors, the Association of Central Government Servants Dislodged from East Pakistan rechristened itself as the East Pakistan Displaced Persons' Association (EPDPA), a registered society with a new office in Vinay Nagar. As an all-volunteer non-profit society, it had the distinction of having its charter drafted by the state's Chief Election Commissioner, Sen Verma (Acharya 1972). By March 1960, Khanna, in his cabinet capacity, informed the parliament about the plan to colonize a part of southeast Delhi for the *baastuhaaraas* (Guha 1973). He also eyed the general elections due in 1962, for which, the stakes escalated when his rival refugee leader from the Right-wing Bharatiya Jana Sangh, Balraj Madhok, clinched the New Delhi parliamentary seat in a 1961 by-election (Smith 2015, 94). On behalf of the city's Bengali migrants, Guha pledged "unflinching support" to Khanna's electoral campaign, provided the constituency's demands were favorably met by his ministry (Guha 1973).

The 212-acre land[10] reserved for the colony was rigidly rocky with afforested patches. Quite disconnected from the Lutyens' core, it bordered the vast Jahapanah forest on Delhi's south. Its early inhabitants could "often hear wolves howling in the night" (Misra 2015). After Ila Pal Choudhury left Delhi, Sen Verma steered the EPDPA and pushed state organs to advance the colony's construction. The Life Insurance Corporation of India, for instance, granted the required loans for the infrastructural works as well as to potential allottees for the purchase of plots. The Vice-chairman of the Delhi Development Authority – the city's urbanization arm – Subodh Gopal Basu Mullick turned out to be another *Ghoti* with a soft corner for *Baangaal* migrants. On Sen Verma's request, he crucially ensured a simplified certification of allottees. Many of the Bengali migrants, though gainfully employed in Delhi, could hardly substantiate their long severed links with East Pakistan with documented proof. Basu Mullick's solution cut past bureaucratic strangleholds and permitted the acceptance of plain affidavits attested by his office as valid declarations of identification (Acharya 1972).

In the 1962 general elections, Mehr Chand Khanna won his parliamentary post from the prestigious New Delhi seat. In the decade that followed, 2,000 families claimed roots in East Pakistan before state officials to secure modest plots for *pucca* dwellings at subsidized rates within the colony that, in its early days, became affectionately – at times, pejoratively – identified in and around India's national capital as "Delhi's Bengali colony" or the "EPDP colony." After long deliberations by the EPDPA[11], on 22 December 1972, "Chittaranjan Park" was finalized as the colony's name as a tribute to Chittaranjan Das, the Indian freedom movement's Bengali stalwart (Khadilkar 1972). The name reportedly had the personal endorsement of then Prime Minister, Indira Gandhi (Acharya 1972; Editor 1972).

The question of whether a colony carved within a city for an ethnic community qualifies as a bordered space – such as the city itself – may be addressed here. A city can well be imagined, or even witnessed, as a space intended for certain groups or classes of inhabitants, separated from its surrounding rural or sub-urban stretches by an informal border stitched together via toll plazas and signboards demarcating city limits. Likewise, within a city, while most neighborhoods, colonies, and blocks may be inter-meshed by a network of streets, cross-streets, bridges, and commutation infrastructure, some others, especially those along its periphery, may also be separated from the rest of the city by less physical and more imagined barriers. Rajaram (2014, 33), studying cities as sites of colonial administration, for instance, exemplifies 1910s' Kuala Lampur as a pro-totype of this, with "spaces not only of inequality, but of deliberate and sustained neglect [...] exist[ing] alongside broad avenues and quite stunning colonial buildings." Even when the infrastructural inequalities may not be too stark, a portion of a city, despite formally being part of it, may be separated from the rest of the urban landscape by being identified with and frequented by only those affiliated to a particular ethnic – racial, linguistic, caste – or class category. This imagined separation of a part of a city from its rest may be seen as an exercise in borderscaping too, and considering Chittaranjan Park's initial mono-ethnic composition – as "Delhi's Bengali colony" – it does qualify as a bordered space, both phys-ically and imaginatively.

With that said, there are at least two notable contradictions to the perceived homogen-eity associated with the colony. First, tall figures of West Bengali origin in Delhi, like Sinha, Pal Choudhury, Guha, and Basu Mullick, pillared the movement for Chittaranjan Park on their influential shoulders, contrasting the pale attitude of West Bengal's political establishment towards the migrants. This bonhomie of the *Ghotis* (West Bengalis) with the *Baangaals* (East Bengalis) in Delhi was quite opposed to the harmless yet tra-ditionally assertive rivalry that prevails in the Bengal region between the two sub-commu-nities for cultural supremacy, as the variances in their praxes range from dialects and eating preferences to the football clubs they cheer. These micro differences of identity were overshadowed, however, by the broader affinity of the two sub-communities to a uni-fying sense of Bengali-ness within a city like Delhi, which saw neither sub-group as an organic constituent. This may be seen as an application of Arjun Appadurai's notion of deterritorialization, which argues that the globalization of communities involving their socio-spatial separation from their roots leads to a "paradox of constructed primordial-ism," whereby, as cultures transcend past borders, "sameness and difference [...] canniba-lize one another," and ethnic allegiances become adaptive.[12]

Second, Nakatani (2015) shows that Chittaranjan Park did not remain homogenous to its East Bengali residents for long. Its "single *Durga Puja* [the festive Bengali worship of the Hindu goddess, *Durga*] split into four [by] 1977" and became "linked up with commerci-alism in the urban environment," often drawing sponsorship from other affluent commu-nities. As festivals "became impersonal," the colony, too, expanded in the 1990s, opening up 714 new plots for allotment that invited buyers from post-partition generations of *Baangaal* as well as *Ghoti bhadraloks*. Soon, the fresh plots also drew buyers from other communities. More recently, with Delhi's growing saturation, the communitarian hom-ogeneity of Chittaranjan Park has only diluted further, as many original allottees – tied to their plots by long-term leases – have allowed real estate developers to vertically expand their residences with plush ready-to-move-in independent apartments, which are largely sold irrespective of ethnicity to whoever pays the right price. Thus, within four decades of its creation as a colony for landless partition-affected migrants from East Pakistan, Chittaranjan Park began to lose its homogeneity. Its image as a bordered Bengali-only space has fast been eroding since.

## V. Conclusion

With sedans parked at its porches, Chittaranjan Park has matured into a residential enclave suited to elite *bhadralok* status, with its apartments sought by raring businessmen and retiring bureaucrats alike, irrespective of ethnicity. It attempts to uphold a lot of its Bengali cultural essence – the exiled Bangladeshi author, Taslima Nasreen, visits the colony when in Delhi to buy the supplies suited to her *Baangaal* palate (Das 2016) – despite its demographic transition. Chittaranjan Park's present-day ambience of modernity has relegated its past to a footnote in popular memory, with the movement behind its birth being unknown to many of its residents. While ample colonies of Delhi, such as Lajpat Nagar, Old Rajinder Nagar, Tilak Nagar, and Model Town, are fondly regarded as spatial benefactors that embraced desperate refugees of the partition from West Pakistan, Chittaranjan Park is devoid of such an identity. The larger regret, in hindsight, is that the partition-affected migrants of Bengal had to struggle with a lobbying movement for a slice of settlement in the national capital of the nation-state whose citizenship they so painstakingly chose. Contrastingly, the state largely took *suo moto* action for the resettlement of West Pakistani refugees, as they braved the bloodbath and made it to Delhi. Since a nascent Delhi, at the time, was far from the space crunch that it faces today, it could well have absorbed far more Bengali migrants languishing in camps and slums, if the Indian state had so intended. Moreover, despite popular notions about the city's composition, Delhi was home to a sizable number of Bengali families well before 1947, as testified by two of the oldest colonial-era schools of the city, which impart education in Bengali.[13] That the demand for Chittaranjan Park garnered state interest a decade after the partition only reflects poorly on the policy priorities of India's then Ministry of Rehabilitation.

Chittaranjan Park, nevertheless, became a shining example of faithful camaraderie between the *Ghoti* Bengalis of West Bengal and their *Baangaal* counterparts of East Bengal, proving that the partition failed to drive a wedge between them. Shattering class barriers, the movement for the colony brought elite *Ghoti bhadraloks* wielding enough influence in Delhi – especially MPs and bureaucrats – closer to those of their less privileged *Baangaal* subordinates who gazed anxiously at their losses in East Pakistan. Despite its initial disdain, nevertheless, the Indian state exceeded expectations to grant settlement space to not just its own East Bengali officials, but to anybody who could claim their ancestry and prove their employment status. The highs and lows of the movement for the colony's formation were significantly influenced by the deeds of the political elite for and against the cause, from Mehr Chand Khanna and Atulya Ghosh to Arun Chandra Guha and Lala Achint Ram. The demand for the colony may have drowned had the matter not escalated as high as to the then ruling party's working committee. The progress that followed exemplified civil-state harmony, as the Indian state honored its commitment and settled over 2,000 partition-affected Bengali families in New Delhi between March 1960 and December 1972, despite the period encapsulating immense socio-political and economic strife for India, including three full-scale wars, the premature demise of two prime ministers, a currency devaluation, famines, and scarcity shocks. Chittaranjan Park has grown to become more accommodative, accepting new residents irrespective of ethnicity and shedding its tag of a bordered urban space of exclusivity for Bengalis.

## Notes

1. In Pierre Nora's (1989) conception, a *lieux de memoire* or memory space is an entity, tangible or intangible, which is enshrined as a symbol of a community's or a nation's history in its collective memory.

SOUTH ASIA

2. For an example of such a list, see Rediff (2013).
3. For a detailed investigation of the lives of the 3440 displaced Bengali families shifted to the Andaman and Nicobar Islands, see Sen (2011, 219–244).
4. In the industries within the Calcutta Metropolitan District of the time, only 48.7% employees were classified as "Bengali" in 1959. 23 per cent of "all earners" in the city were skilled, while only 12% were unskilled. See Lubell (1974, 40–54).
5. The average cost of living in 1947 was Rs. 132, Rs. 285, Rs. 316, and Rs. 335 at Delhi, Bombay, Madras, and Calcutta respectively, compared to the corresponding base costs of 1939. See EW (1949, 22–23).
6. See Annexure 1, "Interview of Mr. AK Guha."
7. Madan Lal Khurana, a student leader of the Jan Sangh in the 1950s, grew in stature to earn the moniker of the "Lion of Delhi" and become the city's Chief Minister by the 1990s. See Rediff (2003).
8. Sekhar Bandopadhyay (2004, 193–196) and Joya Chatterji (1994, 191–203 and 240–241) have discussed the role and plight of Bengal's underprivileged, especially the *Namashudras*, during the partition.
9. At the time, in the absence of the Staff Selection Commission (SSC) – which came up only in 1975 – the UPSC served as the chief agency for state recruitment in India, including for middle-level (Group/Grade B) posts.
10. See Annexure 1. "Interview of Mr. AK Guha."
11. Many members of the EPDPA, led by its then secretary, Bimal Bhushan Chakraborty, unsuccessfully pressed for the colony to be named *Purbachal* (Land of the East). "Chittaranjan Park" was eventually accepted unanimously. See *Purbachal'er Katha's* Editor (1972) and Acharya (1972).
12. Appadurai (1990) sees diasporic groups harbor an "intensified sense of […] attachment" for their homeland, to satisfy which, international host-home networks are established for helping them retain their primordial socio-political roots despite being spatial distanced from them.
13. In Delhi, the Raisina Bengali Senior Secondary School on Mandir Marg and the Bengali Senior Secondary School on Civil Lines began flourishing by the 1930s.

## Disclosure statement

No potential conflict of interest was reported by the author.

## References

Acharya, D.P. 1972. EPDP Association'er Iti-britto [The Journey of the EPDP Association]. *Purbachal'er Katha* (EPDPA [Translated from Bengali]), October.
Alluri, Aparna, and Gurman Bhatia. 2016. The Decade that Changed Delhi. *Hindustan Times and Dawn: 1947 Archive*. 2016. http://www.hindustantimes.com/static/partition/delhi/ (accessed April 19, 2017).
Anderson, Benedict. 1983. *Imagined Communities: Reflections on the Origin and Spread of Nationalism*. London: Verso.
Appadurai, Arjun. 1990. Disjuncture and Difference in the Global Cultural Economy. *Theory, Culture, and Society* 7, no. 2: 295–310.
Bandopadhyay, Sekhar. 2004. *Caste, Culture, and Hegemony: Social Dominance in Colonial Bengal*. London: Sage.
Bandopadhyay, Paritosh. 2016. Smriti'r Nimontron'e: Chittaranjan Park [Down Memory Lane: Chittaranjan Park]. *56th Foundation Day Newsletter* (EBDPA [Translated from Bengali]), April.
Basu, Jayanti, and Alan Roland. 2013. *Reconstructing the Bengal partition: The Psyche Under a Different Violence*. Calcutta: Bhatkal and Sons.

Bhattacharya, Snigdhendu. 2011. Ghost of Marichjhapi Returns to Haunt. *Hindustan Times*, April 25. http://www.hindustantimes.com/kolkata/ghost-of-marichjhapi-returns-to-haunt/story-4v78 MhnW2IZVCQMPfDObqO.html (accessed April 19, 2017).

Bhaumik, Subir. 2008. Internal Displacement in North-East India: Challenges Ahead. In *The Fleeing People of South Asia*, ed. Sibaji Pratim Basu, 249–258. London: Anthem Press.

Butalia, Urvashi. 2017. *The Other Side of Silence: Voices from the Partition of India*. London: Penguin.

Chakrabarty, Bidyut. 2004. *The Partition of Bengal and Assam, 1932–47: Contour of Freedom*. London: Routledge.

Chakraborty, Paulomi. 2014. The Refugee Woman and the New Woman: (En)gendering Middle-class Bengali Modernity and the City in Satyajit Ray's Mahanagar. In *Being Bengali: At Home and in the World*, ed. Mridula Nath Chakraborty, 69–91. New Delhi: Routledge.

Chakraborty, Paulomi. 2018. *The Refugee Woman: Partition of Bengal, Gender, and the Political*. London: Oxford University Press.

Chatterji, Joya. 1994. *Bengal Divided: Hindu Communalism and Partition*. New York: Cambridge University Press.

Chatterji, Joya. 2001. Right or Charity? The Debate Over Relief and Rehabilitation in West Bengal, 1947–50. In *The Partitions of Memory: The Afterlife of the Division of India*, ed. Suvir Kaul, 74–110. New Delhi: Permanent Black.

Chatterji, Joya. 2007. *The Spoils of Partition: Bengal and India, 1947–67*. Cambridge: Cambridge University Press.

Chatterji, Joya. 2016. Dispositions and Destinations in the Bengal Muslim Diaspora, 1947–2007. In *The Bengal Diaspora: Rethinking Muslim Migration*, eds. Claire Alexander, Joya Chatterji, and Annu Jalais, 52–79. New York: Routledge.

Chatterji, Joya. 2018. Secularization and Constitutive Moments: Insights from Partition Diplomacy in South Asia. In *Tolerance, Secularization, and Democratic Politics in South Asia*, eds. Humeira Iqtidar and Tanika Sarkar, 108–133. Cambridge: Cambridge University Press.

Choudhury, Kushanava. 2017. After Partition: Colony Politics and the Rise of Communism in Bengal, August 11. https://www.historyextra.com/period/20th-century/after-partition-colony-politics-and-the-rise-of-communism-in-bengal/ (accessed November 20, 2018).

Das, Nabanita. 2016. Exiled Bangladeshi Author Taslima Nasrin Opens Up on her Delhi connect. *Hindustan Times*, October 29. https://www.hindustantimes.com/books/exiled-bangladeshi-author-taslima-nasrin-opens-up-on-her-delhi-connect/story-krh2slTI82fvED4gwdOQ9O.html (accessed November 20, 2018).

Dasgupta, Priyanka, and TNN. 2018. Times of India. *Every 5th Bengali Speaker Lives outside Bengal*, June 28. https://timesofindia.indiatimes.com/city/kolkata/every-5th-bengali-speaker-lives-outside-bengal/articleshow/64770649.cms (accessed November 18, 2018).

Dasgupta, Abhijit, Masahiko Togawa, and Abul Barkat. 2011. *Minorities and the State: Changing Social and Political Landscape of Bengal*. New Delhi: Sage.

Editor. 1972. Sampadakiya (Editorial). *Purbachal'er Katha* (EPDPA [Translated from Bengali]), October.

EW. 1949. Statistical Summary. *Economic Weekly* 1, no. 10,: 22–23. March.

EW. 1954. East Bengal Refugees. *Economic Weekly*, October 26. http://www.epw.in/system/files/pdf/1954_6/43-44/east_bengal_refugees.pdf (accessed April 19, 2017).

Frasier, Bashabi. 2008. *Bengal Partition Stories: An Unclosed Chapter*. London: Anthem Press.

Ghosh, Arun. 2010. *The Moments of Bengal Partition: Selections from the Amrita Bazar Patrika, 1947–48*. Calcutta: Seribaan.

Ghosh, Vishwajyoti, and Amiya Sen. 2015. A Good Education. In *Partition: The Long Shadow*, ed. Urvashi Butalia, ch. 4. London: Penguin.

Guha, Arun Chandra. 1973. Kalkaji'r Bangali Colony: Chittaranjan Park [Kalkaji's Bengali Colony: Chittaranjan Park]. *Purbachal'er Katha* (EPDPA [Translated from Bengali]), October.

Gujral, Monish. 2004. A legend and the man. In *Moti Mahal's tandoori trail*, ed. Monish Gujral, 1–8. New Delhi: Roli and Janssen.

Houtum, Henk von, Martin van der Velde, and Joren Jacobs. n.d. Demographic and Economic Decline as Symptoms of Peripherality: Plea for the Planning and Design of a Borderscape.

*Nijmegen Center for Border Research*. https://www.academia.edu/2864686/Demographic_and_
economic_decline_as_symptoms_of_peripherality_Plea_for_the_planning_and_design_of_a_
Borderscape (accessed November 20, 2018).

IANS. 2017. Begum Jaan will Renew Focus on Sex Workers: Srijit Mukherji. *Hindustan* Times,
March 13. http://www.hindustantimes.com/bollywood/begum-jaan-will-renew-focus-on-sex-
workers-srijit-mukerji/story-BtGF2RzECOuwfqjmvrbVHP.html (accessed April 19, 2017).

Jaffrelot, Christophe. 1996. *The Hindu Nationalist Movement and Indian Politics*. London: C. Hurst
and Co.

Jaffrelot, Christophe. 2010. *Religion, Caste, and Politics in India*. London: Primus Books.

Jaffrey, Madhur. 2016. *Tandoori Chicken in Delhi: Partition and the Creation of Indian Food*.
New York: Knopf Publishing.

Kanoon, Indian. n.d. The Displaced Persons (Compensation and Rehabilitation) Act, 1954: Bare
Act, doc. 1945893. *Indian Kanoon*. https://indiankanoon.org/doc/1945893/ (accessed April 19,
2017).

Kaul, Suvir. 2001. *The Partitions of Memory: The Afterlife of the Division of India*. New Delhi:
Permanent Black.

Kaur, Ravinder. 2017. *Since 1947: Partition and Punjabi Migrants of Delhi*. New Delhi: Oxford
University Press.

Khadilkar, R.K. 1972. Letter to BB Chakraborty, Secretary, EPDPA, from the Minister for Labour,
Employment, and Rehabilitation. Response to EPDPA/Name/72, Government of India, New
Delhi, December 22.

Lazzirini, Anna. 2015. Metamorphosis of City Borders. In *Borderscaping: Imaginations and
Practicies of Border Making*, eds. Chiara Brambilla, Jussi Laine, James Scott, and Gianluca
Bocchi, 177–186. London: Routledge.

Lubell, Harold. 1974. *Calcutta: Its Urban Development and Employment Prospects*. New Delhi:
Concept Publishing.

Majumdar, Nakuleshwar. 1977. Chittaranjan Park'er Janmakatha [The Tale of Chittaranjan Park's
Birth]. *Purbachal'er Katha* (EPDPA [Translated from Bengali]), October.

Mallick, Ross. 1999. Refugee Resettlement in Forest Reserves: West Bengal Policy Reversal and the.
*Journal of Asian Studies* 58, no. 1: 104–125. February.

Mantri, Rajeev. 2011. India Journal: The Unnecessary Decline of Calcutta. *Wall Street Journal*, April
13. https://blogs.wsj.com/indiarealtime/2011/04/13/india-journal-the-unnecessary-decline-of-
calcutta/ (accessed April 19, 2017).

Menon, Ritu, and Kamla Bhasin. 1998. *Borders and Boundaries: Women in India's Partition*. New
Brunswick: Rutgers University Press.

Misra, Archisman. 2015. Delhi's Bong Paradise: How the 'Bengali Bhadralok' Came to be in CR
Park. *Youth ki Awaaz*, August 7. https://www.youthkiawaaz.com/2015/08/life-in-chittaranjan-
park/ (accessed April 19, 2017).

Nair, Neeti. 2011. *Changing Homelands: Hindu Politics and the Partition of India*. Cambridge:
Harvard University Press.

Nakatani, Tetsuya. 2015. Durga Puja and Neighbourhood in a Displaced Persons' Colony in New
Delhi. In *Cities in South Asia*, eds. Crispin Bates and Minoru Mio. London: Routledge.

Nora, Pierre. 1989. Between Memory and History: Les Lieux de Memoire. Representations, no. 26:
7-24. Spring.

NYT, News Service. 1980. 350 Bengalis are Massacred in Indian Villages. *Pittsburg Post Gazette*,
June 16. https://news.google.com/newspapers?nid=1129&dat=19800616&id=3E4NAAAAIBAJ
&sjid=zm0DAAAAIBAJ&pg=3736,2460642 (accessed April 19, 2017).

PCI. 1951. First Five-year Plan (1951–56): Bare Text. *Planning Commission of India*. http://
planningcommission.nic.in/plans/planrel/fiveyr/1st/1planch38.html (accessed April 19, 2017).

Rai, Satya Mehta. 1986. *Punjab Since Partition*. New Delhi: Durga Publications.

Rajadhyakshal, Madhavi, and TNN. 2013. Delhi World's Second Most Populous Mega-city. *Times
of India*, September 13. http://timesofindia.indiatimes.com/india/Delhi-worlds-second-most-
populous-mega-city/articleshow/22529248.cms (accessed April 19, 2017).

Rajaram, Prem Kumar. 2014. *Ruling the Margins: Colonial Power and Administrative Rule in the Past and Present*. London: Routledge.

Rediff. 2003. The Lion in Winter. *Rediff*, November 24. http://in.rediff.com/election/2003/nov/24os.htm (accessed April 19, 2017).

Rediff. 2013. The Most Touching Films on the Partition. *Rediff*, July 15. http://www.rediff.com/movies/report/slide-show-1-the-most-touching-films-on-the-partition/20130715.htm (accessed April 19, 2017).

Sahni, Diksha, and Nikita Mehta. 2011. Delhi's Refugees: The Story of Bahrisons Bookshop. *Wall Street Journal*, December 12. https://blogs.wsj.com/indiarealtime/2011/12/12/delhis-refugees-the-story-of-bahrisons-bookshop/ (accessed April 19, 2017).

Sen, Uditi. 2011. Dissident Memories: Exploring Bengali Refugee Narratives in the Andaman Islands. In *Refugees and the End of Empire*, eds. P. Pinayi and P. Virdee, 219–243. London: Springer.

Sengupta, Ranjana. 2008. Refugees: Delhi's Last Conquerors. In *Delhi Metropolitan: The Making of an Unlikely City*, ed. Ranjana Sengupta, 68–92. New Delhi: Penguin.

Sengupta, Debjani. 2015. *The Partition of Bengal: Fragile Borders and New Identities*. Cambridge: Cambridge University Press.

Singh, Khushwant. 2011. *The Sunset Club*. New Delhi: Penguin.

Smith, Donald Eugene. 2015. *South Asian Politics and Religion*. New Jersey: Princeton University Press.

Strüver, Anke. 2005. *Stories of the "Boring Border": The Dutch-German Borderscape in People's Minds*. Münster: LIT Verlag Münster.

Tiwari, Saagar. 2010. Developing Bastar: The Dandakaranya Project. In *The Heart of the Matter: Development, Identity, and Violence*, ed. Sagar Kumar, 115–134. New Delhi: Aakar Books.

Trikha, Bhavini, and Lovisha Wadhwa. 2016. Calm and Chaos Coexist in Sarojini Nagar lanes. *Hindustan Times*, July 1. http://www.hindustantimes.com/delhi/calm-and-chaos-coexist-in-sarojini-nagar-lanes/story-VXXMgSN4jVKfyqfyjNITuL.html (accessed April 19, 2017).

Yong, Tan Tai, and Gyanesh Kudaisya. 2004. *The Aftermath of Partition in South Asia*. London: Routledge.

## Annexure 1

Interview of Mr. AK Guha, President, East Bengal Displaced Persons Association

(Conducted with the interviewee's consent at the EBDPA's registered Chittaranjan Park office on 20 February 2017)

**Q1. The association's official website, recalling its heritage, pays tribute to some of its most noted office-bearers. It does not, however, mention about the earliest phase of the movement for Chittaranjan Park in the 1950s. Can you briefly throw some light on how and why the EBDPA, then the EPDPA, came to be formally founded?**

**A.** What is the EBDPA today can be traced to a loose association of a few Bengalis working for the government, at the Lodhi Road observatory, in Delhi. All of them had East Bengali links, but were not necessarily affected directly by the partition. Seeing the government give land allotments to West Pakistani refugees in and around Delhi, Jahnabi Chakraborty rallied several of his East Bengali colleagues, who had no hometowns left for return, into forming an informal pressure group. The group formalized into an association gradually and began a drive to enroll Delhi's East Bengalis, directly displaced or otherwise, to demand a settlement for their own growing community within the city they were employed at. 2000-odd families had enrolled as the first batch of alottees for Chittaranjan Park.

**Q2. How did Chakraborty and his colleagues approach the government? Was the Ministry for Rehabilitation receptive?**

**A.** The 1950s marked the rise of socialist bureaucratization and red tapism in India. So, as implied, the going was tough when it came to convincing the ministry, especially since the people who came up with the proposal were government employees required to obey strict protocols. Once, however, the support of politically connected and active Bengalis – Delhi's important Bengalis – was obtained, the ministry was pushed to take cognizance. The likes of MP Ila Pal Choudhury and her colleague, Aruna Asaf Ali, if I recall correctly, lobbied for the cause directly with Pandit*ji* [Prime Minister Nehru].

**Q3. What did the government do upon taking cognizance of the demand? I am reemphasizing because I have heard that Mehr Chand Khanna, India's rehabilitation minister at the time, was reluctant to act.**

**A.** Yes. Initially, Mehr Chand Khanna had been reluctant. However, with political and public pressure mounting, he, as the minister for rehabilitation, had to act responsibly. As a West Pakistani himself, he could be seen to act partially towards a particular set of refugees. The land finally allotted for a colony for East Bengalis employed in Delhi and affected by the partition in any way measured 212 acres. It was a rocky jungle, which required tremendous development to become habitable. Thus, the Central Public Works Department was also called in. By then, it was already 1969–1970, and the EPDPA became a full-grown registered society. Thereon, dealings with the government became formal and regular.

**Q4. Were the plots uniformly allotted?**

**A.** No. The allottees that had enrolled themselves belonged to various private and public posts, representing varying income groups. Though most belonged to the middle class, a Grade-A government officer on a 275–800 scale of pay could, for obvious reasons, afford a bigger plot than a Grade-B government employee on a 160–330 scale. The former was also entitled to bigger loans from the government. Thus, the plots were of four categories: 160 sq. yards, 220 sq. yards, 320 sq. yards, and even 420 sq. yards. However, by the 1990s, when the colony was expanded to include newer blocks like Pocket 40 and Pocket 52, it was realized that the plots must be cut uniformly to accommodate the optimum number of people.

**Q5. What was your own experience in post-partition Delhi? Why did your family choose to move this far to the national capital?**

**A.** Well, it was the land of opportunity at the time! It still is, to many. My father was directly affected by the partition. We had come to post-1947 India from the troubled area of Barisal and chose to migrate to Delhi by 1950, quite unprepared, but hopeful. We stayed at Rajinder Nagar near Karol Bagh with my maternal uncle, surrounded mostly by Punjabi neighbors. We knew some Bengalis in Timarpur and Gole Market too. Things were not too difficult for outsiders here. I was quickly admitted in a school. Even semi-skilled youth could register their names at a local employment exchange office and attain job offers. Anybody with basic typing skills could be employed for clerical tasks immediately. Most low- and middle-tier jobs, including regarded ones like teaching at schools, were not high-paying. Thus, stable government designations were most sought after, and since the government ran from Delhi, it boasted a demand for skilled staff in the 1950s.

**Q6. You mention Punjabi neighbors. Being a micro-minority of Bengalis in a city increasingly dominated by Punjabis at the time, do you recall any friction between the two communities before Chittaranjan Park was established?**

**A.** Bengalis were scattered across colonies for refugees and government employees across the city, most of which housed a Punjabi- and Hindi-speaking majority. Many Bengalis did feel the pressure of adapting to the new culture, but they managed to fit in well. They had to, in a metropolitan. I was a very young school-goer in the 1950s and stayed out of Delhi in Bihar, Punjab, West Bengal, and Bombay for years due to official postings. However, for whatever time I spent in Delhi, I did not, personally, see any communal or sectarian incidents between the Punjabis and the Bengalis. Chittaranjan Park's Raisina Bengali School, in fact, loved its football rivalries with the DAV Public Schools of Delhi. As people who had lost a lot, the East and the West Pakistanis in Delhi could not afford to lose any more, I guess.

# Index

Note: *Italic* page numbers refer to figures and page numbers followed by "n" denote endnotes.

aesthetic approach 43
Afghan civil war 56
Afghanistan 7, 35, 58, 67, 74–7; Soviet occupation of 54, 56, 58
Afghanistan border 50, 52, 55–9, 61–2
Afghanistan–Pakistan Transit Trade Agreement 55
Afghan militants 55, 59
Afghan refugees 54, 56
agreements 28, 66–71, 74, 76–7, 84, 113; unilateral termination of 70–1
Allama Iqbal 40
Anderson, Benedict 111

Balibar, Etienne 24
Bandopadhyay, Paritosh 114
Bangladesh liberation war 36
Bengali migrants 113, 115–18
Bengali refugees 110–11, 114
Bengalis 7, 45, 108–9, 111, 114, 120
Bengali-speaking Hindus 108, 111
Bengal Partition 110–11
Bhutan 15, 86, 95–7, 99, 101–6; bank in 97, 102–3, 105; border 97
Bhutanese citizens 97, 101–6
Bhutanese currency 100–3
bioregions 84, 91
black money 101, 103–5
Bleiker, Roland 43
bordered space 118–19
bordering practices 22–5, 32
borderland citizens 99, 105–6
borderlanders 12, 17, 23–7, 30–2
borderlands 5–6, 11, 17–18, 105–6
borders 2–8, 10–13, 16–18, 22–32, 34–40, 44–5, 50–8, 61, 69–70, 95–7, 99–102, 106, 110–11; areas 25–6, 30, 100–5; communities 2, 13, 17; disputes 7, 68; fence 26, 28, 30, 51, 57; guards 13, 52–6; inhabitants 27, 87; regions 4–5, 7, 10, 17–18, 25–6, 96–7, 106; reinforcement strategies 50–2, 56; residents 27, 30–2, 87;

studies 4–5, 7–8, 11, 24, 36, 40, 43, 110; vernacularization of 26–7; work 23–6, 28, 30–2; zone 23, 25, 31–2, 87
borderscape 110
Border Security Force (BSF) 24–5, 27–8, 30–1, 45
boundaries 2–5, 7, 17–18, 24–6, 31, 34–8, 46, 50, 57, 66–9, 72, 84, 90–1
boundary lines 31, 68–9
bribery 70, 76–7

Calcutta 108–9, 111–12, 116–17
Chakrabarty, Bidyut 110
Chakraborty, Jahnabi Charan 115
Chakraborty, Paulomi 111
Chatterji, Joya 111
children 30, 37, 40, 57, 61, 114
Chittaranjan Park 7, 108, 110–11, 115, 118–20
cinema 6, 42–3
climate change 82, 84
coercion 69–70, 77
conservation 83–4, 86, 88–90
Cooper, A. 26
corruption 70, 76–7, 98
culture 11, 86, 89
currencies 90, 95–6, 101–2, 104, 106
customary international law 71–2, 77

defensive border strategy 51–2, 54, 61
Delhi, coveted refuge 111–12
demand draft 100, 102–3, 105
demonetization 100–2, 104
disagreement 73–4, 76–7
discursive border 10
disproportionate dividends 112
disputes 7, 67–8, 73–7
Durand agreement 58, 66–70, 76–7
Durand dispute 73, 75
Durand line 3, 7, 35, 58, 66–71, 74–7
Durand Treaty 71, 74, 77
duress 67, 69

128 INDEX

East Pakistan 7, 111–12, 115, 118–20
economic coercion 70, 76–7
economic forces 15
environment 28, 82–3, 87, 89; environmental
identity 92n13
Eschbach, Karl 52
exchange rate 95–7, 99, 101, 106

First Five-Year Plan 115
foreign exchange 98, 105
Frasier, Bashabi 110

Gandhi, Indira 118
Gandhi, M.K. 39
Ghobar, M. G. M. 69
Ghosh, Amitav 109
Ghosh, Arun 110
Ghosh, Vishwajyoti 109
Ghoti Bengalis 120

hard borders 3, 34–6
Hutchinson, D.N. 75

India 3–4, 6–7, 15–16, 18, 22–4, 26–31, 34–7,
39–47, 51, 53–4, 66–7, 69, 71, 82, 85–7, 96–7,
99–100, 102–6, 109–13, 118
India-Bangladesh border 4, 13
India–Bhutan currency arrangement 96
Indian army 4, 27, 30–1, 44
Indian currency 100–3
India-Nepal borders 3
Indian Independence Act 72, 77
Indian rupee 95–6, 102–4
Indians 10–11, 16, 32, 36, 41, 44–6, 96–7, 100–3,
105–6, 110–11
Indian textbooks 41–2
India-Pakistan borders 6
India–Pakistan relations 34–7, 41–2, 44–5
India's border discourse 12–13
Indo-Bhutan borderlands 96, 103, 105–6
Indo-Bhutanese border towns 95
informal exchange rate system 96–9, 103–6
international disputes 74–5
International Monetary Fund 95
interrelated territorialities 14, 18

Jaffrey, Madhur 109
Jaisalmer District 6, 22
Johnson, Corey 26
Jones, Reece 26

Kailash Sacred Landscape 83; conservation
initiative 7, 81–92
Kakar, Hassan 69
Kargil War 30, 44
Karzai, Hamid 55
Kaul, Suvir 110
Kaur, Ravinder 109

Kellogg-Briand Pact 75
Khan, Ayub 39
Krakow Protocol 91n1
Kudaisya, Gyanesh 110
Kuriya Bheri 29

Loya Jirga 70, 77
Loyn, D. 68
Lubell, Harold 111

Manila Declaration 75
Marrakesh Agreement 73
Meghdoot 4
mental borders 4–5, 34–8, 40–7
Merrills, J.G. 73
migrants 36, 51, 110–13, 116–17, 119
militants 12, 51–4, 56, 59–61; groups 7, 54, 59–62
militarization 4, 31, 51, 55, 84
military operations 44, 59–61
mountain governance 83–5
Mukherjee, Subroto 116
mundane encounters 26

Nakatani, Tetsuya 119
Namibia 95–6
narratives 15, 23–4, 26–7, 30, 43, 100, 104
national security 4–5, 51, 54, 56–7, 61
Nehru-Liaquat Pact 115
Nepal 3, 6–7, 13–14, 35, 82, 85–7, 95–6
New Delhi 4, 7, 26, 108–9, 118, 120
Newman, D. 25, 37
Ngultrum (BTN) 96–7, 103–6
non-state actors 23–4
North-West border 73

official exchange rate 96
Operation Parakram 30
othering 6, 38, 44
Oztig, L.I. 51–2

Paasi, Anssi 25–6, 37
pacific settlement, disputes 74, 76–7
Pakistan 3, 6–7, 22–3, 25–31, 34–7, 39–47, 50–2,
54–62, 67, 69, 71–7, 109, 112; border discourse
56; border policies 50, 54; borders 22, 36, 43–5,
47, 54; partition 36, 42; relations 34–5, 37,
41–2, 44–5
Pakistan-Afghanistan Frontier Dispute 66
Pakistanis 45–6, 55, 111; army 60–2; authorities
54–6, 60–2; policymakers 52, 56–8, 60; shoot-
to-kill policy 56; Taliban 59; textbooks 38–40
parallel currency markets 97–9, 104–6
parallel informal exchange rate system 95
parallel markets 96–9, 106
partition 3, 22–3, 37, 39, 42, 44, 108–10, 113,
115–16, 120; of India 22, 58, 109–10
partition-affected Bengalis 108, 110
Pashtuns 58–9, 67

## INDEX

peace 35, 46, 56–7, 59, 61, 75, 84
peaceful border 6
peace process 59–61
Perkins, Chris 26
physical borders 23, 38, 44–5, 47

Radcliffe, Sir Cyril 26
Rahman, Amir Abdur 68
Rajaram, Prem Kumar 118
regional borders 37
regional integration 35–6
Rehabilitation 111–16, 120
Royal Monetary Authority of Bhutan (RMA) 97, 101–2
Rumford, Chris 23–4, 26, 31

Sahlins, Peter 25
Saikal, Amin 68
securitized borders 35, 38, 47
security dynamics 7, 50, 52, 58, 61–2
Sen, Amiya 109
Sengupta, Ranjana 113
settlement obligation 73
Sharma, Ankur 7
shoot-to-kill policies 51–3, 56, 61
Singh, Khushwant 109
Strüver, Anke 110
sub-national actors 88
suboptimal subregionalism 12
Subrahmanyam, Sanjay 16

Taliban 52, 54–5, 58–60; militants 55–6, 59
Tate, G. P. 68
territoriality 7, 16–17, 22, 82, 84, 86

textbooks 34, 36–42, 47
Tibet 13–16, 85
titled India-China Borderlands 6
Tiwari, Saagar 113
transboundary conservation 83–4
transboundary cooperation 83, 85, 88
transboundary protected areas (TBPAs) 83–4, 88, 90
trans-Himalayan borderlands 10, 14
trans-Himalayan trade flows 14
trans-Himalayan trader 13–14, 16
trans-territoriality 81, 87
treaties 67, 69–74, 76–7
Tripura 113–14

UN Charter on pacific settlement 75
unilateral termination, agreement 70–1
United Nations Environment Programme (UNEP) 83–5, 90–1
Urry, J. 24
US-Mexico border 5

Vienna Convention on the Law of Treaties 1969 (VCLT) 67, 69–72, 76–7

war 3, 6, 12, 23, 27, 29, 31, 37, 44, 59
West Bengal 86, 111, 113–14, 116–17, 119–20
West Pakistan 109–10, 113, 115–17, 120
Woolsey, L. H. 70

Yong, Tan Tai 110

Zia-ul-Haq 39